PROTESTANTISM AND CAPITALISM

The Weber Thesis and Its Critics

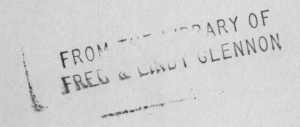

PROBLEMS IN EUROPEAN CIVILIZATION

PROTESTANTISM
AND
CAPITALISM

The Weber Thesis and Its Critics

EDITED WITH AN INTRODUCTION BY

Robert W. Green

PENNSYLVANIA STATE UNIVERSITY

D. C. HEATH AND COMPANY · BOSTON

Englewood · Indianapolis · Dallas · Burlingame · Atlanta

Table of Contents

Introduction

DID the Protestant Reformation, and especially its Calvinist branch, have a decisive influence upon the development of modern capitalism? For more than half a century this question has been the focal point of a scholarly controversy which had its beginning in 1904–5 with the publication by the famous German sociologist, Max Weber, of two articles entitled "Die protestantische Ethik und der Geist des Kapitalismus" [The Protestant Ethic and the Spirit of Capitalism].[1] Together with a supplementary article, "Die protestantische Sekten und der Geist des Kapitalismus" [The Protestant Sects and the Spirit of Capitalism], which appeared in 1906, these articles, with some additional footnotes, now constitute the first studies in Max Weber's collected essays on the sociology of religion.[2]

In these articles Weber admitted his debt to the great economic historian, Werner Sombart, who, in his well-known study, Der Moderne Kapitalismus, published in 1902, has stressed the importance of what he called "the spirit of capitalism" [der Geist des Kapitalismus] as a guiding force in the evolution of modern capitalism. Accepting Sombart's hypothesis that there was such a thing as a "spirit of capitalism" and that its role had been crucial to the development of the modern capitalistic economy, Weber then went on to speculate as to the origin or source of this special "spirit." In his essay Weber proposed the tentative thesis that this crucial element had ap-

peared as a kind of by-product of the religious ethic of Calvinism.

Almost immediately following their first appearance, these articles attracted the interest of scholars in several different fields because, in its various aspects, the Weber hypothesis cut across the areas of a number of separate scholarly disciplines. Since Weber was himself a sociologist, and in this instance he seemed to be attempting to apply a sociological method to an historical problem, both sociologists and historians became concerned. Because capitalism was involved, economic historians were aroused; and the role Weber assigned to Protestantism drew the attention of both Catholic and Protestant theologians. Some of these scholars attacked Weber's position; some supported it; some seemed willing to accept a modified or cautiously qualified version of it. Beyond that, however, if one may judge by what they have written, the authors who commented upon Weber's work, whether supporting or attacking it, seem frequently to have misunderstood or misinterpreted either Weber's method or his conclusions, or both.

As a study of the present state of scholarly opinion on the questions raised and the answers given by Weber, clearly the first task of this volume is to present the Weber thesis, and the first extract is Weber's own statement of the purpose of his study taken from his introduction to The Protestant Ethic and the Spirit of Capitalism. Space is lacking, of course, in a volume of this length, to include Weber's entire work; and so the second selection, an article by Kemper Fullerton from the Harvard Theological Review, is included because it offers the

[1] Archiv für Sozialwissenschaft und Sozialpolitik, Volumes XX and XXI.
[2] Max Weber, Gesammelte Aufsätze zur Religionssoziologie, 3 vols. (Tubingen, 1920–1921).

reader an excellent summary of Weber's argument. The interested student, nevertheless, is emphatically urged to read all of *The Protestant Ethic and the Spirit of Capitalism,* and better still, to go on to the supplementary essay, "Die protestantische Sekten und der Geist des Kapitalismus," and, hopefully, even to Weber's additional articles in volumes XXV, XXVI, XXX, and XXXI of the *Archiv für Sozialwissenschaft und Sozialpolitik.*

The views Weber presented in these essays were not slow to provoke responses from other writers. In 1909 a German scholar, F. Rachfall, attacked the Weber thesis by arguing that capitalism was much older than Protestantism and that other factors were far more important than Protestantism in bringing about the development of modern capitalism. (This line of attack has since been used by other scholars, some of whose writings appear in this booklet.) Just three years later, however, there appeared Ernst Troeltsch's extremely impressive work, *Die sozialen Lehren der christlichen Kirchen und Gruppen* (published in an English translation by Olive Wyon in 1931 as *The Social Teaching of the Christian Churches*). Troeltsch, who was concerned with the whole past development of the Christian social ethic, accepted Weber's view of the relationship of Protestantism to capitalism; and his support for the Weber thesis was so effectively expressed that it has sometimes even been referred to as the Weber-Troeltsch thesis. The third extract in this volume is taken from that part of *The Social Teaching of the Christian Churches* which bears most directly on Weber's theories about the role of Calvinism.

Troeltsch's support must have been particularly welcome to Weber because, meanwhile, Werner Sombart had been hard at work; and the conclusions he presented in 1913 could hardly have been comforting to the author of *The Protestant Ethic and the Spirit of Capitalism.* In the second edition of *Der Moderne Kapitalismus* Sombart had

concluded that the evolution of modern capitalism had begun earlier than he had previously believed, which gave added weight to Rachfall's criticism of Weber's theories. In 1911 Sombart published *Die Juden und das Wirtschaftsleben* (translated into English as *The Jews and Modern Capitalism*) in which he argued that the social attitudes and economic practices associated with Judaism had been the primary source of the spirit of capitalism. As a result of this treatise, Sombart found himself the target of a critical barrage, one of the chief critics being Max Weber; but Sombart, undaunted, in 1913 proceeded to publish an entire book devoted to the study of the spirit of capitalism. This work, entitled *Der Bourgeois* was translated into English in 1915 with the title, *The Quintessence of Capitalism*. The fourth selection has been taken from this book; and the reader may notice that although Sombart's view of the problem and his method of treating it are very similar to Weber's, their conclusions almost completely disagree.

By the time *The Quintessence of Capitalism* had joined the lengthening shelf of studies on the relationship of Protestantism to capitalism, the problem had become a sort of scholarly melee. Anyone who criticized the Weber thesis, for example, could be fairly confident that he himself would be criticized in turn; but the critic — or the critic-of-the-critic — might be either pro-Weber or anti-Weber, historian or economist, sociologist or theologian, Catholic or Protestant, Jew or agnostic, Christian socialist or Marxist. Furthermore, the valuations placed upon the Weber thesis by many of the authors seemed to reflect with unfortunate frequency the economic orientation or the religious affiliation (or lack of it) of the writer involved. If the critic was an admirer of capitalism, he might maintain his particular religious faith had stimulated its development. If, on the other hand, the critic was hostile to capitalism, he perhaps would disavow any possibility that his religion had provided an impetus to capitalistic evolution. The Weber thesis, as a result, has become, in some instances, the victim of partisan contention.

The remaining extracts which make up this book have been selected from the wealth of material produced by this controversy. In order to present in one volume anything approaching an adequate statement in their own words of the authors' views in the context in which they were expressed, the number of selections had to be, of course, severely restricted. The particular extracts included were chosen because they seemed especially representative, not only of the varied opinions about the thesis, but also because they constitute a cross section of the different scholarly disciplines whose members have taken part in the dispute.

Religion and the Rise of Capitalism, an unusually well-known scholarly work, by R. H. Tawney is the source of the fifth selection in this volume. Tawney's famous study was published in 1926 and represents the view of an economic historian. While Tawney accepted Weber's view that there was a causal relationship between the Protestant Reformation and the rise of capitalism, Tawney nevertheless insisted that Weber's emphasis on the unique role of Calvinism in generating the new spirit of capitalism was inadequate to explain the broad overall relationship between Protestantism and capitalism. Tawney tended to place more emphasis on the causative role of the whole Protestant movement as well as general political, social, and economic conditions during the sixteenth and seventeenth centuries.

Not everyone, by any means, has been satisfied with Tawney's approach to the problem, and the next selection comes from the pen of a theologian. Winthrop S. Hudson, in an article entitled "Puritanism and the Spirit of Capitalism" which appeared in the journal, *Church History,* criticizes Weber's concept of Calvinism as oversimplified and considers Tawney's characterization of Puritanism to be a distortion, the more dangerous because it is so subtly accomplished. Hudson, the reader will observe, was particularly concerned about the manner in which Tawney made use of the writings of seventeenth century Puritan preachers to support his argument.

Quite in agreement with Hudson's view that Weber's thesis was oversimplified was Henri Sée, a French economic historian from whose very considerable body of writings on the development of modern capitalism the next extract in this volume is taken. Sée, however, maintained that the oversimplification applied to the economic portion of Weber's argument as well as the theological. On the other hand, Sée, it will be seen, while he offered additional arguments in opposition to Weber's views, was on the whole favorably impressed by the Tawney thesis.

In 1933, six years after the article by Henri Sée appeared, another economic historian joined the fray. This was H. M. Robertson, whose *Aspects of the Rise of Economic Individualism* bears the subtitle, "A Criticism of Max Weber and His School." Robertson did not hesitate to challenge both Tawney and Weber and based his argument on both historical and economic evidence. As the reader peruses the eighth selection in this study, taken from Robertson's work, he will observe the author's emphasis on material rather than spiritual factors as the crucial elements in the development of modern capitalism.

But Robertson was by no means to have the last word. In his *Cattolicismo e protestantismo nella formazione storica del capitalismo* (translated into English in 1935 as *Catholicism, Protestantism and Capitalism*) Amintore Fanfani, an Italian economist, brought some new arguments into the controversy. Fanfani analysed the whole issue once again; and, employing an erudite exposition of Catholic teachings, presented a series of conclusions quite different from those offered previously. The ninth excerpt offers the reader an opportunity to examine Fanfani's views.

The next to last extract has been taken from the work of Albert Hyma, who does not completely agree with Fanfani and has been an outspoken critic of the conclusions drawn by Weber, Troeltsch, and Tawney. Hyma is an historian, a specialist in the study of northern humanism and the Reformation. In a whole series of books and articles which have appeared over the last twenty years, Hyma has vigorously attacked the Weber thesis chiefly on historical grounds. Especially critical of Weber's characterization of Calvinism, he has offered extensive documentary evidence (only a small part of which could be included here) to support his interpretation of the economic views of the leading reformers, both in England and on the continent. The main burden of his attack has been to show that Protestantism was in no way progressive, among religious faiths, in its teachings on economic behavior; and, therefore, in this respect could have had no decisive effect on the development of modern capitalism.

The last selection presented here is from an article by a sociologist, Ephraim Fischoff. "The Protestant Ethic and the Spirit of Capitalism: the History of a Controversy" appeared in the journal, *Social Research,* in 1944. While the reader may be somewhat surprised at the careful qualifications Fischoff draws around the Weber thesis, he can hardly overlook the unusually judicious appraisal which this writer has made of the controversy. It is not only the evidence and the conclusions of various writers which Fischoff weighs, but their methods as well.

The selections offered here are really only an introduction to the study of this dispute, if only for the reason that so many writers have taken part in the controversy. The sheer mass of material on this question might tempt the less conscientious student to dismiss the whole question as a hopelessly fruitless academic squabble. But such an indictment is hardly just. The gathering of evidence by partisans of both sides has led to the discovery and careful consideration of an impressive amount of information about both the Reformation and the nature and development of modern capitalism. Recognizing the vital importance of both Protestantism and capitalism as forces shaping modern civilization, many thoughtful individuals have been led by this debate to further reflection on the methods best suited to the study and analysis of this sort of phenomena. Not least important is the fact that this controversy highlights an even broader and more serious question: what is, or should be, the proper relation between man's moral philosophy and his economic behavior? The surviving documents of the sixteenth and seventeenth centuries seem to indicate that this was considered a question of compelling relevance then. Is it any less relevant in our own time?

The Conflict of Opinion

In fact, the *summum bonum* of this ethic, the earning of more and more money, combined with the strict avoidance of all spontaneous enjoyment of life, is completely devoid of any eudæmonistic, not to say hedonistic, admixture. It is thought of so purely as an end in itself, that from the point of view of the happiness of, or utility to, the single individual, it appears entirely transcendental and absolutely irrational. Man is dominated by the making of money, by acquisition as the ultimate purpose of his life. Economic acquisition is no longer subordinated to man as the means for the satisfaction of his material needs. This reversal of what we should call the natural relationship, so irrational from a naïve point of view, is evidently as definitely a leading principle of capitalism as it is foreign to all peoples not under capitalistic influence. At the same time it expresses a type of feeling which is closely connected with certain religious ideas. If we thus ask, *why* should "money be made out of men," Benjamin Franklin himself, although he was a colorless deist, answers in his autobiography with a quotation from the Bible, which his strict Calvinistic father drummed into him again and again in his youth: "Seest thou a man diligent in his business? He shall stand before kings" (Prov. xxii. 29). The earning of money within the modern economic order is, so long as it is done legally, the result and expression of virtue and proficiency in a calling; and this virtue and proficiency are, as it is now not difficult to see, the real Alpha and Omega of Franklin's ethic. . . .

— MAX WEBER

But Weber's second criterion of the capitalist spirit is too narrow. It leads inevitably to the defect which I feel vitiates his whole argument; he hardly considers any capitalist other than the Puritan capitalist who seeks wealth for the fulfillment of his "calling."
This added refinement is quite superfluous. A realist like Marx, who originated the discussions on capitalism, would no doubt have been greatly astonished if he had been asked to consider only those whose money-making activities were promoted by religious or quasi-religious ends to be possessed of the true capitalistic spirit. This is what we are asked to do.

— H. M. ROBERTSON

No one has ever asserted that Capitalism is the direct product of Calvinism. We can, however, say that both possessed a certain affinity for each other, that Calvinistic ethic of the "calling" and of work, which declares that the earning of money with certain precautions is allowable, was able to give it an intellectual and ethical backbone, and that, therefore, thus organized and inwardly supported it vigorously developed, even though within the limits of anti-mammon.

— ERNST TROELTSCH

His [Weber's] gravest weaknesses in his own special field, where alone criticism is relevant, are not those on which the most emphasis has usually being laid. The Calvinist applications of the doctrine of the "Calling" have, doubtless, their significance; but the degree of influence which they exercised, and their affinity or contrast with other versions of the same idea, are matters of personal judgement, not of precise proof. . . . His account of the social theory of Calvinism, however, if it rightly under-lined some points needing emphasis, left a good deal unsaid. . . . Though some recent attempts to find parallels to that theory in contemporary Catholic writers have not been very happy, Weber tended to treat it as more unique than it was. More important, he exaggerated its stability and consistency. Taking a good deal of his evidence from a somewhat late phase in the history of the movement, he did not emphasize sufficiently the profound changes through which Calvinism passed in the century following the death of Calvin.

— R. H. TAWNEY

Our outline of Catholic social ethics will have made it clear that Catholics, so long as they held closely to the social teachings of the Church, could never act in favour of capitalism. Certainly no one can deny that such men as the Bardi, Pitti, Datini, acted in a capitalistic manner, and, though baptized Christians, introduced a capitalistic mode of life among their Catholic contemporaries. But we deny that in so doing they were acting in conformity with Catholic social ethics. Although they were baptized, we cannot take their action as a ground for judging the action of Catholics and the progress of capitalism. Otherwise, our task would soon end with the conclusion that since capitalism was born in a Europe that was still wholly Catholic, Catholics indis-putably fostered its growth. Instead, we interpret the facts — of which we propose to give a brief survey — in quite another manner.

— AMINTORE FANFANI

One might wonder . . . whether Calvin was a Calvinist; . . . for both John Wesley and Benjamin Franklin are quoted to show what Calvinism was.

— ALBERT HYMA

THE AUTHOR DEFINES HIS PURPOSE

MAX WEBER

Max Weber studied law as a young man and became a jurist. His career was altered, however, by the appearance of an article he wrote on German agricultural labor which led to his appointment to the faculty of political economy at the University of Freiberg. He began teaching at the University of Heidelberg in 1897 and later joined the faculty of the University of Munich. Early in the twentieth century he developed his ideas on the study of sociology. From Weber's point of view, the discovery of laws is an end in itself in the study of natural sciences; but in sociology, laws are only a means to aid in the study of the causal inter-relationships of historical phenomena. The concepts which the sociologist uses to formulate his working hypotheses are "ideal types," such as the "capitalist" and the "Calvinist." Weber was also deeply interested in tracing what he maintained was the increasing rationalization of human activity. *The Protestant Ethic and the Spirit of Capitalism* is part of Weber's attempt to use his method to explain the causes and inter-action of such seemingly diverse cultural phenomena as capitalism and Protestantism.

A PRODUCT of modern European civilization, studying any problem of universal history, is bound to ask himself to what combination of circumstances the fact should be attributed that in Western civilization, and in Western civilization only, cultural phenomena have appeared which (as we like to think) lie in a line of development having *universal* significance and value.

Only in the West does science exist at a stage of development which we recognize today as valid. Empirical knowledge, reflection on problems of the cosmos and of life, philosophical and theological wisdom of the most profound sort, are not confined to it, though in the case of the last the full development of a systematic theology must be credited to Christianity under the influence of Hellenism, since there were only fragments in Islam and in a few Indian sects. In short, knowledge and observation of great refinement have existed elsewhere, above all in India, China, Babylonia, Egypt. But in Babylonia and elsewhere astronomy lacked — which makes its development all the more astounding — the mathematical foundation which it first received from the Greeks. The Indian geometry had no rational proof; that was another product of the Greek intellect, also the creator of mechanics and physics. The Indian natural sciences, though well developed in observation, lacked the method of experiment, which was, apart from beginnings in antiquity, essentially a product of the Renaissance, as was the modern laboratory. Hence medicine, especially in India, though highly developed in empirical technique, lacked a biological and particularly

From Max Weber, *The Protestant Ethic and the Spirit of Capitalism,* translated by Talcott Parsons (New York, 1930), pp. 13–14, 16–27. By permission of Charles Scribner's Sons, New York and George Allen & Unwin Ltd., London. Copyright 1930.

1

a biochemical foundation. A rational chemistry has been absent from all areas of culture except the West. . . .

And the same is true of the most fateful force in our modern life, capitalism. The impulse to acquisition, pursuit of gain, of money, of the greatest possible amount of money, has in itself nothing to do with capitalism. This impulse exists and has existed among waiters, physicians, coachmen, artists, prostitutes, dishonest officials, soldiers, nobles, crusaders, gamblers, and beggars. One may say that it has been common to all sorts and conditions of men at all times and in all countries of the earth, wherever the objective possibility of it is or has been given. It should be taught in the kindergarten of cultural history that this naive idea of capitalism must be given up once and for all. Unlimited greed for gain is not in the least identical with capitalism, and is still less its spirit. Capitalism *may* even be identical with the restraint, or at least a rational tempering, of this irrational impulse. But capitalism is identical with the pursuit of profit, and forever *renewed* profit, by means of continuous, rational, capitalistic enterprise. For it must be so: in a wholly capitalistic order of society, an individual capitalistic enterprise which did not take advantage of its opportunities for profit-making would be doomed to extinction.

Let us now define our terms somewhat more carefully than is generally done. We will define a capitalistic economic action as one which rests on the expectation of profit by the utilization of opportunities for exchange, that is on (formally) peaceful chances of profit. Acquisition by force (formally and actually) follows its own particular laws, and it is not expedient, however little one can forbid this, to place it in the same category with action which is, in the last analysis, oriented to profits from exchange. Where capitalistic acquisition is rationally pursued, the corresponding action is adjusted to calculations in terms of capital. This means that the action is adapted to a systematic utilization of goods or personal services as means of acquisition in such a way that, at the close of a business period, the balance of the enterprise in money assets (or, in the case of a continuous enterprise, the periodically estimated money value of assets) exceeds the capital, i.e. the estimated value of the material means of production used for acquisition in exchange. It makes no difference whether it involves a quantity of goods entrusted *in natura* [in kind] to a travelling merchant, the proceeds of which may consist in other goods *in natura* acquired by trade, or whether it involves a manufacturing enterprise, the assets of which consist of buildings, machinery, cash, raw materials, partly and wholly manufactured goods, which are balanced against liabilities. The important fact is always that a calculation of capital in terms of money is made, whether by modern book-keeping methods or in any other way, however primitive and crude. Everything is done in terms of balances: at the beginning of the enterprise an initial balance, before every individual decision a calculation to ascertain its probable profitableness, and at the end a final balance to ascertain how much profit has been made. For instance, the initial balance of a *commenda*[1] transaction would determine an agreed money value of the assets put into it (so far as they were not in money form already), and a final balance would form the estimate on which to base the distribution of profit and loss at the end. So far as the transactions are rational, calculation underlies every single action of the partners. That a really accurate calculation or estimate may not exist, that the procedure is pure guesswork, or simply traditional and conventional, happens even today in every form of capitalistic enterprise where the circumstances do not demand strict accuracy. But these are points affecting only the *degree* of rationality of capitalistic acquisition.

[1] A *commenda* was a form of medieval trading association which usually was organized to carry out one sea voyage; when that voyage was completed, the profits were divided among the partners. [Editor's note]

For the purpose of this conception all that matters is that an actual adaptation of economic action to a comparison of money income with money expenses takes place, no matter how primitive the form. Now in this sense capitalism and capitalistic enterprises, even with a considerable rationalization of capitalistic calculation, have existed in all civilized countries of the earth, so far as economic documents permit us to judge — in China, India, Babylon, Egypt, Mediterranean antiquity, and the Middle Ages, as well as in modern times. These were not merely isolated ventures, but economic enterprises which were entirely dependent on the continual renewal of capitalistic undertakings, and even continuous operations. However, trade especially was for a long time not continuous like our own, but consisted essentially in a series of individual undertakings. Only gradually did the activities of even the large merchants acquire an inner cohesion (with branch organizations, etc.). In any case, the capitalistic enterprise and the capitalistic entrepreneur, not only as occasional but as regular entrepreneurs, are very old and were very widespread.

Now, however, the Occident has developed capitalism both to a quantitative extent, and (carrying this quantitative development) in types, forms, and directions which have never existed elsewhere. All over the world there have been merchants, wholesale and retail, local and engaged in foreign trade. Loans of all kinds have been made, and there have been banks with the most various functions, at least comparable to ours of, say, the sixteenth century. Sea loans,[2] *commenda,* and transactions and associations similar to the *Kommanditgesellschaft,*[3] have all been widespread, even as continuous businesses. Whenever money finances of public bodies have existed,

[2] A method used in the Middle Ages to insure against loss at sea without violating regulations concerning usury. [Editor's note]

[3] A form of company between the partnership and the limited liability corporation. At least one of the participants is made liable without limit, while the others enjoy limitation of liability to the amount of their investment. [Translator's note]

money-lenders have appeared, as in Babylon, Hellas, India, China, Rome. They have financed wars and piracy, contracts and building operations of all sorts. In overseas policy they have functioned as colonial entrepreneurs, as planters with slaves, or directly or indirectly forced labour, and have farmed domains, offices, and, above all, taxes. They have financed party leaders in elections and *condottieri* in civil wars. And, finally, they have been speculators in chances for pecuniary gain of all kinds. This kind of entrepreneur, the capitalistic adventurer, has existed everywhere. With the exception of trade and credit and banking transactions, their activities were predominantly of an irrational and speculative character, or directed to acquisition by force, above all the acquisition of booty, whether directly in war or in the form of continuous fiscal booty by exploitation of subjects.

The capitalism of promoters, large-scale speculators, concession hunters, and much modern financial capitalism even in peace time, but, above all, the capitalism especially concerned with exploiting wars, bears this stamp even in modern Western countries, and some, but only some, parts of large-scale international trade are closely related to it, today as always.

But in modern times the Occident has developed, in addition to this, a very different form of capitalism which has appeared nowhere else: the rational capitalistic organization of (formally) free labour. Only suggestions of it are found elsewhere. . . . Even real domestic industries with free labour have definitely been proved to have existed in only a few isolated cases outside the Occident. The frequent use of day labourers led in a very few cases — especially State monopolies, which are, however, very different from modern industrial organization — to manufacturing organizations, but never to a rational organization of apprenticeship in the handicrafts like that of our Middle Ages. . . .

And just as, or rather because, the world has known no rational organization of labour outside the modern Occident, it has known no rational socialism. Of course, there has been civic economy, a civic food-supply policy, mercantilism and welfare policies of princes, rationing, regulation of economic life, protectionism, and *laissez-faire* theories (as in China). The world has also known socialistic and communistic experiments of various sorts: family, religious, or military communism, State socialism (in Egypt), monopolistic cartels, and consumers' organizations. But although there have everywhere been civic market privileges, companies, guilds, and all sorts of legal differences between town and country, the concept of the citizen has not existed outside the Occident, and that of the bourgeoisie outside the modern Occident. Similarly, the proletariat as a class could not exist, because there was no rational organization of free labour under regular discipline. Class struggles between creditor and debtor classes; landowners and the landless, serfs, or tenants; trading interests and consumers or landlords, have existed everywhere in various combinations. But even the Western mediaeval struggles between putters-out and their workers exist elsewhere only in beginnings. The modern conflict of the large-scale industrial entrepreneur and free-wage labourers was entirely lacking. And thus there could be no such problems as those of socialism.

Hence in a universal history of culture the central problem for us is not, in the last analysis, even from a purely economic viewpoint, the development of capitalistic activity as such, differing in different cultures only in form: the adventurer type, or capitalism in trade, war, politics, or administration as sources of gain. It is rather the origin of this sober bourgeois capitalism with its rational organization of free labour. Or in terms of cultural history, the problem is that of the origin of the Western bourgeois class and of its peculiarities, a problem which is certainly closely connected with that of the origin of the capitalistic organization of labour, but is not quite the same thing. For the bourgeois as a class existed prior to the development of the peculiar modern form of capitalism, though, it is true, only in the Western hemisphere.

Now the peculiar modern Western form of capitalism has been, at first sight, strongly influenced by the development of technical possibilities. Its rationality is today essentially dependent on the calculability of the most important technical factors. But this means fundamentally that it is dependent on the peculiarities of modern science, especially the natural sciences based on mathematics and exact and rational experiment. On the other hand, the development of these sciences and of the technique resting upon them now receives important stimulation from these capitalistic interests in its practical economic application. It is true that the origin of Western science cannot be attributed to such interests. Calculation, even with decimals, and algebra have been carried on in India, where the decimal system was invented. But it was only made use of by developing capitalism in the West, while in India it led to no modern arithmetic or book-keeping. Neither was the origin of mathematics and mechanics determined by capitalistic interests. But the *technical* utilization of scientific knowledge, so important for the living conditions of the mass of people, was certainly encouraged by economic considerations, which were extremely favourable to it in the Occident. But this encouragement was derived from the peculiarities of the social structure of the Occident. We must hence ask, from *what* parts of that structure was it derived, since not all of them have been of equal importance?

Among those of undoubted importance are the rational structures of law and of administration. For modern rational capitalism has need, not only of the technical means of production, but of a calculable legal system and of administration in terms of formal rules. Without it adventurous and speculative trading capitalism and all sorts of politically determined capitalisms are possible, but no rational enterprise under individual initiative, with fixed capital and certainty of calculations. Such a legal system and such administration have been available for economic activity in a comparative state of legal and formalistic perfection only in the Occident. We must hence inquire where that law came from. Among other circumstances, capitalistic interests have in turn undoubtedly also helped, but by no means alone nor even principally, to prepare the way for the predominance in law and administration of a class of jurists specially trained in rational law. But these interests did not themselves create that law. Quite different forces were at work in this development. And why did not the capitalistic interests do the same in China or India? Why did not the scientific, the artistic, the political, or the economic development there enter upon that path of rationalization which is peculiar to the Occident?

For in all the above cases it is a question of the specific and peculiar rationalism of Western culture. Now by this term very different things may be understood, as the following discussion will repeatedly show. There is, for example, rationalization of mystical contemplation, that is of an attitude which, viewed from other departments of life, is specifically irrational, just as much as there are rationalizations of economic life, of technique, of scientific research, of military training, of law and administration. Furthermore, each one of these fields may be rationalized in terms of very different ultimate values and ends, and what is rational from one point of view may well be irrational from another. Hence rationalizations of the most varied character have existed in various departments of life and in all areas of culture. To characterize their differences from the viewpoint of cultural history it is necessary to know what departments are rationalized, and in what direction. It is hence our first concern to work out and to explain genetically the special peculiarity of Occidental rationalism, and within this field that of the modern Occidental form. Every such attempt at explanation must, recognizing the fundamental importance of the economic factor, above all take account of the economic conditions. But at the same time the opposite correlation must not be left out of consideration. For though the development of economic rationalism is partly dependent on rational technique and law, it is at the same time determined by the ability and disposition of men to adopt certain types of practical rational conduct. When these types have been obstructed by spiritual obstacles, the development of rational economic conduct has also met serious inner resistance. The magical and religious forces, and the ethical ideas of duty based upon them, have in the past always been among the most important formative influences on conduct. In the studies collected here we shall be concerned with these forces.

Two older essays have been placed at the beginning which attempt, at one important point, to approach the side of the problem which is generally most difficult to grasp: the influence of certain religious ideas on the development of an economic spirit, or the *ethos* of an economic system. In this case we are dealing with the connection of the spirit of modern economic life with the rational ethics of ascetic Protestantism.

CALVINISM AND CAPITALISM:
AN EXPLANATION OF THE WEBER THESIS

KEMPER FULLERTON

Kemper Fullerton was a theologian and a specialist in the study and teaching of the languages of the Old Testament. As a student in both United States and Germany, he held degrees from Princeton University (A.B., M.A., D.D.), was a graduate of Union Theological Seminary in New York, and for several years was a Fellow of Union Theological Seminary at the University of Berlin. The year before he published the article from which this selection is taken, he received an honorary Doctorate of Theology from the University of Tübingen. For many years he was a Professor (and later Professor Emeritus until his death in 1940) of Old Testament Languages and Literature at the Oberlin Graduate School of Theology.

Perhaps in nothing, not even in scientific outlook, is the contrast between the Modern Age and the Middle Ages more striking than in the changed attitude toward money and money-making. In the Middle Ages trade was frowned upon and the money-lender despised. In this attitude church and society generally agreed. The church was always castigating the sin of avarice. The making of money was designated by Thomas Aquinas as "turpitudo," even though he admitted its necessity. The thesis that the shop-keeper could only with difficulty please God was introduced into canon law. Usury, which meant not only extortionate interest but interest of any kind, was prohibited by several councils of the church, and to a usurer the privileges of the sacraments were often denied. Even in those days there were, to be sure, practical qualifications of these theoretical judgments, due to the need of money — a need often as keenly felt by the lords spiritual as by the lords temporal. Nevertheless the generalization is safe that money-making was regarded as socially degrading and morally and religiously dangerous. Today all this is changed. Money-making has become the chief aim of modern civilization. In countless ways, gross or subtle, it determines our lives and thinking. It entices into its service many of the best minds of our college graduates. Even our professions, law, medicine, the ministry (witness the vast development of ecclesiastical advertising), are more and more entangled in its net, while the commercialization of amusements, including our college sports, is notorious.

But at this point a distinction is necessary. The change between the present and the past is not primarily in the greater love of money in the present. In all ages avarice has been found in all classes. Whether it is now more widespread than heretofore is not the important question. That difference, if it exists, would be only quantitative, not qualitative. Nor is the change in the

From Kemper Fullerton, "Calvinism and Capitalism," *The Harvard Theological Review,* XXI (1928), 163–191. By permission of Harvard Divinity School.

method of money-making, its technology, the distinguishing characteristic. Capitalism has existed in one form or another in every age. The real difference, which it is Professor Max Weber's aim to point out and more closely examine in the essay which the present article discusses, is found in what he calls "the spirit of modern capitalism." The difference is psychological, or, more precisely formulated, it is found in a new "ethos" of money-making. What is meant by this spirit of modern capitalism and, an even more interesting question, what is its origin?

Before attempting to answer these questions Weber makes a preliminary historical observation of great interest. He notes that the great trading-classes of the bourgeoisie have been chiefly found in the ranks of Protestantism. The proportion of leading industrialists, traders, financiers, technical experts, is greater among Protestants than among Catholics. The latter have always been more inclined to the handicrafts. The Spaniards early recognized this. They said that heresy (that is, the Calvinism of the Netherlands) furthers the spirit of trade. More specifically, these same classes in the sixteenth and seventeenth centuries were mainly found not merely among the Protestants, but among the Protestants of Calvinistic or Calvinistically allied churches — the Huguenots of France, the great Dutch traders, the Puritans of England. In other words, the growth of capitalism in its modern expression coincided to a remarkable degree with that form of Protestantism which, as contrasted with Lutheranism, Weber calls the "ascetic" form. Montesquieu seems to have recognized this singular coincidence when he said of the Protestant English that "they are superior to all other peoples in three things, piety, trade, and liberty." Is this coincidence merely an historical accident, or is there some inner organic connection between these two phenomena, the rise of modern capitalism (or rather of the spirit of modern capitalism) and the great Protestant "ascetic" movement, dominated very largely by the Calvinistic theology? At first

sight the two seem quite unlike each other and in their existing forms they really are unlike. In order to answer this question Weber next seeks to define more nearly what he means by the spirit of modern capitalism.

He chooses as the starting-point in his analysis of the spirit of modern capitalism Benjamin Franklin's "Advice to a Young Tradesman":

Remember that time is money. He who could make ten shillings a day through his work, but goes walking half the day or idles in his room, even if he spends for his amusement only a sixpence, may not count this alone [as a loss], but he has, in addition, given up five shillings, or rather thrown it away. Remember that credit is money. If anyone leaves money with me after it falls due, he makes me a present of the interest. This amounts to a considerable sum if a man has good credit and makes good use of it. Remember that money can beget money [a theory the reverse of Aristotle's!]. Five shillings turned over become six . . . and so on till they are a hundred pounds sterling. He who kills a sow destroys its progeny till the thousandth generation. He who wastes five shillings murders [note the unconscious choice of an ethical term here!], all that might have been produced by it, whole columns of pounds sterling.

It is not simply the saving of money for the use to which it can afterwards be put that Franklin has in mind. The idea which really lies back of it is that of making money as an end in itself, as a profession, as a "calling," in which all one's best capacities are to be engaged. Franklin quotes Prov. 22, 29, "Seest thou a man diligent [note the word!] in business? he shall stand before kings." Here it is not so much the reward of efficiency as diligence, or the duty of efficiency, in which Franklin is interested. He means to enjoin not the love of money but the obligation to make money. But where an obligation exists, there an ethical element enters in. It is this feeling of responsibility to make money which Weber finds the most significant difference between modern capitalism and the forms of capi-

ethos

talism current in past ages. In other words, the difference lies in the spirit, the peculiar ethos of modern capitalism, defined as a sense of obligation in money-making. When one seriously examines this sense of obligation, the question at once arises, Why does it exist? A reason can be seen for making money in order to provide for a man's family, or to secure prestige and power, or even to lead a life of self-indulgence. But there would seem to be something irrational in a ceaseless drive to make money and ever more money. It is not a native instinct in man. In fact, it has to assert itself against his native instincts. One of the greatest difficulties which capitalism in its modern forms has had to contend with is the frequent lack of this feeling of responsibility among workmen. For the intensification of production a sense of responsibility on the part of workmen is absolutely necessary. But if in an emergency higher wages are offered for increased exertion, workmen will indeed work harder, but are apt to work for only half the time; they prefer to halve their time rather than double their wages. The opposite method, that of starving workmen into harder work by reducing their wages, is even less successful in stimulating productivity. (But Weber notices, in passing, that among working-people of pietistic circles in Germany this feeling of obligation is often highly developed!) This indifference to the obligation to make all the money a workman possibly can is called by Weber "traditionalism," as opposed to the spirit of modern capitalism. Before the modern era this traditionalism prevailed not only among the working classes but among the employing classes as well, and Weber draws a picture of the easy-going life of the trader in earlier times. He felt no particular obligation to increase his trade. He felt no anxiety lest, if his trade did not increase, it would dry up. He did not feel it necessary to turn most of his profits back into his business instead of enjoying himself. An excellent example of the spirit of traditionalism is a bazaar-keeper in Damascus of whom I was told when I was in the Near East. My informant said he always liked to trade with this particular dealer. But there was one difficulty. You never could tell when he would be in his shop. It was his custom in the morning to go to his little booth, but he would shut up shop, no matter what the hour, whenever he thought he had made enough metallik for the day, and would then go home to smoke his narghile and enjoy himself. The mediaeval man, even a man engaged in capitalistic enterprises, would have understood this Damascene shop-keeper's intermittent trading far better than he would the ceaseless drive of my poor friend. He would probably have thought the oriental mode of life much the more rational of the two.

But there is another element in the spirit of modern capitalism upon which Weber comments, besides this feeling of obligation to make more profits. Those who are most permanently successful in modern business life are usually marked by a certain quality of self-discipline or "asceticism." They are not the spenders and wastrels of the world. They live moderate and abstemious lives. They do not seek display. They must, if they are to be permanently successful, win the confidence of their workmen and customers. They must be trustworthy. Though Weber does not refer to them, John D. Rockefeller and Russell Sage are excellent examples of the type he has in mind. Such men must pass self-denying ordinances upon themselves. Free indulgence in ordinary pleasures and recreations is not for them. A measure of rigid self-discipline is necessary to ultimate success. Thus, in addition to the feeling of obligation, Weber's analysis of the spirit of modern capitalism includes this tinge of "asceticism." Sacrifices are entailed. And for what? In order to make ever larger and larger profits! Again the question must be raised: Is there not an element of irrationality in all this, if it be judged by the usual standards of what makes life worth living? How can this curious phenomenon be explained?

It might be thought that because this spirit of capitalism is at present so necessary

Beruf- calling
Calling -toil

in carrying on the capitalistic processes it is therefore a result of these processes, and the explanation might be given that this feeling of obligation is an adjustment of men's minds to the new economic era that was ushered in by the great discoveries of the fifteenth and sixteenth centuries with their stimulation of trade. But Weber points out that capitalistic forms and capitalistic spirit, which so naturally go together, by no means always coincide. The capitalistic spirit, the feeling of obligation in one's business or calling, was prevalent in seventeenth-century New England, which was founded by preachers and university men in the interest of religion, but wanting in the Southern states, which were developed in the interests of business. The same spirit was wanting in Florence in the fourteenth and fifteenth centuries, in spite of a highly developed form of capitalism, but present in the Pennsylvania backwoods of the eighteenth century amid such primitive economic conditions that, because of the lack of gold, trade was almost reduced to barter and banks were in their infancy. Under such conditions Franklin emphasized the moral obligation of making money. Could there be a greater contrast than in this differing attitude toward money-making? Instead of being "turpitudo," money-making is now itself almost a religion. A religion! Might it be that this strange irrational feeling of obligation to make money, though now unconnected with any religious interest, once had a religious sanction which gave it meaning and support?

The reader will recall the observation that the great trading classes arose and became most fully developed among Protestants rather than Catholics. Is there not here a hint of some strange elusive connection between the Protestant form of religion and money-making?

We have now reached a point where we must embark with Weber on a voyage of rediscovery to a world that for most of us has sunk as completely as Atlantis beneath the waves of the sea. His account of this rediscovered world, and the connection

which he establishes between it and the life of our capitalistic culture today, form the most fascinating part of his essay.

In casting about for a clue to the possible solution of the interesting question just raised, Weber lights upon a curious philological fact. He notes that Luther used the German word *Beruf* ("calling") in a sense which it had never before possessed. Nor is there any precise equivalent for it either in antiquity or Catholicism. It appears in Luther's translation of Ecclesiasticus 11, 21, "Trust in the Lord and abide in thy *Beruf*." From this translation and from Luther's use of the word elsewhere it became a standing word in the vocabulary of the Protestant peoples. Now the Greek word which Luther translates "calling" is πόνος, "toil." But to translate this by "calling" is evidently an interpretation rather than a strict translation. What did Luther mean by it? From his use of the term elsewhere it is clear that he is here thinking of the labor of the secular, everyday life as a God-appointed task, a calling. By means of this word a religious significance thus comes to be attached to the secular life, even down to its humblest details. "God accomplishes all things through you," he tells us, "through you he milks the cow and does the most servile works." But more especially still, this conception of the secular life as a God-appointed task necessarily involves the idea that the proper performance of such a secular task is a religious obligation; and the idea of the obligation to live a religious life within the sphere of the secular which is found in Luther's use of the word "calling" is one of the most momentous contributions which the Reformation made to social theory. How significant it is can be fully appreciated only when the Catholic theory is understood which Luther was attacking through the use of this word. One of the fundamental doctrines of Roman Catholicism is the sharp distinction between the laity and "secular" clergy on the one hand and "religious" orders on the other. The adjective, "religious," was applied, not to the former but to the monks and the nuns.

The latter were "religious" in a sense in which others could not be. A different standard of morals was enjoined upon them. The general obligations of a Christian were comprised in what were known as *praecepta evangelica,* or the morals of the Decalogue, which were in turn practically identified with natural-law morality, or the law written upon the conscience of mankind of which St. Paul speaks in the first chapter of Romans. The religious orders, on the other hand, were obligated to follow the *consilia evangelica,* the higher morality of the gospels, specially expressed in the vows of obedience, poverty, and chastity. This latter morality was impossible of fulfilment in the secular life; in order to practise it, men must withdraw from the world. "Come out from among them and be ye separate," is the motto of monasticism. Thus what may be called a double standard of morality came to exist within the church itself.

Luther's conception of the secular life as a "calling" involved a complete break with this theory. For him no distinction was permissible between two standards of morality, *praecepta evangelica,* to be performed within the world, and *consilia evangelica,* which can be fulfilled only apart from the world. All men are equally obligated to fulfil both the commands and the "advices" of the gospel. And this fulfilment is to be accomplished, not in the cloister, apart from the world, but in the sphere of the secular life itself. This does not mean that Luther's attitude was essentially a "world-affirming" attitude. It was not. He was to a very large degree inwardly estranged from the world. His view, as distinguished from the monastic view, may be summed up in the words, "Be ye in the world but not of it." Nevertheless Luther's conception of "calling" was the first and most important step toward a new appraisal of the secular life. For the Catholic, "calling," or "vocation," was to live the religious life apart from the world. "Calling" for Luther was to live the secular life religiously, to serve God within one's calling (*in vocatione*). The final step remained to

be taken, namely, to serve God by one's calling (*per vocationem*). This step Luther does not seem to have taken in any decisive way. In his earlier writings he had a Pauline indifference to the secular life; it was morally and religiously neutral like eating and drinking. Later, through his opposition to monasticism, which he repudiated as egoistic and an evasion of the duties of love to one's neighbor, he came to look upon the secular life as affording opportunities to express this love. Through the various secular activities of our lives we are to serve others.

But as Luther came more and more under the domination of the predestinarian idea, he began to look on "calling" as an opportunity given to man primarily for the purpose of obeying God by humbly and cheerfully acquiescing in that lot in life to which God had assigned him. Not what a man could accomplish through his calling (*per vocationem*) but the spirit of obedience or resignation which he could exhibit within it (*in vocatione*) was Luther's controlling thought in his conception of the secular life. Thus it came to pass that while Luther opened the way for a new appraisal of the secular life by breaking down the Catholic distinction between it and the religious life, he did not himself develop the vast economic possibilities latent in this new appraisal. As a matter of fact he remained a "traditionalist" in his attitude toward money-making, untouched by the spirit of modern capitalism. Through this new estimate of the secular life we begin dimly, though only dimly, to see how it may possibly have come about that Protestants rather than Catholics have been the chief traders and industrialists; the Protestant religion begins to invade the sphere of the secular. But it is yet a far cry from the religious value which Luther set on the sphere of the secular and the utterly irreligious spirit of modern capitalism. Is there any middle term between these two extremes? The Protestants of Calvinistic origin have been the most conspicuous exponents of successful trade. Is the middle term to be found in this branch of Protestantism? To the examination of the great Calvinistic movement, or, more generally stated, of the disciplinary, or "ascetic," movement in Protestantism as distinct from Lutheranism, we must now turn.

While Luther started from the experience of justification by faith, that is, from the human side of experience, Calvin's attempt to restate the Christian religion as against Rome starts from the conception of God. In his view God is absolute Will, and the only absolute that exists. Hence God is the only being who is perfectly free. Therefore what God wills is right, and must be accepted whether we can understand it or not (which is a fundamentally irrational conception of God). This free and righteous will of God expresses itself in Scripture, according to Calvin, in the double decree of election and reprobation. Calvin's treatment of this doctrine is thoroughly intellectualized; its implications are drawn out by logical processes; experience and emotion play little part in his deductions. In other words, Calvinism as a system, though it starts from an irrational conception of God, is worked out in a thoroughly rationalistic way, and this rationalistic note in the system must be constantly borne in mind as we study its practical consequences.

The first great consequence is what may be called an intellectual as well as practical other-worldliness. Man is not the centre of the system, nor is even Christ, but God. In the words of the famous answer to the first question of the Westminster Shorter Catechism, "Man's chief end is to glorify God and enjoy him forever." This aim gives to life its reason, its *rationale*. Anything that diverts the mind from this one supreme aim is a species of idolatry, a worship of the creature rather than the creator. Out of this suspicion of the creature arises the "ascetic" view of life, so characteristic of Calvinism and of the Puritan movement generally, which continued to prevail even after the dogmatic system of Calvinism became seriously impaired. Again, since the individual is elected by the eternal decree

of God, all intermediaries between God and man are, at least theoretically, excluded. No sacramental grace, no priesthood which controls it, no church, no human help of any kind avails here. The soul stands in the presence of its God in awful isolation. Weber calls this the "dis-enchantment of the world," that is, its emancipation from sacramental magic, begun by Old Testament prophecy, supported by the scientific movement of Hellenism, and now culminating in the Calvinistic polemic against Rome. It is at this point that Calvinism distinguishes itself most sharply from Rome.

Because of the elimination of all intermediaries between God and man there arises at the very heart of the Calvinistic system a tremendous emphasis upon individualism. That this individualism has played a noble part in the cause of human liberty is too often forgotten, but logically it is anti-social. It concentrates the attention upon the self, even at times to the extent of avoiding too intimate friendships as a worship of, or reliance upon, the creature. The gentle Baxter warns us that "it is an *irrational* act and not fit for a *rational* creature to love any one farther than *reason* will allow us. . . . It very often taketh up men's minds so as to hinder their love of God." This intense preoccupation with oneself is effectively illustrated in the opening chapter of the Pilgrim's Progress, where the Pilgrim's flight from the City of Destruction is described:

So I saw in my dream that the man began to run. Now he had not run far from his own door when his wife and children, perceiving it, began to cry after him to return; but the man put his fingers in his ears and ran on, crying, "Life! life! eternal life!"

On the other hand, in sharp contrast with this emphasis upon the individual, Calvinism has shown a much greater genius for social organization than Lutheranism, and with its intense individualism has been able to combine an equally intense social activity. The Pilgrim, in order to get to heaven, does not flee to the desert as an anchorite. His way lies, as Weber points out, through Vanity Fair. Not withdrawal from the world, as in monasticism, but struggle with the world is the Calvinistic idea of life. Not, "Come out from among them and be ye separate," but, "Be ye in the world but not of it," is the new battle cry. Weber points out the striking contrast between the Divine Comedy, which closes with the contemplation of the vision of God, and Paradise Lost, at the end of which Adam and Eve go forth, in a kind of triumphant resignation, to battle with the world. In the Puritan poem, what has been called the "mysticism of action" has been substituted for the mysticism of contemplation. And this action is within the world, within society. But how can the intense individualism of Calvinism and its equally intense social activity be combined? The middle term is here the glory of God. That is the aim of society as well as of the individual. Through the improvement of society God is also glorified. And how is this improvement to be accomplished? Through faithfulness in one's calling. This world of ours was so arranged by God as to serve the needs of mankind. In our calling we too are to follow this cosmic hint of God and serve our fellow men.

But at this point Luther's conception of "calling" undergoes in Calvinism a significant transformation. It will be remembered that Luther considered our calling to be the means of expressing either love to our neighbor or our acquiescence in the divine will concerning our lives. In the former case a personal, humane interest in our neighbor was the natural result; in the latter case there develops a rather quietistic attitude toward life. But by the introduction of the greater glory of God as the supreme and absorbing motive of all human endeavor, both these consequences of Luther's conception of calling become modified in very important ways. In the first place, since the work for the regeneration of society is now to be done primarily for the glory of God, the emotional, humanitarian element in what we today call the "social-service ideal" is largely eliminated. The

general good of the many takes the place of personal interest in the individual. Social service becomes, to use Weber's term, "depersonalized." It is social only because it is performed within society. It ministers, indeed, to the good of society, but it is not done primarily for the sake of society. It is done for the glory of God. If it were done for the sake of the individual alone, that would set the creature in place of the creator, and so be a species of idolatry. Two illustrations will make clear what Weber means by a depersonalized social activity. In the life of Adoniram Judson his reflections are recorded after he had tried to evangelize the city of Proom in Burmah and was stoned out of town. His sad comment was that its inhabitants would have the chains of hell fastened upon them more tightly because they had heard the gospel message and refused it. If the purely personal and humanitarian interest had been uppermost, it would probably have prevented Judson from exposing the people of Proom to such a dreadful risk. But as it was, he felt that he was discharging the will of God: "Go ye into all the world, and preach the gospel to every creature." In 1915 the present writer was ordered out of Palestine by the Turks and left the country in company with many members of the religious orders and Protestant missionaries. One of these, a member of the Christian and Missionary Alliance, was asked if he expected to return after the war. He was doubtful about it, and gave as his reason that he had already preached the gospel in all the villages of Palestine and had thus fulfilled the will of God. The heroic but in fact absurd slogan of the Student Volunteer Movement in its earlier stages, "The Evangelization of the World in this Generation," springs from the same depersonalized conception of the social activity of the missionary. The evangelization of the world because God wills it takes the place of the salvation of the world for its own sake. Contrast the appealing close of the book of Jonah.

In the next place, though work for the good of mankind is in a certain measure depersonalized when the motive of love to our neighbor is modulated into the motive of God's glory, there is no lessening of the pressure of work. If God has ordered and arranged this great physical universe for the good of man and through this manifests his glory, it is supremely important to correlate society to the same great end, and this is done through the fulfilment of such duties in our calling as are imposed by the laws of nature. No mere quietistic acceptance of the universe is possible here. The tremendous drive of God's will and God's glory lies back of all work in our calling. The normal result is a tense and ceaseless activity. Thus the new motive of life, to glorify God and enjoy him forever, this completely otherworldly orientation of our existence, leads to a rationalized and a quasi-ascetic view of life in general (we are to enjoy forever God, not creature-pleasures), a depersonalized and therefore rationalized view of love to our neighbor, and ceaseless activity within the sphere of the secular in order to bring the secular within the final aim of life, the glory of God. But this drive toward activity in one's calling which, along with the rationalizing of life, Weber wishes especially to emphasize, is intensified even more directly by another consideration which originates in the heart of the Calvinistic system, namely in the doctrine of election.

The great question for every non-sacramental religion is, How can I be sure that I am saved? or, in the Calvinistic formula, How can I be sure that I am one of the elect? In Roman Catholicism the church could mediate to the believer this assurance through the sacraments, especially the sacrament of penance, but in Calvinism, as we have seen, all authoritative intermediaries are swept aside and the soul is left alone in the presence of its Maker. And its Maker's will is inscrutable. How, then, is the soul to be assured of its election? At first the question was not so insistent in Calvin's own thinking. The promises of God in Scripture and Calvin's own unwavering faith in Christ made doubt impossible. But as Calvinism developed, the question

pressed more and more for an answer. Two answers were given. Assurance can be obtained either from the *testimonium Spiritus Sancti*, the inner consciousness of the individual that the power of God is *in* him, or from the ability consistently to perform good works, the consciousness of the individual that the power of God is working *through* him. In the first case he is conscious that he is a vessel, in the second that he is an instrument. While the first method of assurance was undoubtedly emphasized by Calvin himself and always played, at least theoretically, a part in Calvinistic theology, the second method became the more important in practice. And it is at this point that one of the main differences between Calvinism and Lutheranism emerges. Lutheran piety is more of the passive, contemplative, mystical type. It shares with Catholic mystics the idea of the mystical union with God, in which God enters into the soul, or, rather, in which the soul becomes absorbed in God and thus finds assurance. But Calvinism had a highly transcendentalized conception of God to which the idea of the mystical union was inwardly alien, and, as a highly rationalized system of thought, it was suspicious of the emotional life favored by the idea of the mystical union. Emotions can deceive. For these reasons both the logic and the philosophy of Calvinism worked more and more away from the idea of assurance based upon inward experience, in which there was an important point of contact with the Lutheran conception of the mystical union, and came to rest for the assurance of election upon the outward sensible signs of a pious life. Certitude is to be preserved not so much through the feelings as in action. It is interesting to notice that whereas the Westminster Confession of Faith still relies on the promises of Scripture and the Testimony of the Spirit as the formal grounds of Assurance in the section devoted to that subject (section 18), it is held in section 16, on Good Works, that these *strengthen* assurance. Similarly the Savoy Declaration maintains that Christians are saints "by effectual calling visibly manifested by their profession and walking." Objective, recognizable signs in the Christian's mode of life are now required in addition to inward feeling in order to give assurance. The great scriptural support for this idea is 1 John 2, 3: "Hereby we do know that we know him, if we keep his commandments." Thus once more we arrive at the emphasis upon action which is so characteristic of Calvinism. The will of God, God's own glory which is at the same time the chief end of man, combined with the soul's necessity of gaining an assurance of election, produces a tremendous drive toward action, as contrasted with the contemplative life.

We have now reached the point where the bearing of all this upon the peculiar Calvinistic conception of "calling" may be seen, and at the same time the similarities and differences between Calvinism on the one hand and Roman Catholicism and Lutheranism on the other are most clearly revealed.

(1) Both Calvinism and Catholicism lay great emphasis upon works. Lutheran theologians often twitted the Calvinists with this romanizing insistence upon works. But there was a sharp distinction between the Romanist and the Calvinist doctrine of works. In the former, works are the means of salvation; in the latter, the means of assurance. By faith alone could men be saved — the Calvinist held fast to this great Reformation principle.

(2) But Calvinism followed Luther in ignoring the Catholic distribution of good works between *praecepta evangelica* and *consilia evangelica*. The former, as we have seen, furnished the standards for the laity and secular clergy, the latter for the religious orders. In the case of the laity, Mother Church mercifully took account of the weakness of the flesh. Any defective performance of the "precepts," due to the corruption of man's nature, could be made good by sacramental grace (penance). The consequence was that Catholic lay morality took on, in the Protestant view, a certain casualness. Lapses were easily made good.

It was far otherwise with the performance of the *consilia*. Within the secular life these could be performed only to a limited degree; and so life withdrawn from the world now becomes necessary. But within this withdrawn life itself the sternest self-discipline is required. The whole of it is subjected to the strictest and most constant regulation. The "ascetic" ideal, the necessity of which was waived for the laity, is reserved for the religious orders, and for them not even the sacraments could ameliorate its severity. It is true that here also lapses could be made good by the sacraments, but if "merit" were to be gained, the number of lapses must be reduced as much as possible. Hence the whole monastic life had to be rationalized upon the basis of the "ascetic" ideal. Now when Luther broke down the distinction between the life of the laity and the life of the monks, and contended that the full Christian life could be lived within the sphere of the secular, he did not work out the final consequences of his new position. He did not introduce the rationalized, "ascetic" ideal of monasticism into the secular life. We have seen how in Luther's idea of "calling," that is of the Christian life in the secular sphere, there is expressed either a quietistic acquiescence in the will of God or love to our neighbor. He laid little emphasis on works, much less on a systematized and rationalized life of action. "Tears," he said, "precede works and suffering surpasses doing." His experience of forgiveness and of justification by faith led him to emphasize the inner life of the Christian rather than his outer life. Thus Lutheranism in its main tendency was never ascetic. The piety of the Lutheran was more like the casual piety of the Catholic layman. It was a piety dominated by emotion rather than by reason, and this characteristic was favored also by the considerable measure of sacramentarianism which Luther took over from Catholicism. But in Calvinism all this is reversed. By the ideal of man's chief end as the glorification of God, an ideal that is God-willed, and by the practical necessity of having some means of assurance, a necessity that springs from the doctrine of election when the sacramental approach to God is abandoned, the basis is furnished for a new conception of the secular life. The ideal of discipline, or "asceticism," proper to Catholic monasticism is now transferred to the secular life. Within the sphere of this life lies one's calling (so Luther), but calling now becomes the means of moral discipline (so Calvin). Just as the monk apart from the world must subject the whole of his life to the severest regulation, so now the Calvinist within the world must rigorously discipline himself. His life is to be a rationalized life of systematic self-control. The monk did this to secure a reward. It was a work of supererogation. The Calvinist did it not for reward — that would be to deny the grace of God in election, but in order to secure the sense of assurance that he was elect. Yet this statement is not quite exact. The Calvinist practised self-discipline not even to secure assurance; he practised it for the glory of God, and in the practice of it assurance came. Assurance itself was not the aim but the consequence of this discipline, a kind of by-product, though a by-product of immense importance.

(3) But further, as merit was not secured by the Catholic except through extraordinary effort, through works of supererogation, so *full* assurance did not come to the Calvinist except through perseverance. He must continue in good works if he is to continue in assurance. Thus the Calvinist, as contrasted with the Lutheran, was led again to transfer the Catholic monastic ideal of strict discipline to the secular life, the life of "calling." According to Sebastian Franck the significance of the Reformation is just this, that "every Christian must be a monk *his whole life long*." Instead of the spiritual aristocracy of the monks apart from the world, we now have, as Weber puts it, "a spiritual aristocracy of the elect within the world." We can now understand what the Calvinistic or, more generally, the Puritan conception of "calling" is, and in what respects it resembles or differs from Catholicism and Lutheranism. It is the life

of strict discipline (an idea borrowed from Catholic monasticism) lived in the secular sphere (an idea borrowed from Luther) with the sole intent of glorifying God and with the blessed sense of assurance of election as its reward (the special contribution of Calvinism). We have thus finally arrived at the idea of the service of God through one's calling (*per vocationem*) as contrasted with Luther's idea of this service in one's calling (*in vocatione*). This life of calling must be quasiascetic, for the secular life tempts to the worship of the creature and so would detract from God's glory. This "asceticism" takes the form of the strictest regulation of the whole of life, as in monasticism. Assurance is attained only through perseverance. Life thus becomes thoroughly rationalized, Calvinistic piety at this point contrasting with Lutheran piety. It is rationalized by its aim, the glory of God, and by its method, a life of ceaseless watchful self-control. All this led practically to the development of an immensely intensified moral activity within the sphere of the secular life as the most noticeable characteristic of the Calvinistic churches and of similar Protestantism generally, a moral activity which has probably never been equalled before or since. It is (*a*) this rationalized theory of life, (*b*) this intensified mood for work, and (*c*) the quasiascetic discipline which accompanies both theory and mood that have immediate interest for Weber. Such an immense output of spiritual energy could not fail profoundly to influence subsequent generations. Can it be that these three factors, which grew directly out of the Calvinistic theology in its distinction from Rome on the one hand and from Lutheranism on the other, furnish the key to the development of the spirit of modern capitalism? Do these aspects of Calvinism furnish the middle term between Luther's conception of "calling" performed in the secular life and that conception of money-making as in itself a "calling" which in part constitutes the spirit of modern capitalism?

In the last main section of his essay

Weber undertakes to show how this rationalized, strenuously active, methodically "ascetic" mode of life, represented by the Puritan conception of "calling," furnishes the religious basis of capitalism, without which capitalism would never have attained the control which it now exercises over the minds of men. After all, however blind economists may be to the fact, metaphysical convictions are the only ones which have the power absolutely to dominate men's lives. Economic reasons alone cannot account for the extraordinary power in the western civilization of today which the money-making motive exerts. The whole point of Weber's essay is to show that something deeper, more transcendental, more idealistic, is at work here, and must be reckoned with if the psychology of capitalism, its spirit or temper, is to be adequately explained.

If one looks into Baxter's "The Saints' Everlasting Rest" or his "Christian Directory" or similar pastoral works of the Puritan divines (and it is such practical works rather than the more theoretical dogmatic discussions which reflect the real moral interests of the masses), one is at first sight struck by the suspicious attitude toward riches expressed in all these writings, in full harmony with the similar warnings of the mediaeval church. The possession of riches is regarded as dangerous, and equally so the pursuit of them. Riches tempt to confidence and contentment therein, to laziness and sensuality. The pursuit of them diverts from the main object of life, the glory of God. But in conjunction with all these warnings, and unconsciously confusing them, another note is sounded by these writers. They are constantly exhorting to industry. The saints' everlasting rest is a rest in the next life, not in this one. Here it behooves man to work, and ever more to work.

There are two chief motives given for work. Work is still, as it always has been in the western church, a means of discipline. It is the best prophylactic against what the Puritan called the "unclean life," against the sloth and sensuality which riches so often engender. Work in one's calling is Baxter's prescription against sexual temptation as well as against religious doubts. Again, work is to be done because God commanded it, in other words for his glory. This meant that utilitarian motives were disregarded or at least subordinated. So far as this life is concerned, work becomes an end in itself. It gains a meaning beyond itself only when looked at *sub specie aeternitatis*, from a religious and other-worldly point of view.

It is for action [says Baxter] that God maintaineth us and our activities. Work is the moral as well as the natural end of power. . . . It is action that God is most served and honored by. . . . The public welfare or the good of many is to be valued above our own.

This last sentence sounds like an expression of our own social-service ideal. It must be understood in the light of what has already been said as to the religious, depersonalized interest in public welfare, yet it does form, as Weber suggests, the point of transition from the motive of the glory of God to the utilitarianism of the later liberal theology.

Again Baxter says:

Will not wealth excuse [from work]? Answer: It may excuse you from some sordid sort of work, by making you more serviceable to another, but you are no more excused from the service of work . . . than the poorest man. . . . Though they [the rich] have no outward want to urge them, they have as great a necessity to obey God. . . . God has strictly commanded it [work] to all.

Even Zinzendorf says: "One does not work simply to live, but one lives to work." The great scriptural warrant for the exhortation to work is 2 Thess. 3, 10, "that if any would not work, neither shall he eat." This passage emphasizes not the reward, but the duty, of work. The Puritan will make the most of his calling. A bee-like industriousness is enjoined.

God hath commanded you [urges Baxter]

some way or other to labor for your daily bread and not to live as drones of the sweat of others.

And again:

Be wholly taken up in diligent business of your lawful callings when you are not exercised in the more immediate service of God. . . . Labor hard in your calling. . . . See that you have a calling which will find you employment for all the time which God's immediate service spareth.

The terrific Puritan drive toward intense activity is illustrated in various ways in Baxter's writings. For example, it leads him to elaborate the reasons for various callings. Specialization in callings educates and trains the skill of the laborer, and so enables him to increase his output quantitatively and to better it qualitatively. It thus makes for the common good, which is the good of the most people — ideas these which, as Weber reminds us, strikingly resemble the economic principles of Adam Smith. But it cannot be too often repeated that this apparent utilitarianism of Baxter is not in his case real utilitarianism. It springs out of religious interests, not out of humanitarian or economic interests. It is, so to speak, the "ascetic" rather than the economic use of "calling." Industry in one's calling is the expression of the methodically disciplined life devoted to the glory of God. But, and this is to be remembered in view of what follows, the mood for work in such an "ascetic" Protestantism, although engendered by religious considerations, may easily become diverted to a purely economic interest when once the other-worldly point of view is abandoned.

Again, the emphasis upon activity is indicated by what is said by Baxter and others on the use of time:

Keep up a high esteem of time and be every day more careful that you lose none of your time than you are that you lose none of your gold and silver. And if vain recreations, dressings, feastings, idle talk, unprofitable company or sleep be any of them temptations to rob you of your time, accordingly heighten your watchfulness.

With these warnings of Baxter may be compared that of Matthew Henry: "Those who are prodigal of their time despise their own souls." Sloth becomes one of the deadly sins. It is, so to speak, a continuous sin, and thus interferes in the most dangerous way with the methodically disciplined life. To sleep more than six or at most eight hours is, according to Baxter, morally reprehensible. "Sloth," he says, "destroys the state of grace." We have not yet reached Franklin's "Time is money," but we have arrived at its religious counterpart. Time is infinitely valuable, for every lost hour detracts from the glory of God.

Now all this emphasis upon industry and efficiency in a man's calling insensibly leads to a new attitude toward riches, in sharp contrast with the warnings against them already cited. As a matter of fact, the religious and disciplinary use of one's calling has much the same result as the directly economic exploitation of it. It inevitably leads to the accumulation of riches. It is permissible to change one's calling if the glory of God can be better subserved. Practically this means, if the new calling is a more useful one; and the standards for judging its usefulness are first, its moral character, secondly, the importance of the goods to be produced, and thirdly, its profitableness, for if God who orders our lives provides a chance for profit, he has his own purposes in this, and therefore the chance of profit must be accepted. Thus Baxter says:

When God shows you a way in which you can lawfully make more without danger to your soul or to others than you can in some other way, and when you reject this way and follow the way that brings in less, then you cross one of the purposes of your calling. You refuse to be God's steward and to accept his gifts in order to use them for others when he so demands. Of course [Baxter continues, as though aware of the danger of this advice] you are not to labor to be rich for the purposes of fleshy indulgence, but for God's sake.

To strive for riches as an exercise in one's

calling is thus not only permissible, but commendable.

You may labor in that manner that tendeth most to success and lawful gain. You are bound to improve your talents.

It was frequently argued that to wish to be poor was as absurd as to wish to be sick. As scriptural warrant for all this the parable of the talents did yeoman's service. Thus arises the strange anomaly that the pursuit of riches, which is such a danger to the soul, since it tends to divert it from doing all things to the glory of God, has become, from the standpoint of magnifying one's calling, not only permissible but a duty, and the possession of riches, which tempts to sensuality and sloth, has become a mark of faithfulness in the discharge of one's calling. It is clear that in this whole development the decisive thing is the idea of "calling," that is, of the methodically disciplined mode of life within the sphere of the secular. The more intense the life of calling, the more God is honored; the more consistently such a life is lived, the more sure one can be of salvation. All this works out into an intensified industriousness, into the mood for work, and the natural economic result is riches. The most earnest adherents of the disciplinary ideal of Protestantism thus come to serve the interests of Capitalism. This result must now be studied more in detail.

The direct economic effects of the Puritan mode of life in calling are manifested in two ways. In the first place the "ascetic" mode of life worked powerfully toward the limitation of consumption. The Puritan looked, for example, with suspicion upon fine clothes. He looked with suspicion upon all the enjoyments of the senses as inclining to the worship of the creature. As a protest against the extravagant life of the feudal nobility the Puritan exalted the idea of stewardship. Enjoyment must not cost anything. To spend money upon one's self leads to unfaithfulness in stewardship.

Frugality comes to be a cardinal virtue. Baxter says:

Every penny which is paid upon yourselves or your children or your friends must be done by God's own appointment, and to serve and please him [the glory of God motive]. Watch narrowly, or else that thievish, carnal self will leave God nothing.

Accordingly, what is spent upon oneself must be strictly limited. It also follows that the more property one has, the greater the sense of stewardship. It must be kept unimpaired and even increased, as Jesus taught in the parable of the talents, for this redounds to the glory of God.

In the second place, the intensified activity in one's calling which Puritanism encouraged led to a vastly increased production. Money-making was now freed from the traditional opprobrium which had attached to it. Profits had already been legalized. Calvin himself had seen to that, when, for the first time in history, he had advocated the permissibility of usury (interest). But now profits were looked upon as willed by God, as a mark of his favor and a proof of success in one's calling. The Puritans continued to wage war against the dangers of riches, yet this was not in opposition to rational business, but, as Weber puts it, to irrational consumption, to the extravagance and dissipation which wealth might encourage. Their attack was directed against indulgence in all the external forms of luxury which characterized the feudal aristocracy as a worship of the creature and as opposed to the rational, God-willed use of possessions for the good of the individual and the community. The limit of the permissible in consumption is defined by the word comfort. It was extravagance, display, that was sinful. The ideal of the home takes the place of the feudal ideal of the palace. So far as production was concerned, Puritanism fought against injustice in money-making, against hoarding, against mammonism, the love of riches for their own sake.

But at this point Puritanism found itself

in a dilemma. On the one hand the pursuit of wealth for its own sake was sinful. On the other the religious value set upon constant, systematic, efficient work in one's calling as the readiest means of securing the certainty of salvation and of glorifying God became a most powerful agency in economic expansion. The rigid limitations of consumption on the one hand and the methodical intensification of production on the other could have but one result — the accumulation of capital. But the Puritan attitude to calling, with its almost automatic result in accumulation of riches, was destined to become more influential than the Puritan fear of riches. To a very large extent the disciplinary rationalization of life as "calling" accounts for the spirit of modern capitalism. It is not the accumulation of capital in itself that is the decisive thing, but rather a methodical accumulation of it which is a chief characteristic of modern capitalism. And this methodical accumulation has at least one of its main motives in the Calvinistic conception of life as calling. Wherever the Puritan theory of life was held, it strengthened the tendency toward a rationalized, bourgeois, economic mode of life. The Puritan, as Weber expresses it, "stood at the cradle of the economic man." Weber clinches his argument by the following remarkable paragraph from one of John Wesley's sermons:

I fear whenever riches have increased, the essence of religion has decreased in the same proportion. Therefore I do not see how it is possible in the nature of things for any revival of true religion to continue long. For religion must necessarily produce both industry and frugality, and these cannot but produce riches. But as riches increase, so will pride, anger, and love of the world in all its branches. How then is it possible that Methodism, that is, a religion of the heart, though it flourishes now like a green bay tree, should continue in this state? For the Methodists in every place grow diligent and frugal. Consequently they increase in goods. Hence they proportionately increase in pride, in anger, in the desire of the flesh, the desire of the eyes, and the pride of life. So, although the form of religion remains, the spirit is swiftly vanishing away. Is there no way to prevent this continued decay of pure religion? We ought not to prevent people from being diligent and frugal; we must exhort all Christians to gain all they can and to save all they can, that is, in effect, to grow rich. What way can we take that our money-making may not sink us to the nethermost hell? There is one way, and there is no other under heaven. If those who gain all they can and save all they can will also give all they can [the 'ascetic' motive], then, the more they gain the more they will grow in grace and the more treasure they will lay up in heaven.

To this passage I would add another taken from one of the last sermons preached by Wesley before his death:

After you have gained all you can and saved all you can, spend not one pound, one shilling, one penny, to gratify either the desire of the flesh, the desire of the eyes, or the pride of life, or for any other end than to please and glorify God [note the usual motive]. Having avoided this rock on the right hand, beware of that on the left. Hoard nothing. Lay up no treasure on earth; give all you can, that is, all you have. I defy all men upon earth, yea all angels in heaven, to find any other way to extract the poison from riches. . . . You who receive 500 pounds a year and spend only 200, do you give back 300 to God? If not, you certainly rob God of that 300. . . . Nay, may I not do what I will with my own? Here lies the ground of your mistake. It is not your own. It cannot be, unless you are lord of heaven and earth.

In these citations we have in a nutshell most of those fundamental ideas of Protestant "asceticism" which Weber has been describing. Wesley correctly foresaw the dangers which would befall the church through the very virtues which Puritanism emphasized. What he did not foresee was the cosmic extent of these dangers. He did not foresee a world so dominated by money-making that its whole organization is determined by this one great aim. And now we are prepared to understand the way in which Protestant "asceticism" became transformed into the spirit of modern capitalism.

As the great economic movements of the

seventeenth, eighteenth, and nineteenth centuries developed through the increasing exploitation of the New World, Africa, and Asia, through the consequent growth of foreign trade, and through the rise of industrialism, the making of profits became an end in itself. *But before this was accomplished religion had consecrated money-making.* As Weber says, "What the great religious epoch of the seventeenth century bequeathed to its utilitarian heir was above all else a gloriously, one might even say a pharisaically, good conscience in money-making."

Is it merely a coincidence [asks the Quaker Rowntree] or is it a consequence that the lofty profession of spirituality made by the Friends has gone hand in hand with shrewdness and tact in the transaction of mundane affairs? Real piety favors the success of the trader by insuring his integrity [faithfulness in calling] and fostering habits of prudence and forethought, important items in obtaining that standing and credit in the commercial world which are requisite for the steady accumulation of wealth.

The relationship of the Puritan self-disciplined and methodical life, as seen in the words "integrity," "prudence," "forethought," to the methodical life of business, as seen in the phrase, "the steady accumulation of wealth," could not be more tellingly, because unconsciously, expressed. Every vestige of the old ecclesiastical theory that a tradesman could scarcely please God now disappeared, and the specifically bourgeois ethic represented in Franklin's maxims arose. No longer was money-making a means, by which the assurance of salvation could be secured or God be glorified. It had become an end in itself. The methodical "asceticism" of the Puritan, his thrift and frugality, are now employed in a business interest. Baxter and Wesley exhorted their hearers to save in order not to rob God, and the habit of frugality was established; Franklin exhorts his young tradesman to save in order to accumulate capital. Puritanism had led to the rationalization of life as calling. Then a tragic thing happened. Capitalism saw the business significance of calling, removed the transcendental, otherworldly motive, and transformed "calling" into a job. . . .

THE ECONOMIC ETHIC OF CALVINISM

ERNST TROELTSCH

Ernst Troeltsch was a lecturer at Göttingen University, a Professor of Theology at Bonn University and later at Heidelberg. He finished his career (he died in 1923) at the University of Berlin. It was at Heidelberg that Troeltsch was in close association with Max Weber while he was writing *The Social Teaching of the Christian Churches.* Troeltsch's purpose in this work was to determine how far the origin, growth, and modifications of Christianity, "as well as the arrest of that growth in modern times," were sociologically determined. All religious, dogmatic, and theological factors he considered as reflex functions of the sociological conditions under which they arose.

T HE BEGINNINGS of the economic ethic of Calvinism were insignificant, but it developed into a factor of the greatest historical importance, both in the development of the modern economic spirit and in that of Calvinism itself.

From the outset, in its main features the economic ethic of Calvinism was also related to the corresponding aspects of Lutheranism. The Calvinistic ethic shared the Lutheran view about work, to which it assigned a high value, regarding it as the practical exercise of a calling appointed by God, and therefore as Divine worship; it also regarded it as a method of self-discipline and of diverting evil desires. Both Calvin and Luther advocated labour as a universal duty, and abolished monasticism and mendicancy. The Calvinistic economic ethic also agreed with the Lutheran ethic in its "anti-Mammon" spirit, its urgent desire for modesty and moderation, its observance of distinctions in rank, its campaign against luxury, which in this respect was prosecuted with unexampled severity by laws against luxury, and which was supported ecclesiastically by the moral tribunal. Calvin also believed that poverty fostered the Christian virtues more effectively than wealth, and he launched out into violent denunciations of the great commercial cities like Venice and Antwerp. In spite of all this, however, Calvin influenced the "Reformed" economic ethic from the very beginning in such a way that, as in the political sphere, it developed an utterly different spirit from that which animated the Lutheran ethic, both in its primitive and in its present form. This took place, however, without any special and conscious intention on Calvin's part. To a very large extent indeed, the direction in which this ethic evolved was determined by the conditions which governed the practical situation in Geneva.

This was the decisive turning-point: Calvin was convinced that this "anti-Mammon" Christian spirit could express itself and maintain its existence within the sphere of a society which was based essentially upon a money economy, upon trade and industry. Unlike Lutheranism in similar

From Ernst Troeltsch, *The Social Teaching of the Christian Churches,* translated by Olive Wyon, 2 vols. (New York, 1950), II, 641–650, 808–809, 812–815. By permission of the Macmillan Company, New York, and George, Allen and Unwin Ltd., London. Copyright, 1931.

circumstances, Calvin did not hark back to the agrarian patriarchal form of life as the ideal with its closely knit self-contained family life, based as far as possible on primitive methods of production, but he recognized industrial production based on a money economy as the natural foundation and form of professional work alongside of agrarian labour. Calvin himself had a great deal to do with questions of industrial production, and he quite approved of the fact that greater profits were made in trade than in agriculture, since they were simply the reward of carefulness and industry. It is, of course, true that he urged the abolition of certain kinds of business which were questionable from the Christian point of view, such as the manufacture of playing-cards, but in general he was in favour of movement and progress. It was at Calvin's instigation that, with the aid of a State loan, the manufacture of cloth and velvet was introduced into Geneva as a home industry, in order to give work to the poor and unemployed. Later on, when this industry had to be given up on account of the competition of Lyons, the manufacture of watches was introduced with the same aim. He had no desire merely to uphold existing customs and methods of gaining a livelihood. He never denied the necessity for the mobility of an economic system based on industry and trade. All this, however, was due to the Genevan situation and the Genevan atmosphere, which even affected his correspondence; his letters, indeed, deal constantly with the interests of finance, trade, and industry (from the point of view of the manual labourer).

As a jurist and a townsman, from the beginning he may have felt differently about these things than Luther who was a monk, but from the sources it is plain that, in any case, in Geneva he could not think or feel otherwise, if he were to have a practical influence, and that he accepted this necessity without scruple or difficulty. The reason why Calvin was able to accept this situation as he did was probably due to the peculiar character of his practical active ethic, which embraced the whole sphere of public life, and which set in the forefront those elements of behaviour which were practically possible to achieve, while the radical commandments about love and suffering were relegated to the background. If Luther had lived in Geneva under the same conditions we can hardly imagine that he would have thought and felt otherwise than in Wittenberg. If Geneva had been a specially large and active commercial town it is of course probable that even Calvin would have felt it much more difficult to submit to the claims of Capitalism. In Geneva, however, which was surrounded by hostile and rival neighbours, and whose territory was very small, the conditions were narrow and provincial. But it was precisely in this form that Calvin found Capitalism acceptable, as a calling which suited the existing conditions in the city, and which was capable of being combined with loyalty, seriousness, honesty, thrift, and consideration for one's neighbour. It was just because the economic conditions at Geneva were so bourgeois, and on such a small scale, that Capitalism was able to steal into the Calvinistic ethic, while it was rejected by the Catholic and the Lutheran ethic.

That is officially expressed, properly speaking, in the important fact that Calvin and the Calvinistic ethic rejected the canonical veto on usury and the scholastic theory of money, and on the contrary supported a doctrine of money, credit, and usury which were nearer to the modern economic idea, with limitations, certainly, with which we shall have to deal presently. In this Calvin abandoned the purely consumer's standpoint of the previous Christian ethic, and recognized the productive power of money and of credit. Calvin's cooperation with the economic administration of the State, and his conception of the importance of a social life which was well ordered from the economic point of view, for the holy community, shows that he felt an inner connection between economic progress and moral elevation. Calvin's successors at Geneva went forward in the path which he had traced.

Beza and the *Vénérable Compagnie* devoted much detailed care and thought to questions of economic prosperity and efficiency. They also watched to see that wealth was rightly distributed, and that proper relief was given to the poor, and work to the unemployed. In questions of this kind the Government of the State continually turned to them for their opinions and advice. They took an interest in taxation and in State loans, and in the rate of interest, which was always fixed with their approval. They gave their judgment in favour of the erection of a State Bank, both in order to bring to the State the gain of exchange of business and to create cheap credit for the trades which were needing assistance.

Thus this economic practice of Geneva became the starting-point from which Capitalism was incorporated into the Calvinistic ethic all over the world, though with caution and under certain limitations. Conditions among the French Huguenots, in the Netherlands, and in England, each with their own characteristics, also helped to adjust modern business life to the religious point of view. One very important aspect of the situation is the fact that the Calvinists in France and England, and at the outset also in the Netherlands, and, above all, during their period of exile on the Lower Rhine, as minorities were forced out of public life and official positions in the State; they were thus obliged, in the main, to go into business life. Apart from this, however, the Calvinists displayed a strong tendency in this direction, even in circumstances which were not particularly favourable to business life; their industrious habits, their detachment from the world, and their rational and utilitarian spirit certainly strengthened this tendency.

The economic situation in Geneva, however, contained the germ of logical developments which went beyond the intention of Calvin and the Genevese. Once Capitalism had been accepted, even with many precautions, given the right *milieu*, everywhere it led to results which increased its power; while the specifically Calvinistic habits of piety and industry justified its existence and helped to increase its strength, which gave it in the Calvinistic communities a special character and a peculiar intensity.[1] The exhortation to continual industry in labour, combined with the limitation of consumption and of luxury, produced a tendency to pile up capital, which for its part — in the necessity of its further utilization in work and not in enjoyment — necessitated an

[1] No one has ever asserted that Capitalism is the direct product of Calvinism. We can, however, say that both possessed a certain affinity for each other, that Calvinistic ethic of the "calling" and of work, which declares that the earning of money with certain precautions is allowable, was able to give it an intellectual and ethical backbone, and that, therefore, thus organized and inwardly supported it vigorously developed, even though within the limits of anti-mammon. "There is no doubt that where an economic system and a 'spirit' with which it has a certain affinity meet, there ensues a development along uniform lines which is also inwardly unbroken (that is, where the spirit and the economic system agree, which is not always the case), of the kind which I had begun to analyse (that is, like the Calvinistic development.)" The conjunction of these two elements itself is an historic accident, as I have said already in describing the similarly comparatively close affinity between the mediaeval system and the Catholic ethic. But out of such accidents (*Weber: Schlusswort, XXXI, p. 580*): "Humanity which through the meeting of religious and economic elements was created"; *p. 583:* "Protestant asceticism created for it (bourgeois capitalism) a positive ethic, a soul which needed that restless activity in order that 'spirit' and 'form' might be one"; *p. 588:* A current of psychic elements which arose from a very specific moral and religious source, combined with capitalistic possibilities of development from which the great historical developments proceed. The Christian ethic only attained a great actual importance for world-history when it was supported by an "accident" of this kind. In itself alone, when it did not receive this support, it simply remained in the realm of theory. The combination of these elements then reacted, however, upon the religious and ethical spirit, as I prove in both instances. In the history of the Christian ethic there have only been two "accidents" of this kind, the medieval system and the Calvinistic system, whose expansion through the bourgeois sect will be demonstrated in the next section. There are other certainly often finer and deeper conceptions of the Christian Ethos to whom an historic influence of this kind was denied, because they were not favoured by such an "accident" or in their very nature were unable to find such support. If I speak here of "accident," this is naturally meant logically, i.e. that here there is no immanent development, not that these things have happened *sine Deo*.

ever-increasing turnover. The duty of labour, coupled with the ban on luxury, worked out "economically as the impulse to save," and the impulse to save had the effect of building up capital. To what extent these developments took place everywhere is a separate question. Upon the whole, however, this result belonged to the very nature of the case, and it is the general opinion that this is what actually took place among the most important Calvinistic peoples.

This, however, is not the main point at issue. The contribution of Calvinism to the formation of the Capitalist system itself is not the most important aspect of the question. This only becomes clear when, with Weber and Sombart, we inquire into the ethical "spirit" and the world outlook, or the "economic temper" which gave the system its firm hold over the minds of men, and which, in spite of its opposition to natural human instincts, has been able to strike root in human minds as a firm conviction. Economic traditionalism, interrupted by unscrupulous individuals who are simply out for gain, is much more in line with ordinary human instincts than the concrete and abstract dominion of labour and profit, as ends in themselves, the continual increase of work produced by every fresh profit from labour. It is here that we perceive the importance (together with the related, yet different, effects of Judaism) which the peculiar Calvinistic type of the inward ethical attitude has gained towards the performance of labour in business life, and its religious estimate of the earning of money. The Protestant ethic of the "calling," with its Calvinistic assimilation of the Capitalist system, with its severity and its control of the labour rendered as a sign of the assurance of election, made service in one's "calling," the systematic exercise of one's energies, into a service both necessary in itself and appointed by God, in which profit is regarded as the sign of the Divine approval. This conception of the "calling" and of labour, with its taboo on idleness of every kind, with its utilization of every

chance of gain, and its confidence in the blessing of God, now, however, to a great extent approached the commercial professions and the business of making money. It laid the foundation of a world of specialized labour, which taught men to work for work's sake, and in so doing it produced our present-day bourgeois way of life, the fundamental psychological principles which gave it birth, which, however, it was not bound to perpetuate once this way of life had become the constitution of the modern world.

Thus there arose a current — definite, particularly powerful, and influential — of the bourgeois capitalistic spirit, which was pre-eminently typical of the bourgeois way of life in general. This was the predominance of labour and of the "calling," of industry for its own sake, a process of objectifying work and the results of work, which was only possible where work was exalted by means of an ascetic vocational ethic of that kind, into the sphere of that which is *necessary in itself* by means of the underlying religious conception. Calvinism, which in its early days included a good many groups of the aristocracy, was at first indifferent to social questions, but in the course of the political development in various countries it became bourgeois; this social transformation, however, was entirely in line with certain elements in its spirit. . . .

The significant point which is important even today for our subject is this: that in these Christian circles, and in them alone, was it possible to combine modern economic activity with Christian thought, and, indeed, that down to the present day it is possible to do this with a clear conscience. In this connection we only need to recall the circumlocutions with which Catholicism tries to make this modern form of economic life tolerable, and how, at bottom, it continually attempts to restrain it, or the revulsion with which early Lutheranism and contemporary German Conservatism officially regard Capitalism. Seen in this light, the significance of this new Calvinistic form of Christianity for the whole modern development, and especially for the position of Protestantism within it, becomes plain. It is the only form of Christian social doctrine which accepts the basis of the modern economic situation without reserve. The reason for this does not lie in any supposed "greater insight" into the essence of the economic processes, but in the fact that here the super-idealistic and Pietistic hindrances in the fundamental ethical idea have fallen away, which would have otherwise hindered or restrained this development; because, on the contrary, the Calvinistic ethic contains energies which directly further this economic development.

Whether a Christian ethic of this kind, contrasted with that of Catholicism and of Lutheranism, is entirely an advantage, whether it is not tinged rather strongly with the spirit of "business" and the avidity of a materialistic outlook on life, is another question. The main point is that it is peculiar to the leading modern nations, or at least to majority groups amongst them, and that it here effects an adjustment to the modern economic world which has not been achieved by the Christian piety of other nations.

The Christian element in this Calvinistic justification of Capitalism would, however, be greatly misunderstood if one did not at the same time remember the limits with which the real Christian idea of love here also surrounds the ethic of industry, and which have continued to exert a beneficent influence right down to the present day, wherever, in all capitalistic labour, the main Calvinistic ideas have remained vitally alive. Labour is asceticism, an asceticism which is absolutely necessary. Profit is the sign of the blessing of God on the faithful exercise of one's calling. But labour and profit were never intended for purely personal interest. The capitalist is always a steward of the gifts of God, whose duty it is to increase his capital and utilize it for the good of Society as a whole, retaining for himself only that amount which is necessary to provide for his own needs. All surplus wealth should be used for works of public utility, and

especially for purposes of ecclesiastical philanthropy. Thus the Genevese assessed themselves to the furthest possible limit for special cases of need, and gave regularly in support of the local poor as well as for the numerous refugees. The charitable activity of the Church which was exercised by the board of deacons was part of the requirement of the Church-order instituted by God, was organized with great energy, and, with the aid of voluntary gifts which were often amazingly large, it was able to cope with the demands made upon it. This is the origin of the practice known among us through the example of American millionaires — in which even men who have become quite indifferent to religion will give a large portion of their profits for public purposes. The actual theory and practice of money and interest has also been determined by this spirit of philanthropy.

Only "productive credit" for business purposes is allowed, not "usury credit," which is simply used for living on interest. From poor men, or people who have been otherwise harassed by misfortune, no interest is to be taken; loans also were not to be refused for lack of securities. Arrangements of that kind are only to be carried out with reference to the good of the community as a whole. The debtor ought to gain just as much from the money as the creditor. The law of cheapness ought to prevail everywhere, in accordance with the principle of the Gospel and of the Natural Law, that "whatsoever ye would that they should do unto you, do ye also unto them." Finally, the rate of interest ought not to exceed a maximum, which is to be legally fixed according to the needs of the situation. This was the theory. In Geneva practical life was regulated in accordance with these principles. The fight against usury and the exploitation of the poor fill the protocols of the Council and of the Consistory, and these Christian-Social elements of Calvinistic doctrine have also left their mark upon ethics. Thus we can understand how it is that within Calvinism, in the face of the modern development of Capitalism, there

has always been, and still is, a tendency to merge into a form of Christian Socialism. We have already seen that a Socialism of this kind was contained, from the very outset, in the Genevan ideal of the Holy Community. It was continued in the "communities under the Cross," where the religious idea developed freely. How far it helped to determine the State legislation of Calvinistic countries has still to be discovered.

The great English system of legislation which deals with the poor, with workmen and with wages — in the guild-professional sense and, above all, with respect to education for work — bore traces of its spirit. In opposition to the "Manchester" conception of the State and of economics, Carlyle deliberately asserted the old Puritan ideas. The Christian Socialism of the English people at the present day is essentially of Calvinistic origin, and the activity of the American churches is often of a Christian Socialist kind directed against the abuses of Capitalism. In Switzerland, in the Netherlands, in England, and in America there are today Socialist clergy, whereas within the sphere of Lutheranism such a phenomenon is regarded as an offence against the sacred foundation of the Divine order, as taking part in purely secular matters, as a reprehensible revolutionary spirit, and a human intervention in the order of Providence; among us social heresies are more dangerous and more objectionable than doctrinal heresies. The meaning of that is, however, that Calvinism is in closer agreement with modern tendencies of social life than Lutheranism, or than Catholicism, which, at least in the Latin lands of its origin, likewise holds these heresies at arm's length. This also is the basis of that intense self-consciousness of Calvinism, the sense that it is the only form of Christianity adapted to modern life, because, on the one hand, it is able to justify modern forms of economic production before the tribunal of conscience, and because, on the other hand, by means of Christian Socialism, it strives to rectify the abuses of the system when

they occur. It is very conscious of representing "modern Christianity"—not because it is in touch with modern theological thought (for its theological tendency inclines to conservatism, and it is only its overwhelmingly practical character which leads to dogmatism being relegated to a secondary position), but because it is in harmony with the political and economic way of life, and understands how to further and yet to define its problems, whereas it considers that Lutheranism is philosophically diseased, unpractical, and remote from the problems of ordinary life. . . .

It has already been made abundantly clear that Lutheranism taught that labour in a calling was both a service rendered to God and an outward expression of brotherly love. On the other hand, by its emphasis upon the purely inward aspect of religion, its lack of a clear standard of moral behaviour, and its acquiescence in the conditions of life which were created by Natural Law, but were often extremely unchristian, it was not able, on its own initiative, to bring about a coherent and systematic transformation of social life in general. Neither in theory nor in its attitude to life does it possess a systematic ethic. Again and again Lutheranism casts aside its asceticism (which it also possesses as the corollary of the doctrine of Original Sin), and gives itself up to repose in the blessedness of the Divine Mercy, and to the thankful enjoyment of Divine gifts in all that is good and beautiful, and whenever it becomes dubious about the world and about sin it withdraws into the refuge of its inner happiness of justification through faith.

Catholicism, on the other hand, likewise values the cosmos of the vocational system as the means of natural existence appointed by Natural Law. But this system of callings is applicable to the conditions of natural existence, and is thus merely the lower degree of that higher supernatural ethic, which inwardly is no longer connected with the claims of the active life, but which in the life of contemplation attains the highest degree of supernature or grace.

Ascetic Protestantism, however, regards the "calling" as a proof, and the ardent fulfilment of one's professional duty as the sign and token of the state of grace. Accordingly it gathers all the work of the "calling" into a coherent system of the utmost concentration of human faculties on the aim of the "calling," which is appointed to the individual through his providential position within the system. The principles and ideals of Ascetic Protestantism may therefore be summarized thus: the inner severance of feeling and enjoyment from all the objects of labour; the unceasing harnessing of labour to an aim which lies in the other world, and therefore must occupy us till death; the depreciation of possessions, of all things earthly, to the level of expediency; the habit of industry in order to suppress all distracting and idle impulses; and the willing use of profit for the religious community and for public welfare; these principles, which may vary in detail, are all in the main similar in character, and to a considerable extent also they have been and are being realized. . . .

The economic ethic, finally, teaches (likewise from the general Christian point of view) that labour is the result of the Fall, and is to be regarded as the penalty and the discipline of sin. But this idea is here developed into that of a rational, systematic discipline of labour, evolved, above all, in Puritanism, and thence taken over in a more or less logical manner; this ethic regards laziness and idleness as the source of all evil, and the result of a failure to impose discipline. With this systematic view of work (to which, incidentally, other than Puritan motives were sometimes added, as, for instance, among the Quakers the waiting and self-preparation for the Divine illumination), a strong and systematic impulse was given to production, while, on the other hand, with the same asceticism there is united a considerable limitation of consumption and a complete avoidance of all luxury (at least, of all that is obvious and that ministers to vanity and arrogance). It is only at this point that we see the full effect of that which has already been described as the favourable ethical disposition of Calvinism for bourgeois Capitalism. Thus this economic ethic became middle-class, one might almost say lower middle-class-capitalist, and it bore all the signs of the results of the capitalistic attitude towards life: systematic division of labour, emphasis upon specialization, the feeling for advantage and profit, the abstract duty of work, the obligation towards property as towards something great, which ought to be maintained and increased for its own sake. The owner of wealth or property is "the Lord's Steward," and administers a Divine gift which has been entrusted to him. An ethic of this kind placed at the disposal of the nascent modern bourgeois Capitalism both energetic and courageous *entrepreneurs,* and men who were willing to endure exploitation if only they could get work. This ethic differs from the Capitalism of antiquity and of the later Middle Ages by those very features which have just been described, and alongside of it the other existing kinds of Capitalism, of course, must not be overlooked.

This type of Capitalism, however, preserves its special Christian character by its taboo on pleasure-seeking and self-glorification, the sense of the duty of work for the service of God, strict honesty and reliability, the humane obligation to make provision for the workers and to give respect to employers, and the extensive use of wealth for philanthropic ends.

The system of fixed prices, the standardization and classification of goods according to their quality, the building up of business upon the strictest formal honesty, the principle "honesty is the best policy" — all arose at this point. It is the expression of a spiritual and moralistic opposition to the guild system and to unfair dealing in individual cases; it means that the life of business is constructed upon the calculation of the individual in relation to an abstract circle of purchasers, and upon the absolute necessity for correctness and honesty as regards estimates and deliveries. The inscription on the Bremen Exchange, which states that the merchant is the most honest man, should be interpreted from this point of view. The justification for the economic life lies in its value to the community, and in this sense it can be considered a blessing; in itself, however, the ideal attitude is that of the man whose spirit is inwardly entirely independent of possessions. It is even possible to go a step farther and to exalt poverty, which preserves from the dangers of wealth, just as, on the other hand, wealth, used in a Christian way, preserves the community from misery and want. Thus here also there is no idea of equality. This is prevented by the whole idea of Providence, and above all, where it was still a vital force, by the idea of Predestination. The conception is always that of a cosmos direced by God, in which the Christian Ethos only works itself out through reciprocal activities, division of labour, a variety of gifts and capacities. Thus, as Calvinism and the sects are of one mind on the question of the development of a voluntary Church, and on the question of separation between Church and State, so also their views coincide in the economic ethic of secular asceticism which determines the ethic of Ascetic Protestantism, renouncing its greater earlier freedom: Calvinism reaches this point of view under the urgent sense of need to prove in daily life the reality of its faith, and it therefore produces the systematic asceticism of labour; the passive, persecuted sect comes to this point by giving up its hostility towards the world, and by fusing its ascetic detachment from the world with the Protestant idea of the "calling." Further, both movements shared the following experience: on account of their Nonconformity and their freedom from the State, they were forcibly excluded from all official positions in the State and from its dignities; thus they were thrust out of the ruling classes and obliged to join the bourgeois middle class; this still further intensified the bourgeois capitalist element.

Agriculture was not excluded, but it was only practised by the people of this class by farming, and by trading in property in land; but it has nothing to do with the feudal ownership of land.

Thus the difference between this ethic and that of the theoretical traditional economic ethic of Catholicism is clear. In this ethic, work and possessions belong to the natural sphere alone; the desire for gain does not directly concern the religious ethic at all; gain is regarded merely as a method of providing for one's needs according to one's rank in Society; whatever is earned beyond that should be used for charity; the most genuine charity, however, is actually exercised by those who possess nothing at all, by those who stand outside the ordinary work of the world altogether.

The difference between this economic ethic and that of Lutheranism is equally clear. Lutheranism, it is true, makes the task of earning a living part of the "calling" to brotherly love, but, in spite of this, it gives preference to the callings which belong to a settled order of Society consisting of agricultural labourers, manual workers, and officials; Capitalism and the calculating spirit which is continually striving to make more money is regarded by Lutheranism with detachment and extreme misgiving.

But even contrasted with primitive Calvinism, to which, with its State Church point of view, all methods of gaining a livelihood were of equal importance, which had not developed the asceticism of labour to this extent, and which had no trace of the lower middle-class spirit at all — this was something new. This was the result of that asceticism in which the Puritan, legalistic, organizing Calvinism came into contact with those sects which were comparatively ready to accept secular civilization; it was also the result of the social and political situation in which both Calvinism and the sects found themselves over against the official world.

THE ROLE OF RELIGION IN THE
FORMATION OF THE CAPITALIST SPIRIT

WERNER SOMBART

Werner Sombart was the son of a self-made industrialist and land-owner and began his career, after studying at the universities of Berlin and Pisa, as a counselor to the Bremen Chamber of Commerce. In 1890, however, he accepted a teaching position at the University of Breslau and remained in the academic profession the remainder of his life. In 1917 he joined the faculty of the University of Berlin, becoming an emeritus professor in 1931. He was well known for his vigor and lucidity in the classroom but was internationally known for his many publications on the economic development of Europe. Continuing to write almost until the year of his death (1941), he published many articles and over twenty books, many of which were translated into other languages. (For example, *Der proletarische Sozialismus,* a two volume work published in 1929, was translated into twenty-four languages). Some of Sombart's views have been presented to many American students through F. L. Nussbaum's *A History of the Economic Institutions of Modern Europe* (1933) and the article, "Capitalism," which Sombart wrote for the *Encyclopedia of Social Sciences.*

Religious systems and churches are able to influence economic life in different ways, particularly by their power of directing the mind to this goal or that. Sometimes their influence may be direct, sometimes very roundabout. It may check certain tendencies or give them an impetus. It is not surprising therefore that the history of the capitalist spirit should be inextricably bound up with the history of churches and religious systems. . . .

The capitalist spirit received a set-back at the hands of Catholicism in Spain. There religious interests developed to the exclusion of all others. The reason for this is plain, and historians have not overlooked it. The history of the Iberian peninsula for a thousand years and more was the story of the struggle between Christianity and Islam. The Mahometan domination resulted in giving the Spanish Christians one great aim in life — the expulsion of the Moors. . . . It is said that no less than 3,700 battles were waged against the Moors before they were finally expelled. But even after that the ideal of Christian chivalry predominated in Spain, so much so that it characterized all the Spanish colonial enterprises and coloured the home policy of the crown. Feudalism and fanaticism intertwined to form a special outlook on life, which maintained itself as long as it could, but was wholly out of place in the modern period of history. The national hero of Spain is probably the most uncapitalist type in the annals of the world. Who does not know him — the last knight-errant, the kindly and attractive Don Quixote?

Whether Catholicism stood in the way of the capitalist spirit in Ireland it is not

From Werner Sombart, *The Quintessence of Capitalism,* translated by M. Epstein (New York, 1915), pp. 236–262. By permission of E. P. Dutton & Co. Copyright 1915.

easy to say. But certain it is that in all other countries its influence was most beneficial to capitalist growth, which it assisted and accelerated. Such was the case in an especial degree in Italy, which played the first role in the history of early capitalism. . . .

There is no doubt that the popes and their financial policies contributed much to the establishment of capitalism, and thus to the expansion of the capitalist spirit. . . . The system of papal taxation, which extended to the whole of the then known world (especially from the 13th century on), called into existence an upper class of powerful international bankers, who acted like yeast on the capitalist dough.

What is of far greater significance, and what I propose to review, is the influence exercised by the Catholic Church on the capitalist spirit by reason of its doctrines.

Of course, not all the doctrines of Catholicism will come into our survey. To consider them all would be to make our labour much more difficult than it need be. It would also distract us from the root of the matter, which is the influence of religion in any period on the mind of man in his capacity of economic agent. Religious and metaphysical hair-splitting are quite unnecessary for the solution of the problem; all that is needed is just to view the practical rules of everyday life and common religious exercises. There is no need for our purpose, so it seems to me, to go into the philosophical and theological depths of the problem. Deep ploughing is not always a necessity of successful tillage. If, therefore, I remain on the surface of things, it is because I believe that the causes and their effects will be best apparent there.

The doctrines of the Catholic Church were embodied in medieval scholasticism as formulated by Thomas Aquinas. Ever since the 14th century this religious system has been recognized as official by the Church of Rome. Its main characteristic is that it unites the two currents of thought found in Christianity from its very beginning—the Pauline and Augustinian doctrines of love and the legalism of the Law.

Thomas Aquinas did away with the opposition between the Law and the Gospels, and his theory of legal ethics is what we must turn to.

The fundamental idea of the ethical system is the rationalization of life. Reason, everlasting and divine, that governs nature and the universe—Reason must regulate the world by the senses and control the passions and appetites. "Sin in human affairs is what is contrary to the dictates of reason," says Aquinas. Or again, "the more necessary a thing is, the more should reference be had to the demands of Reason." The sexual passion is most necessary for the common good; consequently it should most stringently be held in sway, in accordance with the dictates of reason. Virtue is nought else but the maintenance of the equilibrium in all things, as reason demands; its essence consists in making the desires of the senses subservient to reason, so that no passions out of all accord with reason may spring up.

In the natural world with its appetites and desires a moral, rational world is built up of the Biblical Laws. This new world, born of freedom, Aquinas puts on an equality with the decalogue, although elements of Hellenistic philosophy formed part and parcel of it in later times. The goal set by Aquinas for all men is to live in accord with reason. What means to that end does he suggest? The fear of God. The fear of God sets a man thinking; it forces him to review his conduct; it makes a rational being of him.

Now bear in mind that the very idea of rationalizing life was in itself a great impetus to the growth of capitalism. Acquisitiveness and economic rationalism are in reality the result of applying to economic life the rule of religion. Before capitalism could develop it was needful to root up natural man with all his passions, to replace the primitive and original outlook by specifically rationalist habits of mind, to turn topsy-turvy all the values of life. The *homo capitalisticus*, that artificial and artistic creation, was the result. Whatever other forces may have helped the growth of economic rationalism, there can be no doubt that one of its mightiest supports came from the fact that rationalism was inculcated by the Church, which desired to influence the whole of life in the same direction as the capitalist spirit influenced economic activities. Even were we to suppose that economic interests were not without influence on ecclesiastical ethics, the view would still hold good that economic rationalism was bound to profit by forming part of such a thoroughly rationalist body of rules, supported moreover by the all-embracing power of the Church.

The influence of religious doctrines on the economic outlook must have been immense, seeing that they affected the mind in just such ways as were beneficial to capitalism. Take the behest of Christian ethics that the erotic appetite should be held in check. No one perceived more than St. Thomas that middle-class virtues would thrive only where the sexual life of man was controlled. He knew only too well that extravagance, the deadly sin of the bourgeois outlook, went as a rule hand in hand with an advanced attitude toward love. Extravagance in other things usually meant extravagance in voluptuousness. He knew also that luxury and debauchery are twin sisters. Accordingly, he taught that who so lived in purity and moderation was hardly likely to be subject to the sin of prodigality, and besides would manage his affairs economically. What bearing had this on capitalism? The abstemious liver was sure to make an energetic undertaker.[1]

Moderation of appetite was thus the foundation for a larger structure. To begin with, if you ordered your passions aright you would the more easily be able to order aright the whole of life and be economical in material things. Reason and order in worldly affairs was a cardinal doctrine in Christian ethics.

But above all else the Schoolmen praised economy, which they termed *liberalitas.*

Liberalitas represents the right middle policy which avoids the two extremes of avarice and prodigality; it denotes a proper balancing of income and expenditure; it teaches the art of using the goods of the world aright; it inculcates the true love of money and opulence. The prodigal loves money too little, the miser too much. In Aquinas's condemnation of too great an expenditure, especially when it tends to make you live beyond your means, there is implied the duty of saving; and his dwelling upon the evil consequences of extravagance implies a recommendation of the bourgeois economy based on income, and a condemnation of the seigniorial economy based on expenditure.

But extravagance is not the only enemy of middle class virtues condemned by Christian ethics and accounted sinful. There are others, chief among them being idleness, which is the beginning of all evil. The idler commits a sin because he wastes time which is exceedingly precious; he is lower than the beasts for even brute creation is industrious; in nature nothing idles. Particularly eloquent in his plea for filling up every minute is St. Antonine of Florence, who brushes aside the excuse of idlers that they are intent on divine contemplation, that they follow Mary rather than Martha. Narrow is the gate of those who can see God, he says, and few be they who enter in thereby. Consequently the great mass of people must be active and busy.

Honesty no less than industry and frugality was also taught by the Schoolmen, more especially commercial honesty, which, as we have seen, forms a good part of the capitalist spirit. Commercial honesty owes much to the teaching of the Church. Within the bounds of the city, where your neighbour's eye might be looking, or the gild brethren watching, you could not help being honest in your business. But when markets extended beyond the city, what but the conscience of the tradesman could keep him straight? That was where the Church came in, for it was its business to stir up the individual conscience. It did so by

[1] By the term "undertaker," as used in this extract, the translator means "entrepreneur," an employer who, seeking profit, assumes the risks of management and investment. [Editor's note]

condemning all manner of cheating as one of the mortal sins. How great the influence of the Church was in this respect appears from a remark of Alberti's, who ascribes the success of his family not only to business acumen but also to their commercial honesty, for which God Almighty had rewarded them. . . .

St. Antonine of Florence was especially concerned with the intellectual fault of *acidia,* which may be best translated "moral laziness." In his view moral laziness leads to negligence, idleness, unreliability, stupidity, time-wasting, and imprudence. . . .

Imagine how valuable this training was from the point of view of capitalism. The Church fathers certainly did not think of the capitalist undertaker, but he more than any other profited much by the practice of these virtues of intellectual energy. They are the very qualities needed for success as an undertaker, and here was the Church backing them up with all its authority. . . .

I am aware that my view of the influence of the Church's teaching on capitalism is opposed to the prevailing one. Not only has the latter not observed that the ethics of Thomas Aquinas are very favorably disposed to the capitalist spirit, but it has also been suggested that numerous maxims and prescriptions in it show that scholasticism was actually opposed to the new type of man who came into being in the capitalist age. A renewed study of the sources has convinced me that the accepted views are incorrect. The opinions of the Schoolmen, especially of the later ones, concerning wealth and its acquisition, and more particularly their views on usury, far from being a hindrance to the growth of the capitalist spirit, were in reality an impetus of no small weight.

Nor is there anything remarkable about that. For what manner of people were the Schoolmen? It is a mistake to think of them as mild bookworms, unlearned in the ways of the world . . . engaged in hair splitting and endless repetitions concerning unrealities. Many of the lesser lights do indeed fit into this picture. But the great minds never.

. . . St. Thomas, . . . Antonine of Florence, . . . Bernard of Siena, . . . Cardinal Cajetan . . . and many more . . . were neither without knowledge of the world nor were they unworldly. As a matter of fact these later Schoolmen had more sympathy for and understanding of capitalism than the 17th century zealot preachers of Puritanism. How much practical knowledge is to be found in the *Summa* of St. Antonine! It is the work of one of the most wideawake men of his time, who walked through the streets of Florence with his eyes open, who was acquainted with the thousand and one business tricks of his fellow-citizens, who was not unlearned in transport insurance nor in the nature of bills of exchange, who knew all about the silk industry and woolmaking.

What, then, was the attitude of these men to the new economic order and its spirit?

Let us first turn to the teachings of the Schoolmen in regard to poverty and wealth. The old Christian ideal of poverty which the early Fathers valued so much, and which the first secretaries not only preached but practiced, appears in the later Schoolmen to have vanished altogether. It is of little moment whether the pious Christian be poor or rich; what is of consequence is what use he makes of his poverty or his riches. The wise man does not flee from opulence or from poverty as such; he discountenances and avoids the misuse of either. . . .

To be wealthy was always looked upon by the Schoolmen as an act of God. But what of becoming wealthy, what of acquiring wealth? On this point the views did not always accord. St. Thomas holds the static conception of society, that which characterized social conditions in the pre-capitalist era. Every man had his niche wherein he stayed to the end of his days. He had his calling and his status and the income in accord with that. All change, all development, all progress were inward processes and were conceivable only as regards man's relation to the Deity. Consequently the amount of wealth of every person was a fixed quantity. He was as rich as his status required.

But such a view could not possibly be maintained in the revolutionary 14th and 15th centuries. . . . For if you followed it to its logical conclusion, it meant that no one should rise above his station, . . . once a peasant always a peasant, once a craftsman always a craftsman — "which is absurd," as Cardinal Cajetan concludes in his criticism of Aquinas's opinions. Clearly, he holds, every man ought to have the possibility of working himself up and becoming richer than he was. And these are his reasons. If anyone has special gifts which enable him to rise beyond his station, he ought also to be allowed to acquire the means appropriate for the higher status. This version of the matter opened wide the doors for the capitalist undertakers, . . . the men who had a keen eye for business and other large enterprises. These could acquire gain and accumulate capital as much as they wanted with the full approval of Mother Church.

As much as they wanted? There were limitations, of course. Their acquisitions had to be made in accordance with reason, and the means they adopted for reaching their goal had to be such as were not in conflict with morality. . . . In a word, unscrupulous and unbounded acquisitiveness has always been condemned by Catholic teachers of morality down almost to this very day. By so doing they lent their support to the conception of the old-fashioned bourgeois, which prevailed to the end of the period of early capitalism, but which, it must be added, was not averse to profits honestly gotten. It was not so much the quantity of profit that the Church teachers were concerned with as the mental attitude of the capitalist undertaker. What they wanted to prevent, and no doubt succeeded in preventing, was the utter transvaluation of all values, such as that which characterizes our own age.

A warm sympathetic understanding of the expansion of economic life in their age and country rings true in all that the later Italian Schoolmen wrote touching economic questions. In other words, capitalism appealed to them. It was on that account that they clung to the teaching of the canon law concerning usury. For what did the prohibition of usury mean to the Catholic moralists of the 15th and 16th centuries? Expressed in modern terms it denoted: Don't prevent money from becoming capital.

At first sight this may seem paradoxical. Yet the more carefully I study the sources the more convinced I become that the prohibition of usury gave a mighty impetus to the expansion of the capitalistic spirit. I am surprised that no one has noticed this before. Possibly one reason is that the specialists who have hitherto devoted themselves to scholastic philosophy were not economists and lacked that knowledge of affairs which Bernard of Siena and Antonine of Florence both possessed.

The conception of capital in St. Thomas's writings is in the germinating stage. But even he differentiates between borrowing for unproductive purposes (the simple loan) and borrowing for productive objects (capital), and goes so far as to say that while to receive payment for the first is wrong, to receive payment for the second is perfectly legitimate. Antonine of Florence and Bernard of Siena appear to understand the essence of capitalism in its completeness. Indeed, they use the term "capital," and what they have to say about it political economy has learned afresh from Karl Marx. Incidentally it may be noted that Antonine, with a fullness of knowledge, indicated the importance of a speedy turnover for increasing profits. But we are more interested in his clear demarcation between the investment of capital (*ratio capitalis*) and the simple loan of money (*ratio mutui*). In the second case money is barren, in the first it is productive, "possessing in that capacity not merely the character of money or of a commodity, but something more — the power of creation, which we term 'capital.' "

What is the attitude of the Church

authorities to interest and profit? Payment for simple lending they forbade, but a share of the surplus which capital created they allowed in all cases, whether it flowed from commerce or from the work of a middleman or from transport insurance or from a joint-stock, or in any other way. Only one condition is postulated: the capitalist must himself participate in the undertaking. If he remains in the background, if he will not venture his money, if he lacks the spirit of enterprise, let him have no profit. It is clear from this that before a man might receive interest he had to be prepared to bear the losses as well as provide the initial capital. Hence a joint-stock company had to limit its liabilities; bank deposits could not yield interest; you were not allowed to lend a craftsman a sum of money at a fixed rate (seeing that you eliminated risk); a partnership might be entered into only if all the partners agreed to share the losses.

It is clear that these pious men were anxious to spur on enterprise. What they rewarded was industry, the mother of all profit. Money in itself was just barren dross. Only when industry — undertaking — is applied to it does it become fruitful, and then only the surplus is lawful. The Schoolmen hated nothing so much as idleness, and their theory of interest bears witness to the fact. For if a man lends out money at interest without himself being an undertaker of some sort, he is an idler, who may not therefore receive his reward in the form of interest, even if the money borrowed is productive capital. This holds good so long as others and not the lender apply it productively. A passage in Antonine's writings is characteristic. It is there pointed out that the *nobili* who will not work, but put their money in other people's businesses without also sharing their risks, are receiving usury pure and simple.

The doctrine of lawful profit and that of the intellectual virtues thus coalesce. The burden of both is the same: energetic undertaking is a delight unto the Lord, but an extravagant nobility, stay-at-home slack-ers, and idle usurers are an abomination unto His soul.

Protestantism has been all along the line a foe to capitalism, and more especially to the capitalist economic outlook. How could it be otherwise? Capitalism is something worldly, something for this life on earth, and the more man's gaze is directed to the joys of existence here below, the more devotees will capitalism enroll. But for that reason it will be hated and condemned of all who regard our life here as only a preparation for life hereafter. The increasing intensity of religious feelings necessarily results in an increasing indifference to economic activities, and an increasing indifference to economic activities means a weakening and dissolution of the capitalist spirit. This actually happened at the Reformation. The reform movement gave a fillip to the inner life, and intensified the craving for metaphysics in men. Consequently capitalism was prejudiced in proportion as the reform doctrines spread.

In Lutheranism this tendency was strengthened by Luther's own devotion to the economic conditions that prevailed in the early Middle Ages with the self-supporting peasant and craftsman. That is why Luther's philosophy is far behind that of the Schoolmen. It may be said with certainty that in those countries where Lutheranism triumphed the influence of religion on economic affairs, in so far as it was effective, made not for the growth, but most decidedly for the retardation, of capitalist tendencies. But other forms of Protestantism, and Calvinism in particular, were no different in this respect. In Calvinist lands the Church was distinctly hostile to capitalism, and the assumption is not far-fetched that the new faith was on the whole more harmful than helpful to the growth of the capitalist spirit.

This view, I know, is contrary to that generally prevailing, which holds that Calvinism, especially in its Anglo-Scottish guise of Puritanism, aided capitalist development, if, indeed, it did not give it birth. It remains for me therefore to demonstrate the anti-capitalist direction of Calvinist-Puritanical ethics. I shall limit my consideration to English and Scotch sources, seeing that it is commonly accepted that Puritanism helped capitalism in Great Britain more than anywhere else.

At the outset let us note that the early Christian ideal of poverty came to the fore once again in Puritan ethics. Riches and their acquisition were regarded in much the same fashion as the Gospels speak of them, and the aversion to earthly goods was more marked than in scholasticism. In principle, the Puritans and the Schoolmen were agreed. For both, riches and poverty were of no consequence whatever for the soul's salvation. But whereas we observed a certain inclination on the part of the School-men to riches, among the Puritans the consensus of opinion is more sympathetic to poverty. In other words, reason in both schools is indifferent to poverty and wealth alike, but the feelings of the doctors sway them in opposite directions. The Schoolmen were for wealth, the Puritans for poverty. Hence it is that the condemnation of riches in Baxter's *Directory* occupies ever so much more space than in the *Summae theologicae* of the Catholic writers. . . .

Baxter summarizes the evil consequences of the love of money under ten headings, viz., it draws the heart away from God; it stops the ear to His word; it makes impossible holy meditation and conference; it steals the needful from preparing for death; it generates spite between neighbors and wars between nations; it is the source of all unrighteousness and oppression; it destroys charity and good works; it disordereth and profaneth families; it is the very price that the devil gives for souls; and it distracts from communion with God.

If wealth is thus frowned upon, how much more its acquisition, especially by means of capitalist undertaking. Here, too, the Gospel provides a watchword: "Take no thought for the morrow." . . .

I have hitherto quoted Baxter because he is the typical representative of the Puritan moral teachers. All of them, however, were inimical to acquisitiveness; all of them are everlastingly asking, Why care for earthly goods? Why take thought for tomorrow? The words are almost identical with those of Baxter. . . .

It was only to be expected that this condemnation of all earthly goods was paralleled by a strong recommendation to turn the mind to God. Every moment spent not in the service of God is lost. Every hour spent in prayer, in attention to sermons, in holy ceremonies, is fruitful of treasures that cannot be compared with money. Time is only wasted with "excess of worldly cares and business." Men so occupied are full of mundane thoughts from early morn till late at night. The world leaves them no time for earnest communion, and robs them of precious moments which belong to God and their immortal souls — moments for prayer, reading, or conference on holy matters.

For many a year life was moulded in accordance with views such as these, especially in Scotland, the stronghold of Puritanism. Which means that the greater part of men's waking hours were spent in church or in preparation for the Church services. Markets were forbidden to be held, certainly in the 17th century, on Saturdays, Sundays, and Mondays. There were week-day services, morning and evening, in all the churches; sermons were delivered twice and even three times a week; in the year 1650 an address was given every afternoon. In 1653 a weekly programme was instituted for religious exercises. For Wednesdays, fasting and eight hours' prayer and preaching; for Saturdays, two or three sermons; for Sundays, twelve hours' service in church; for Mondays, three or four sermons.

To flee from the world — that was the ideal of every word, of every action of the pious Puritan of those days. There had been nothing like it since the early Christian sects. Nevertheless, Puritanism did not altogether suppress the capitalist spirit.

Indeed, certain of its aspects unconsciously facilitated its growth. Puritanism served the interests of its arch-enemy, capitalism, in that it took up and developed the ethical principles of scholasticism passionately and with a singleness of purpose.

Puritanism re-echoed the old watch-words: Rationalize life; keep the passions under control; let reason dominate the natural inclinations. "Take nothing and do nothing merely because the sense or appetite would have it, but because you have reason so to do." These words of Baxter appear again and again insistently. Once more the master-sin is sensuality, flesh-pleasing or voluptuousness. Isaac Barrow's treatise *Of Industry* sums up the fundamental teaching of Puritanism. "We should govern and regulate according to very strict and severe laws all the faculties of our soul, all the members of our body, all internal motions and all external actions proceeding from us; we should check our inclinations, curb our appetites and compose our passions; we should guard our hearts from vain thoughts and bad desires; we should bridle our tongues from evil and from idle discourses; we should order our steps in the straight way of righteousness, not deflecting to the right hand or to the left."

Conduct of this kind was held to lead to grace, and every individual had to keep close watch on himself if he would retain that grace. So the habit was formed of fashioning the whole of life on the basis of reason, in accordance with the will of God. Not that the average man ever gave the theory of it a thought. Sufficient for him that the minister proclaimed God's desire for a particular conduct of life, which to the pious was just the sum total of a number of behests. These he obeyed according to the measure of the fear of God within him. He was no different in this respect from the good Catholic, who had likewise to plague himself with self-control. If anything, the Puritan was stricter in his observance. Now, as the doctrines of scholasticism and Puritanism were identical in their terms, the sternness of the Puritan can be accounted for only by the deeper religious feelings of the 17th-century man.

It is curious how the single virtues are recommended to the faithful by the Puritan preachers and the Catholic doctors in exactly the same way, word for word. Life was to be ordered aright, so both demanded; and the middle-class virtues which each proclaimed were identical.

First as to industry: "By industry we understand a serious and steady application of mind, joined with a rigorous exercise of our active faculties in prosecution of any reasonable, honest, useful design in order to accomplish or attain some considerable good; as, for instance, a merchant is industrious, who continueth intent and active in driving on his trade for acquiring wealth." Industry is desired of God. All gifts, of course, come from Him, but His will is that we should attain them by work. We are therefore to be industrious. That is the burden of Isaac Barrow's dissertation, which quotes the Old Testament freely. "Shall we alone be idle, while all things are so busy? We may easily observe every creature about us incessantly working toward the end for which it was designed, indefatigably exercising the powers with which it is endowed; diligently observing the law of its creation. . . ." Is not this the repetition of what St. Antonine wrote? And this likewise? "Idleness is indeed the nursery of sins, which as naturally grow up therein as weeds in a neglected field or insects in a standing puddle: 'Idleness teaches much evil' (Eccles. xxxiii. 27)."

Next, employ your time usefully; games, gaming, hunting, and masked balls are evil things and should be avoided.

Thirdly, in both codes sensuality and drunkenness are of the Devil, and are deadly sins. Possibly there was greater control of these things in the Puritan countries in the 17th century than in the Italian cities in the 15th. . . . Purity among the Anglo-Saxons became prudery. It is not too much to say that Puritanism is responsible for the humbug and hypocrisy in sexual matters in old England no less than in New England across the Atlantic. . . .

Fourth in order comes economy, a master virtue with the Schoolmen and the Puritans alike. In 17th-century Scotland the preachers reintroduced sumptuary laws, insisting that there should be strict economy in clothing, in house-room, and at celebrations of weddings and the like. . . .

But all Protestant sects took an extremist view of economy, so much so that we are perhaps on the track of one — the only one — point of divergence in the social ethics of the Puritans and the Schoolmen. It can best be expressed by saying that Puritanism utterly crushed the least sign of any artistic longing for sensuous magnificence and grandeur. Far otherwise was the outlook of scholasticism. Its beauty was that it sprang from a deeply artistic temperament. Even yet we may perceive in it the heavenly spirit of the Augustinian outlook on life. . . .

All this sense of the artistic expresses itself in the recognition as a virtue of high rank of something which finds no place whatever in any of the systems of Protestant ethics. I refer to what the Schoolmen called *magnificentia,* which denoted the striving to accomplish what is great and glorious. In the first place, you think of the Church and public life. But you are by no means to exclude a love of the ornate from your own life, whether it be for special occasions, as, for example, a wedding-feast, or for constant enjoyment, as, for example, your home. And of course in works of art this love of beauty and magnificence must most certainly express itself.

The Protestants had lost all sense of beauty; *magnificentia* found no place in their ethical and religious system, well-suited as it was to their cold, drab, whitewashed, pictureless kirks, that took the place of the noble Gothic piles with their "storied windows richly dight casting a dim religious light." Indeed in Puritan ethics the very opposite of *magnificentia,* miser-

liness, became one of the cardinal virtues. The Schoolmen, on the other hand, had condemned it as a deadly sin. . . .

Nevertheless, to change parsimony into miserliness was one of the chief services rendered to capitalism by Puritan and Quaker ethics, unless it be held that the removal of the ban on interest was a greater service. This I myself doubt. We have already observed that the medieval prohibition of interest was really a blessing in disguise for the capitalist spirit. Consequently the attitude of the later moralists to interest and usury was of little moment.

But there are a number of things for which Puritanism was certainly not responsible. First and foremost, it had nothing to do with middle-class virtues as such, seeing that when Puritanism arose these had been in existence for several centuries. Does not Alberti know them all to perfection? If any religious system is to be made responsible for them, it must be Catholicism. Protestantism merely took over what the Schoolmen had created.

Nor do I think Puritanism accountable for the boundless development of acquisitiveness, and the senseless desire to make money anyhow, which characterizes the capitalist spirit at its zenith. Puritan preachers were totally averse to all money-getting. In so far as they did reckon with natural acquisitiveness and the desire for riches, there was always the condition, implied or expressed, that riches were not to be regarded as an end in themselves. Wealth could be justified only when it was spent in ways pleasing to God, and so long as it did not endanger the salvation of the undertaker. Here again we meet with the precisely similar language of the Schoolmen. Baxter is not opposed to riches, but they must only be used for doing good — "in the service of God, in beneficence to our neighbour, in advancing public good. . . . That you make not riches your chief end: riches for our fleshly ends must not ultimately be intended or sought. But — in subordination to higher things they may. Then your end must be, that you may be better provided to do God service, and may do the more good with what you have. You may labour to be rich for God, though not for the flesh and sin."

In the third place, unscrupulous money-getting cannot be laid at the door of Puritanism. Like scholasticism it preached the need for honourable ways in business. . . . Moreover, Puritanism clung to the doctrine of "just price" current among the School-men. And what does "just price" mean but the subjection of the market to the laws of righteousness and the cheapening of wares? Free competition Puritanism condemned utterly. "It is a false rule of them that think their commodity is worth as much as any one will give. But it is taken for granted in the market that every man will get as much as he can have and that 'Caveat emptor' is 'the only security.' It is not so among Christians, nor infidels who profess either truth or common honesty."

Finally, I doubt very much whether Puritanism was the cause of the great undertakings that appeared later in Puritan countries. Puritanism hardly encouraged far-sighted and adventurous enterprises; shopkeeping was the most it could achieve.

Your Scotchman is a Puritan. But to regard as Puritan men like Cecil Rhodes and the really great undertakers who came to the fore in England and America in the 19th century, that is hardly warranted by the facts. It would be but a narrow conception of the capitalist spirit thus to see its various manifestations springing from Puritanism. The truth is that our latter day "merchant adventurers" are all made of very different stuff; their progenitors were the Raleighs, the Cavendishes, the Drakes, the Fuggers, and the rest of them, who, born before Puritanism became a force, were immune from the abstruse stuff which a ghost like Mr. Baxter crammed into the *Christian Directory*.

It cannot be denied, of course, that there were some great capitalist undertakers among the Puritans. But whether they owed their greatness to Puritan ethics is doubtful. It was more probably much more due to their racial qualities or to fortune's guiding hand. One factor, and the only one, may have helped the capitalist spirit, and that was the subjection of the undertaker to the laws of Puritan ethics. But deep this influence could never have been.

RELIGION AND THE RISE OF CAPITALISM

R. H. TAWNEY

One of the best known English economists and economic historians, R. H. Tawney graduated from Balliol College, Oxford; and, after teaching at Glasgow University and Oxford University, moved to the Chair of Economic History at the London School of Economics. Tawney has been a leading member of the British Labour Party since its earliest years and could hardly be said to be friendly to capitalism. No mere propagandist for the Labour Party, however, he has written an impressive group of scholarly books in addition to *Religion and the Rise of Capitalism*, among which are *The Acquisitive Society* and *The Agrarian Problem in the Sixteenth Century*.

Like the rise of the great industry three centuries later, the economic revolution which accompanied the Renaissance gave a powerful stimulus to speculation. Both in Germany and in England, the Humanists turned a stream of pungent criticism on the social evils of their age. Mercantilist thinkers resharpened an old economic weapon for the armoury of princes. Objective economic analysis, still in its infancy, received a new impetus from the controversies of practical men on the rise in prices, on currency, and on the foreign exchanges. . . .

That the problems of a swiftly changing economic environment should have burst on Europe at a moment when it was torn by religious dissensions more acute than ever before, may perhaps be counted as not least among the tragedies of its history. But differences of social theory did not coincide with differences of religious opinion, and the mark of nearly all this body of teaching, alike in Germany and in England, is its conservatism. Where questions of social morality were involved, men whose names are a symbol of religious revolution stood, with hardly an exception, on the ancient ways, appealed to mediaeval authorities, and reproduced in popular language the doctrines of the Schoolmen.

A view of the social history of the sixteenth century which has found acceptance in certain quarters has represented the Reformation as the triumph of the commercial spirit over the traditional social ethics of Christendom. Something like it is of respectable antiquity. As early as 1540 Cranmer wrote to Oziander protesting against the embarrassment caused to reformers in England by the indulgence to moral laxity, in the matter alike of economic transactions and of marriage, alleged to be given by reformers in Germany. By the seventeenth century the hints had become a theory and an argument. Bossuet taunted Calvin and Bucer with being the first theologians to defend extortion, and it only remained for a pamphleteer to adapt the indictment to popular consumption, by writing bluntly that "it grew to a proverb that usury was the brat of heresy." That the revolt from Rome synchronized, both in Germany and in England, with a period of

From *Religion and the Rise of Capitalism* by R. H. Tawney, pp. 79–80, 82–85, 102–108, 110–111, 112–114, 213, 218–227, 231–236, 239–243, 246–249, 277–280. Copyright, 1926, by Harcourt, Brace and Company, Inc.; renewed by R. H. Tawney. Used by permission of the publishers, Harcourt, Brace and Company, Inc., and John Murray and Company, Ltd.

acute social distress is undeniable, nor is
any long argument needed to show that,
like other revolutions, it had its seamy side.
What is sometimes suggested, however, is
not merely a coincidence of religious and
economic movements, but a logical connection between changes in economic organization and changes in religious doctrines. It is
implied that the bad social practice of the
age was the inevitable expression of its
religious innovations, and that, if the reformers did not explicitly teach a conscience-
less individualism, individualism was, at
least, the natural corollary of their teaching.
In the eighteenth century, which had as
little love for the commercial restrictions of
the ages of monkish superstition as for their
political theory, that view was advanced as
eulogy. In our own day, the wheel seems
almost to have come full circle. What was
then a matter for congratulation is now
often an occasion for criticism. There are
writers by whom the Reformation is
attacked, as inaugurating a period of unscrupulous commercialism, which had previously been held in check, it is suggested,
by the teaching of the Church.

These attempts to relate changes in social
theory to the grand religious struggles of
the age have their significance. But the
obiter dicta of an acrimonious controversy
throw more light on the temper of the
combatants than on the substance of their
contentions, and the issues were too complex to be adequately expressed in the
simple antitheses which appealed to partisans. If capitalism means the direction of
industry by the owners of capital for their
own pecuniary gain, and the social relations
which establish themselves between them
and the wage-earning proletariat whom
they control, then capitalism had existed on
a grand scale both in mediaeval Italy and
in mediaeval Flanders. If by the capitalist
spirit is meant the temper which is prepared
to sacrifice all moral scruples to the pursuit
of profit, it had been only too familiar to
the saints and sages of the Middle Ages.
It was the economic imperialism of Catholic
Portugal and Spain, not the less imposing,

if more solid, achievements of the Protestant
powers, which impressed contemporaries
down to the Armada. It was predominantly
Catholic cities which were the commercial
capitals of Europe, and Catholic bankers
who were its leading financiers.

Nor is the suggestion that Protestant
opinion looked with indulgence on the
temper which attacked restraints on economic enterprise better founded. If it is
true that the Reformation released forces
which were to act as a solvent of the traditional attitude of religious thought to social
and economic issues, it did so without
design, and against the intention of most
reformers. In reality, however sensational
the innovations in economic practice which
accompanied the expansion of financial
capitalism in the sixteenth century, the
development of doctrine on the subject of
economic ethics was continuous, and, the
more closely it is examined, the less foundation does there seem to be for the view that
the stream plunged into vacancy over the
precipice of the religious revolution. To
think of the abdication of religion from its
theoretical primacy over economic activity
and social institutions as synchronizing
with the revolt from Rome, is to antedate a
movement which was not finally accomplished for another century and a half, and
which owed as much to changes in economic and political organization, as it did
to developments in the sphere of religious
thought. In the sixteenth century religious
teachers of all shades of opinion still
searched the Bible, the Fathers and the
Corpus Juris Canonici for light on practical
questions of social morality, and, as far as
the first generation of reformers was concerned, there was no intention, among
either Lutherans, or Calvinists, or Anglicans, of relaxing the rules of good conscience, which were supposed to control
economic transactions and social relations.
If anything, indeed, their tendency was to
interpret them with a more rigorous severity,
as a protest against the moral laxity of the
Renaissance, and, in particular, against the
avarice which was thought to be peculiarly

the sin of Rome. For the passion for regeneration and purification, which was one element in the Reformation, was directed against the corruptions of society as well as of the Church. Princes and nobles and business men conducted themselves after their kind, and fished eagerly in troubled waters. But the aim of religious leaders was to reconstruct, not merely doctrine and ecclesiastical government, but conduct and institutions, on a pattern derived from the forgotten purity of primitive Christianity. . . .

The most characteristic and influential form of Protestantism in the two centuries following the Reformation is that which descends, by one path or another, from the teaching of Calvin. Unlike the Lutheranism from which it sprang, Calvinism, assuming different shapes in different countries, became an international movement, which brought, not peace, but a sword, and the path of which was strewn with revolutions. Where Lutheranism had been socially conservative, deferential to established political authorities, the exponent of a personal, almost a quietistic, piety, Calvinism was an active and radical force. It was a creed which sought, not merely to purify the individual, but to reconstruct Church and State, and to renew society by penetrating every department of life, public as well as private, with the influence of religion.

Upon the immense political reactions of Calvinism, this is not the place to enlarge. As a way of life and a theory of society, it possessed from the beginning one characteristic which was both novel and important. It assumed an economic organization which was relatively advanced, and expounded its social ethics on the basis of it. In this respect the teaching of the Puritan moralists who derive most directly from Calvin is in marked contrast with that both of mediaeval theologians and of Luther. The difference is not merely one of the conclusions reached, but of the plane on which the discussion is conducted. The background, not only of most mediaeval social theory, but also of Luther and his English contemporaries, is the traditional stratification of rural society. It is a natural, rather than a money, economy, consisting of the petty dealings of peasants and craftsmen in the small market town, where industry is carried on for the subsistence of the household and the consumption of wealth follows hard upon the production of it, and where commerce and finance are occasional incidents, rather than the forces which keep the whole system in motion. When they criticize economic abuses, it is precisely against departures from that natural state of things — against the enterprise, the greed of gain, the restless competition, which disturb the stability of the existing order with clamorous economic appetites — that their criticism is directed. . . .

For Calvin, and still more his later interpreters, began their voyage lower down the stream. Unlike Luther, who saw economic life with the eyes of a peasant and a mystic, they approached it as men of affairs, disposed neither to idealize the patriarchal virtues of the peasant community, nor to regard with suspicion the mere fact of capitalist enterprise in commerce and finance. Like early Christianity and modern socialism, Calvinism was largely an urban movement; like them, in its earlier days, it was carried from country to country partly by emigrant traders and workmen; and its stronghold was precisely in those social groups to which the traditional scheme of social ethics, with its treatment of economic interests as a quite minor aspect of human affairs, must have seemed irrelevant or artificial. As was to be expected in the exponents of a faith which had its headquarters at Geneva, and later its most influential adherents in great business centres, like Antwerp with its industrial hinterland, London, and Amsterdam, its leaders addressed their teaching, not of course exclusively, but none the less primarily, to the classes engaged in trade and industry, who formed the most modern and progressive elements in the life of the age.

It is in the light of that change of social perspective that the doctrine of usury associated with the name of Calvin is to be interpreted. Its significance consisted, not in the phase which it marked in the technique of economic analysis, but in its admission to a new position of respectability of a powerful and growing body of social interests, which, however irrepressible in practice, had hitherto been regarded by religious theory as, at best, of dubious propriety, and, at worst, as frankly immoral. Strictly construed, the famous pronouncement strikes the modern reader rather by its rigour than by its indulgence. "Calvin," wrote an English divine a generation after his death, "deals with usurie as the apothecarie doth with poyson." The apologetic was just, for neither his letter to Oecolampadius, nor his sermon on the same subject, reveals any excessive tolerance for the trade of the financier. That interest is lawful, provided that it does not exceed an official maximum, that, even when a maximum is fixed, loans must be made *gratis* to the poor, that the borrower must reap as much advantage as the lender, that excessive security must not be exacted, that what is venial as an occasional expedient is reprehensible when carried on as a regular occupation, that no man may snatch economic gain for himself to the injury of his neighbour — a condonation of usury protected by such embarrassing entanglements can have offered but tepid consolation to the devout money-lender.

Contemporaries interpreted Calvin to mean that the debtor might properly be asked to concede some small part of his profits to the creditor with whose capital they had been earned, but that the exaction of interest was wrong if it meant that "the creditor becomes rich by the sweat of the debtor, and the debtor does not reap the reward of his labour." There have been ages in which such doctrines would have been regarded as an attack on financial enterprise rather than as a defence of it. Nor were Calvin's specific contributions to the theory of usury strikingly original. As a hard-headed lawyer, he was free both from the incoherence and from the idealism of Luther, and his doctrine was probably

regarded by himself merely as one additional step in the long series of developments through which ecclesiastical jurisprudence on the subject had already gone. In emphasizing the difference between the interest wrung from the necessities of the poor and the interest which a prosperous merchant could earn with borrowed capital, he had been anticipated by Major; in his sanction of a moderate rate on loans to the rich, his position was the same as that already assumed, though with some hesitation, by Melanchthon. The picture of Calvin, the organizer and disciplinarian, as the parent of laxity in social ethics, is a legend. Like the author of another revolution in economic theory, he might have turned on his popularizers with the protest: "I am not a Calvinist."

Legends are apt, however, to be as right in substance as they are wrong in detail, and both its critics and its defenders were correct in regarding Calvin's treatment of capital as a watershed. What he did was to change the plane on which the discussion was conducted, by treating the ethics of money-lending, not as a matter to be decided by an appeal to a special body of doctrine on the subject of usury, but as a particular case of the general problem of the social relations of a Christian community, which must be solved in the light of existing circumstances. The significant feature in his discussion of the subject is that he assumes credit to be a normal and inevitable incident in the life of society. He therefore dismisses the oft-quoted passages from the Old Testament and the Fathers as irrelevant, because designed for conditions which no longer exist, argues that the payment of interest for capital is as reasonable as the payment of rent for land, and throws on the conscience of the individual the obligation of seeing that it does not exceed the amount dictated by natural justice and the golden rule. . . . But capital and credit are indispensable; the financier is not a pariah, but a useful member of society; and lending at interest, provided that the rate is reasonable and that loans are made freely to the poor, is not *per se* more extortionate than any other of the economic transactions without which human affairs cannot be carried on. That acceptance of the realities of commercial practice as a starting-point was of momentous importance. It meant that Calvinism and its offshoots took their stand on the side of the activities which were to be most characteristic of the future, and insisted that it was not by renouncing them, but by untiring concentration on the task of using for the glory of God the opportunities which they offered, that the Christian life could and must be lived....

It was that revolution in the traditional scale of ethical values which the Swiss reformers desired to achieve; it was that new type of Christian character that they laboured to create. Not as part of any scheme of social reform, but as elements in a plan of moral regeneration, they seized on the aptitudes cultivated by the life of business and affairs, stamped on them a new sanctification, and used them as the warp of a society in which a more than Roman discipline should perpetuate a character the exact antithesis of that fostered by obedience to Rome. The Roman Church, it was held, through the example of its rulers, had encouraged luxury and ostentation: the members of the Reformed Church must be economical and modest. It had sanctioned the spurious charity of indiscriminate almsgiving: the true Christian must repress mendicancy and insist on the virtues of industry and thrift. It had allowed the faithful to believe that they could atone for a life of worldliness by the savourless formality of individual good works reduced to a commercial system, as though man could keep a profit and loss account with his Creator: the true Christian must organize his life as a whole for the service of his Master. It had rebuked the pursuit of gain as lower than the life of religion, even while it took bribes from those who pursued gain with success: the Christian must conduct his business with a high seriousness, as in itself a kind of religion.

Such teaching, whatever its theological merits or defects, was admirably designed to liberate economic energies, and to weld into a disciplined social force the rising *bourgeoisie,* conscious of the contrast between its own standards and those of a laxer world, proud of its vocation as the standard-bearer of the economic virtues, and determined to vindicate an open road for its own way of life by the use of every weapon, including political revolution and war, because the issue which was at stake was not merely convenience or self-interest, but the will of God. Calvinism stood, in short, not only for a new doctrine of theology and ecclesiastical government, but for a new scale of moral values and a new ideal of social conduct. Its practical message, it might perhaps be said, was *la carrière ouverte* — not *aux talents,* but *au caractère.* ...

The two main elements in this teaching were the insistence on personal responsibility, discipline and asceticism, and the call to fashion for the Christian character an objective embodiment in social institutions. Though logically connected, they were often in practical discord. The influence of Calvinism was not simple, but complex, and extended far beyond the circle of Churches which could properly be called Calvinist. Calvinist theology was accepted where Calvinist discipline was repudiated. The bitter struggle between Presbyterians and Independents in England did not prevent men, to whom the whole idea of religious uniformity was fundamentally abhorrent, from drawing inspiration from the conception of a visible Christian society, in which, as one of them said, the Scripture was "really and materially to be fulfilled." Both an intense individualism and a rigorous Christian Socialism could be deduced from Calvin's doctrine. Which of them predominated depended on differences of political environment and of social class. It depended, above all, on the question whether Calvinists were, as at Geneva and in Scotland, a majority, who could stamp their ideals on the social order, or, as in England, a minority, living on the defensive beneath the suspicious eyes of a hostile Government.

In the version of Calvinism which found favour with the English upper classes in the seventeenth century, individualism in social affairs was, on the whole, the prevalent philosophy. It was only the fanatic and the agitator who drew inspiration from the vision of a New Jerusalem descending on England's green and pleasant land, and the troopers of Fairfax soon taught them reason. But, if the theology of Puritanism was that of Calvin, its conception of society, diluted by the practical necessities of a commercial age, and softened to suit the conventions of a territorial aristocracy, was poles apart from that of the master who founded a discipline, compared with which that of Laud, as Laud himself dryly observed, was a thing of shreds and patches. As both the teaching of Calvin himself, and the practice of some Calvinist communities, suggest, the social ethics of the heroic age of Calvinism savoured more of a collectivist dictatorship than of individualism. The expression of a revolt against the mediaeval ecclesiastical system, it stood itself, where circumstances favoured it, for a discipline far more stringent and comprehensive than that of the Middle Ages. If, as some historians have argued, the philosophy of *laissez faire* emerged as a result of the spread of Calvinism among the middle classes, it did so, like tolerance, by a route which was indirect. It was accepted less because it was esteemed for its own sake, than as a compromise forced upon Calvinism at a comparatively late stage in its history, as a result of its modification by the pressure of commercial interests, or of a balance of power between conflicting authorities. . . .

"The triumph of Puritanism," it has been said, "swept away all traces of any restriction or guidance in the employment of money."[1] That it swept away the restrictions imposed by the existing machinery is true; neither ecclesiastical courts, nor High

Commission, nor Star Chamber, could function after 1640. But, if it broke the discipline of the Church of Laud and the State of Strafford, it did so but as a step towards erecting a more rigorous discipline of its own. It would have been scandalized by economic individualism, as much as by religious tolerance, and the broad outlines of its scheme of organization favoured unrestricted liberty in matters of business as little as in the things of the spirit. To the Puritan of any period in the century between the accession of Elizabeth and the Civil War, the suggestion that he was the friend of economic or social license would have seemed as wildly inappropriate as it would have appeared to most of his critics, who taunted him, except in the single matter of usury, with an intolerable meticulousness. . . .

The attempt to crystallize social morality in an objective discipline was possible only in a theocracy; and, still eloquent in speech, theocracy had abdicated in fact, even before the sons of Belial returned to cut down its groves and lay waste its holy places. In an age when the right to dissent from the State Church was still not fully established, its defeat was fortunate, for it was the victory of tolerance. It meant, however, that the discipline of the Church gave place to the attempt to promote reform through the action of the State, which reached its height in the Barebones Parliament. Projects for law reform, marriage reform and financial reform, the reform of prisons and the relief of debtors, jostled each other on its committees; while outside it there were murmurs among radicals against social and economic privilege, which were not to be heard again till the days of the Chartists, and which to the conservative mind of Cromwell seemed to portend mere anarchy. The transition from the idea of a moral code enforced by the Church, which had been characteristic of early Calvinism, to the economic individualism of the later Puritan movement took place, in fact, by way of the democratic agitation of the Independents. Abhorring the whole mecha-

[1] Cunningham, *The Moral Witness of the Church on the Investment of Money and the Use of Wealth,* 1909, p. 25.

nism of ecclesiastical discipline and compulsory conformity, they endeavoured to achieve the same social and ethical ends by political action.

The change was momentous. If the English Social Democratic movement has any single source, that source is to be found in the New Model Army. But the conception implied in the attempt to formulate a scheme of economic ethics — the theory that every department of life falls beneath the same all-encompassing arch of religion — was too deeply rooted to be exorcised merely by political changes, or even by the more corroding march of economic development. Expelled from the world of fact, where it had always been a stranger and a sojourner, it survived in the world of ideas, and its champions in the last half of the century laboured it the more, precisely because they knew that it must be conveyed to their audiences by teaching and preaching or not at all. Of those champions the most learned, the most practical, and the most persuasive was Richard Baxter.

How Baxter endeavoured to give practical instruction to his congregation at Kidderminster, he himself has told us. "Every Thursday evening my neighbours that were most desirous and had opportunity met at my house, and there one of them repeated the sermon, and afterwards they proposed what doubts any of them had about the sermon, or any other case of conscience, and I resolved their doubts." Both in form and in matter, his *Christian Directory, or a Summ of Practical Theologie and Cases of Conscience* is a remarkable book. It is, in essence, a Puritan *Summa Theologica* and *Summa Moralis* in one; its method of treatment descends directly from that of the mediaeval *Summae,* and it is, perhaps, the last important English specimen of a famous *genus*. Its object, as Baxter explains in his introduction, is "the resolving of practical cases of conscience, and the reducing of theoretical knowledge into serious Christian practice." Divided into four parts, Ethics, Economics, Ecclesiastics, and Politics, it has as its purpose to establish the rules of a

Christian casuistry, which may be sufficiently detailed and precise to afford practical guidance to the proper conduct of men in the different relations of life, as lawyer, physician, schoolmaster, soldier, master and servant, buyer and seller, landlord and tenant, lender and borrower, ruler and subject. Part of its material is derived from the treatment of similar questions by previous writers, both before and after the Reformation, and Baxter is conscious of continuing a great tradition. But it is, above all things, realistic, and its method lends plausibility to the suggestion that it originated in an attempt to answer practical questions put to its author by members of his congregation. Its aim is not to overwhelm by authority, but to convince by an appeal to the enlightened common sense of the Christian reader. It does not overlook, therefore, the practical facts of a world in which commerce is carried on by the East India Company in distant markets, trade is universally conducted on credit, the iron manufacture is a large-scale industry demanding abundant supplies of capital and offering a profitable opening to the judicious investor, and the relations of landlords and tenants have been thrown into confusion by the fire of London. Nor does it ignore the moral qualities for the cultivation of which an opportunity is offered by the life of business. It takes as its starting-point the commercial environment of the Restoration, and its teaching is designed for "Rome or London, not Fools' Paradise."

Baxter's acceptance of the realities of his age makes the content of his teaching the more impressive. The attempt to formulate a casuistry of economic conduct obviously implies that economic relations are to be regarded merely as one department of human behaviour, for which each man is morally responsible, not as the result of an impersonal mechanism, to which ethical judgments are irrelevant. Baxter declines, therefore, to admit the convenient dualism, which exonerates the individual by representing his actions as the outcome of uncontrollable forces. The Christian, he insists, is committed by his faith to the acceptance of certain ethical standards, and these standards are as obligatory in the sphere of economic transactions as in any other province of human activity. To the conventional objection that religion has nothing to do with business — that "every man will get as much as he can have and that *caveat emptor* is the only security" — he answers bluntly that this way of dealing does not hold among Christians. Whatever the laxity of the law, the Christian is bound to consider first the golden rule and the public good. Naturally, therefore, he is debarred from making money at the expense of other persons, and certain profitable avenues of commerce are closed to him at the outset. "It is not lawful to take up or keep up any oppressing monopoly or trade, which tends to enrich you by the loss of the Commonwealth or of many."

But the Christian must not only eschew the obvious extortion practised by the monopolist, the engrosser, the organizer of a corner or a combine. He must carry on his business in the spirit of one who is conducting a public service; he must order it for the advantage of his neighbour as much as, and, if his neighbour be poor, more than, for his own. He must not desire "to get another's goods or labour for less than it is worth." He must not secure a good price for his own wares "by extortion working upon men's ignorance, error, or necessity." When prices are fixed by law, he must strictly observe the legal maximum; when they are not, he must follow the price fixed by common estimation. If he finds a buyer who is willing to give more, he "must not make too great an advantage of his convenience or desire, but be glad that [he] can pleasure him upon equal, fair, and honest terms," for "it is a false rule of them that think their commodity is worth as much as any one will give." If the seller foresees that in the future prices are likely to fall, he must not make profit out of his neighbour's ignorance, but must tell him so. If he foresees that they will rise, he may hold his wares back, but only — a somewhat

embarrassing exception — if it be not "to the hurt of the Commonwealth, as if . . . keeping it in be the cause of the dearth, and . . . bringing it forth would help to prevent it." If he is buying from the poor, "charity must be exercised as well as justice"; the buyer must pay the full price that the goods are worth to himself, and, rather than let the seller suffer because he cannot stand out for his price, should offer him a loan or persuade some one else to do so. In no case may a man doctor his wares in order to get for them a higher price than they are really worth, and in no case may he conceal any defects of quality; if he was so unlucky as to have bought an inferior article, he "may not repair [his] loss by doing as [he] was done by, . . . no more than [he] may cut another's purse because [his] was cut." Rivalry in trade, Baxter thinks, is inevitable. But the Christian must not snatch a good bargain "out of greedy covetousness, nor to the injury of the poor . . . nor . . . so as to disturb that due and civil order which should be among moderate men in trading." On the contrary, if "a covetous oppressor" offer a poor man less than his goods are worth, "it may be a duty to offer the poor man the worth of his commodity and save him from the oppressor."

The principles which should determine the contract between buyer and seller are applied equally to all other economic relations. Usury, in the sense of payment for a loan, is not in itself unlawful for Christians. But it becomes so, when the lender does not allow the borrower "such a proportion of the gain as his labour, hazard, or poverty doth require, but . . . will live at ease upon his labours"; or when, in spite of the borrower's misfortune, he rigorously exacts his pound of flesh; or when interest is demanded for a loan which charity would require to be free. Masters must discipline their servants for their good; but it is "an odious oppression and injustice to defraud a servant or labourer of his wages, yea, or to give him less than he deserveth." As the descendant of a family of yeomen, "free," as he says, "from the temptations of poverty and riches," Baxter had naturally strong views as to the ethics of landowning. Significantly enough, he deals with them under the general rubric of "Cases of oppression, especially of tenants," oppression being defined as the "injuring of inferiors who are unable to resist or to right themselves." "It is too common a sort of oppression for the rich in all places to domineer too insolently over the poor, and force them to follow their wills and to serve their interest, be it right or wrong. . . . Especially unmerciful landlords are the common and sore oppressors of the countrymen. If a few men can but get money enough to purchase all the land in a county, they think that they may do with their own as they list, and set such hard bargains of it to their tenants, that they are all but as their servants. . . . An oppressor is an Anti-Christ and an Anti-God . . . not only the agent of the Devil, but his image." As in his discussion of prices, the gist of Baxter's analysis of the cases of conscience which arise in the relations of landlord and tenant is that no man may secure pecuniary gain for himself by injuring his neighbour. Except in unusual circumstances, a landlord must not let his land at the full competitive rent which it would fetch in the market: "Ordinarily the common sort of tenants in England should have so much abated of the fullest worth that they may comfortably live on it, and follow their labours with cheerfulness of mind and liberty to serve God in their families, and to mind the matters of their salvation, and not to be necessitated to such toil and care and pinching want, as shall make them liker slaves than free men." He must not improve (i.e. enclose) his land without considering the effect on the tenants, or evict his tenants without compensating them, and in such a way as to cause depopulation; nor must a newcomer take a holding over the sitting tenant's head by offering "a greater rent than he can give or than the landlord hath just cause to require of him." The Christian, in short, while eschewing "causeless, perplexing, melancholy scruples, which would stop a man in

the course of his duty," must so manage his business as to "avoid sin rather than loss," and seek first to keep his conscience in peace.

The first characteristic to strike the modern reader in all this teaching is its conservatism. In spite of the economic and political revolutions of the past two centuries, how small, after all, the change in the presentation of the social ethics of the Chistian faith! A few months after the appearance of the *Christian Directory*, the Stop of the Exchequer tore a hole in the already intricate web of London finance, and sent a shiver through the money-markets of Europe. But Baxter, though no mere antiquarian, discourses of equity in bargaining, of just prices, of reasonable rents, of the sin of usury, in the same tone, if not with quite the same conclusions, as a mediaeval Schoolman, and he differs from one of the later Doctors, like St. Antonino, hardly more than St. Antonino himself had differed from Aquinas. Seven years later Bunyan published *The Life and Death of Mr. Badman*. Among the vices which it pilloried were the sin of extortion, "most commonly committed by men of trade, who without all conscience, when they have an advantage, will make a prey of their neighbour," the covetousness of "hucksters, that buy up the poor man's victual wholesale and sell it to him again for unreasonable gains," the avarice of usurers, who watch till "the poor fall into their mouths," and "of those vile wretches called pawnbrokers, that lend money and goods to poor people, who are by necessity forced to such an inconvenience, and will make by one trick or another the interest of what they so lend amount to thirty and forty, yea sometimes fifty pounds by the year." As Christian and Christiana watched Mr. Badman thus bite and pinch the poor in his shop in Bedford, before they took staff and scrip for their journey to a more distant City, they remembered that the Lord himself will plead the cause of the afflicted against them that oppress them, and reflected, taught by the dealings of Ephron the son of Zohar, and of David with Ormon the Jebusite, that there is a "wickedness, as in selling too dear, so in buying too cheap." Brother Berthold of Regensburg had said the same four centuries before, in his racy sermons in Germany. The emergence of the idea that "business is business," and that the world of commercial transactions is a closed compartment with laws of its own, if more ancient than is often supposed, did not win so painless a triumph as is sometimes suggested. Puritan as well as Catholic accepted without demur the view which set all human interests and activities within the compass of religion. Puritans, as well as Catholics, essayed the formidable task of formulating a Christian casuistry of economic conduct.

They essayed it. But they succeeded even less than the Popes and Doctors whose teaching, not always unwittingly, they repeated. And their failure had its roots, not merely in the obstacles offered by the ever more recalcitrant opposition of a commercial environment, but, like all failures which are significant, in the soul of Puritanism itself. Virtues are often conquered by vices, but their rout is most complete when it is inflicted by other virtues, more militant, more efficient, or more congenial, and it is not only tares which choke the ground where the good seed is sown. The fundamental question, after all, is not what kind of rules a faith enjoins, but what type of character it esteems and cultivates. To the scheme of Christian ethics which offered admonitions against the numberless disguises assumed by the sin which sticketh fast between buying and selling, the Puritan character offered, not direct opposition, but a polished surface on which these ghostly admonitions could find no enduring foothold. The rules of Christian morality elaborated by Baxter were subtle and sincere. But they were like seeds carried by birds from a distant and fertile plain, and dropped upon a glacier. They were at once embalmed and sterilized in a river of ice. "The capitalist spirit" is as old as history, and was not, as has sometimes been said,

the offspring of Puritanism. But it found in certain aspects of later Puritanism a tonic which braced its energies and fortified its already vigorous temper. At first sight, no contract could be more violent than that between the iron collectivism, the almost military discipline, the remorseless and violent rigours practised in Calvin's Geneva, and preached elsewhere, if in a milder form, by his disciples, and the impatient rejection of all traditional restrictions on economic enterprise which was the temper of the English business world after the Civil War. In reality, the same ingredients were present throughout, but they were mixed in changing proportions, and exposed to different temperatures at different times. Like traits of individual character which are suppressed till the approach of maturity releases them, the tendencies in Puritanism, which were to make it later a potent ally of the movement against the control of economic relations in the name either of social morality or of the public interest, did not reveal themselves till political and economic changes had prepared a congenial environment for their growth. Nor, once those conditions were created, was it only England which witnessed the transformation. In all countries alike, in Holland, in America, in Scotland, in Geneva itself, the social theory of Calvinism went through the same process of development. It had begun by being the very soul of authoritarian regimentation. It ended by being the vehicle of an almost Utilitarian individualism. While social reformers in the sixteenth century could praise Calvin for his economic rigour, their successors in Restoration England, if of one persuasion, denounced him as the parent of economic license, if of another, applauded Calvinist communities for their commercial enterprise and for their freedom from antiquated prejudices on the subject of economic morality. So little do those who shoot the arrows of the spirit know where they will light. . . .

The England of Shakespeare and Bacon was still largely mediaeval in its economic organization and social outlook, more interested in maintaining customary standards of consumption than in accumulating capital for future production, with an aristocracy contemptuous of the economic virtues, a peasantry farming for subsistence amid the organized confusion of the open-field village, and a small, if growing, body of jealously conservative craftsmen. In such a society Puritanism worked like the yeast which sets the whole mass fermenting. It went through its slack and loosely knit texture like a troop of Cromwell's Ironsides through the disorderly cavalry of Rupert. Where, as in Ireland, the elements were so alien that assimilation was out of the question, the result was a wound that festered for three centuries. In England the effect was that at once of an irritant and of a tonic. Puritanism had its own standards of social conduct, derived partly from the obvious interests of the commercial classes, partly from its conception of the nature of God and the destiny of man. These standards were in sharp antithesis, both to the considerable surviving elements of feudalism in English society, and to the policy of the authoritarian State, with its ideal of an ordered and graded society, whose different members were to be maintained in their traditional status by the pressure and protection of a paternal monarchy. Sapping the former by its influence, and overthrowing the latter by direct attack, Puritanism became a potent force in preparing the way for the commercial civilization which finally triumphed at the Revolution.

The complaint that religious radicalism, which aimed at upsetting the government of the Church, went hand in hand with an economic radicalism, which resented the restraints on individual self-interest imposed in the name of religion or of social policy, was being made by the stricter school of religious opinion quite early in the reign of Elizabeth. Seventeenth-century writers repeated the charge that the Puritan conscience lost its delicacy where matters of business were concerned, and some of them were sufficiently struck by the phenomenon to attempt an historical explanation of it.

The example on which they usually seized — the symbol of a supposed general disposition to laxity — was the indulgence shown by Puritan divines in the particular matter of moderate interest. It was the effect, so the picturesque story ran, of the Marian persecution. The refugees who fled to the Continent could not start business in a foreign country. If, driven by necessity, they invested their capital and lived on the proceeds, who could quarrel with so venial a lapse in so good a cause? Subsequent writers embellished the picture. The redistribution of property at the time of the Dissolution, and the expansion of trade in the middle of the century, had led, one of them argued, to a great increase in the volume of credit transactions. The opprobrium which attached to loans at interest — "a sly and forbid practice" — not only among Romanists and Anglicans, but among honest Puritans, played into the hands of the less scrupulous members of "the faction." Disappointed in politics, they took to money-lending, and, without venturing to justify usury in theory, defended it in practice. "Without the scandal of a recantation, they contrived an expedient, by maintaining that, though usury for the name were stark naught, yet for widows, orphans and other impotents (therein principally comprising the saints under persecution) it was very tolerable, because profitable, and in a manner necessary." Naturally, Calvin's doctrine as to the legitimacy of moderate interest was hailed by these hypocrites with a shout of glee. "It took with the brethren like polygamy with the Turks, recommended by the example of the divers zealous ministers, who themselves desired to pass for orphans of the first rank." Nor was it only as the apologist of moderate interest that Puritanism was alleged to reveal the cloven hoof. Puritans themselves complained of a mercilessness in driving hard bargains, and of a harshness to the poor, which contrasted unfavourably with the practice of followers of the unreformed religion. "The Papists," wrote a Puritan in 1653, "may rise up against many of this generation. It is a sad thing that they should be more forward upon a bad principle than a Christian upon a good one."

Such, in all ages, is history as seen by the political pamphleteer. The real story was less dramatic, but more significant. From the very beginning, Calvinism had comprised two elements, which Calvin himself had fused, but which contained the seeds of future discord. It had at once given a whole-hearted *imprimatur* to the life of business enterprise, which most earlier moralists had regarded with suspicion, and had laid upon it the restraining hand of an inquisitorial discipline. At Geneva, where Calvinism was the creed of a small and homogeneous city, the second aspect had predominated; in the many-sided life of England, where there were numerous conflicting interests to balance it, and where it was long politically weak, the first. Then, in the late sixteenth and early seventeenth centuries, had come the wave of commercial and financial expansion — companies, colonies, capitalism in textiles, capitalism in mining, capitalism in finance — on the crest of which the English commercial classes, in Calvin's day still held in leading-strings by conservative statesmen, had climbed to a position of dignity and affluence.

Naturally, as the Puritan movement came to its own, these two elements flew apart. The collectivist, half-communistic aspect, which had never been acclimatized in England, quietly dropped out of notice, to crop up once more, and for the last time, to the disgust and terror of merchant and landowner, in the popular agitation under the Commonwealth. The individualism congenial to the world of business became the distinctive characteristic of a Puritanism which had arrived, and which, in becoming a political force, was at once secularized and committed to a career of compromise. Its note was not the attempt to establish on earth a "Kingdom of Christ," but an ideal of personal character and conduct, to be realized by the punctual discharge both of public and private duties. Its theory had

been discipline; its practical result was liberty.

Given the social and political conditions of England, the transformation was inevitable. The incompatibility of Presbyterianism with the stratified arrangement of English society had been remarked by Hooker. If the City Fathers of Geneva had thrown off by the beginning of the seventeenth century the religious collectivism of Calvin's régime, it was not to be expected that the landowners and *bourgeoisie* of an aristocratic and increasingly commercial nation, however much Calvinist theology might appeal to them, would view with favour the social doctrines implied in Calvinist discipline. In the reign of the first two Stuarts, both economic interests and political theory pulled them hard in the opposite direction. "Merchants' doings," the man of business in Wilson's *Discourse upon Usury* had observed, "must not thus be overthwarted by preachers and others, that cannot skill of their dealings." Behind the elaborate facade of Tudor State control, which has attracted the attention of historians, an individualist movement had been steadily developing, which found expression in opposition to the traditional policy of stereotyping economic relations by checking enclosure, controlling food supplies and prices, interfering with the money-market and regulating the conditions of the wage contract and of apprenticeship. In the first forty years of the seventeenth century, on grounds both of expediency and of principle, the commercial and propertied classes were becoming increasingly restive under the whole system, at once ambitious and inefficient, of economic paternalism. It was in the same sections of the community that both religious and economic dissatisfaction were most acute. Puritanism, with its idealization of the spiritual energies which found expression in the activities of business and industry, drew the isolated rivulets of discontent together, and swept them forward with the dignity and momentum of a religious and a social philosophy.

For it was not merely as the exponent of certain tenets as to theology and church government, but as the champion of interests and opinions embracing every side of the life of society, that the Puritan movement came into collision with the Crown. In reality, as is the case with most heroic ideologies, the social and religious aspects of Puritanism were not disentangled; they presented themselves, both to supporters and opponents, as different facets of a single scheme. "All that crossed the views of the needy courtiers, the proud encroaching priests, the thievish projectors, the lewd nobility and gentry . . . whoever could endure a sermon, modest habit or conversation, or anything good — all these were Puritans." The clash was not one of theories — a systematic and theoretical individualism did not develop till after the Restoration — but of contradictory economic interests and incompatible conceptions of social expediency.

. . . What in Calvin had been a qualified concession to practical exigencies, appeared in some of his later followers as a frank idealization of the life of the trader, as the service of God and the training-ground of the soul. Discarding the suspicion of economic motives, which had been as characteristic of the reformers as of mediaeval theologians, Puritanism in its later phases added a halo of ethical sanctification to the appeal of economic expediency, and offered a moral creed, in which the duties of religion and the calls of business ended their long estrangement in an unanticipated reconciliation. Its spokesmen pointed out, it is true, the peril to the soul involved in a single-minded concentration on economic interests. The enemy, however, was not riches, but the bad habits sometimes associated with them, and its warnings against an excessive preoccupation with the pursuit of gain wore more and more the air of afterthoughts, appended to teaching the main tendency and emphasis of which were little affected by these incidental qualifications. It insisted, in short, that money-making, if

not free from spiritual dangers, was not a danger and nothing else, but that it could be, and ought to be, carried on for the greater glory of God.

The conception to which it appealed to bridge the gulf sprang from the very heart of Puritan theology. It was that expressed in the characteristic and oft-used phrase, "a Calling." The rational order of the universe is the work of God, and its plan requires that the individual should labour for God's glory. There is a spiritual calling, and a temporal calling. It is the first duty of the Christian to know and believe in God; it is by faith that he will be saved. But faith is not a mere profession, such as that of Talkative of Prating Row, whose "religion is to make a noise." The only genuine faith is the faith which produces works. "At the day of Doom men shall be judged according to their fruits. It will not be said then, Did you believe? but, Were you doers, or talkers only"? The second duty of the Christian is to labour in the affairs of practical life, and this second duty is subordinate only to the first. "God," wrote a Puritan divine, "doth call every man and woman . . . to serve him in some peculiar employment in this world, both for their own and the common good. . . . The Great Governour of the world hath appointed to every man his proper post and province, and let him be never so active out of his sphere, he will be at a great loss, if he do not keep his own vineyard and mind his own business."

From this reiterated insistence on secular obligations as imposed by the divine will, it follows that, not withdrawal from the world, but the conscientious discharge of the duties of business, is among the loftiest of religious and moral virtues. "The begging friars and such monks as live only to themselves in no one thing to further their own subsistence or the good of mankind . . . yet have the confidence to boast of this their course as a state of perfection; which in very deed, as to the worthiness of it, falls short of the poorest cobbler, for his is a calling of God, and theirs is none." The idea was not a new one. Luther had advanced it as a weapon against monasticism. But for Luther, with his patriarchal outlook on economic affairs, the calling means normally that state of life in which the individual has been set by Heaven, and against which it is impiety to rebel. On the lips of Puritan divines, it is not an invitation to resignation, but the bugle-call which summons the elect to the long battle which will end only with their death. "The world is all before them." They are to hammer out their salvation, not merely *in vocatione*, but *per vocationem*. The calling is not a condition in which the individual is born, but a strenuous and exacting enterprise, to be undertaken, indeed, under the guidance of Providence, but to be chosen by each man for himself, with a deep sense of his solemn responsibilities. "God hath given to man reason for this use, that he should first consider, then choose, then put in execution; and it is a preposterous and brutish thing to fix or fall upon any weighty business, such as a calling or condition of life, without a careful pondering it in the balance of sound reason."

Laborare est orare. By the Puritan moralist the ancient maxim is repeated with a new and intenser significance. The labour which he idealizes is not simply a requirement imposed by nature, or a punishment for the sin of Adam. It is itself a kind of ascetic discipline, more rigorous than that demanded of any order of mendicants — a discipline imposed by the will of God, and to be undergone, not in solitude, but in the punctual discharge of secular duties. It is not merely an economic means, to be laid aside when physical needs have been satisfied. It is a spiritual end, for in it alone can the soul find health, and it must be continued as an ethical duty long after it has ceased to be a material necessity. Work thus conceived stands at the very opposite pole from "good works," as they were understood, or misunderstood, by Protestants. They, it was thought, had been a series of single transactions, performed as compensa-

tion for particular sins, or out of anxiety to acquire merit. What is required of the Puritan is not individual meritorious acts, but a holy life — a system in which every element is grouped round a central idea, the service of God, from which all disturbing irrelevances have been pruned, and to which all minor interests are subordinated.

His conception of that life was expressed in the words, "Be wholly taken up in diligent business of your lawful callings, when you are not exercised in the more immediate service of God." In order to deepen his spiritual life, the Christian must be prepared to narrow it. He "is blind in no man's cause, but best sighted in his own. He confines himself to the circle of his own affairs and thrusts not his fingers in needless fires. . . . He sees the falseness of it [the world] and therefore learns to trust himself ever, others so far as not to be damaged by their disappointment." There must be no idle leisure; "those that are prodigal of their time despise their own souls." Religion must be active, not merely contemplative. Contemplation is, indeed, a kind of self-indulgence. "To neglect this [i.e. bodily employment and mental labour] and say, 'I will pray and meditate,' is as if your servant should refuse your greatest work, and tye himself to some lesser, easie part. . . . God hath commanded you some way or other to labour for your daily bread." The rich are no more excused from work than the poor, though they may rightly use their riches to select some occupation specially serviceable to others. Covetousness is a danger to the soul, but it is not so grave a danger as sloth. "The standing pool is prone to putrefaction: and it were better to beat down the body and to keep it in subjection by a laborious calling, than through luxury to become a cast-away." So far from poverty being meritorious, it is a duty to choose the more profitable occupation. "If God show you a way in which you may lawfully get more than in another way (without wrong to your soul or to any other), if you refuse this, and choose the less gainful way, you cross one of the ends of your Calling, and you refuse to be God's steward." Luxury, unrestrained pleasure, personal extravagance, can have no place in a Christian's conduct, for "every penny which is laid out . . . must be done as by God's own appointment." Even excessive devotion to friends and relations is to be avoided. "It is an irrational act, and therefore not fit for a rational creature, to love any one farther than reason will allow us. . . . It very often taketh up men's minds so as to hinder their love to God." The Christian life, in short, must be systematic and organized, the work of an iron will and a cool intelligence. Those who have read Mill's account of his father must have been struck by the extent to which Utilitarianism was not merely a political doctrine, but a moral attitude. Some of the links in the Utilitarian coat of mail were forged, it may be suggested, by the Puritan divines of the seventeenth century. . . .

The springs of economic conduct lie in regions rarely penetrated by moralists, and to suggest a direct reaction of theory on practice would be paradoxical. But if the circumstances which determine that certain kinds of conduct shall be profitable are economic, those which decide that they shall be the object of general approval are primarily moral and intellectual. For conventions to be adopted with whole-hearted enthusiasm, to be not merely tolerated, but applauded, to become the habit of a nation and the admiration of its philosophers, the second condition must be present as well as the first. The insistence among men of pecuniary motives, the strength of economic egotism, the appetite for gain — these are the commonplaces of every age and need no emphasis. What is significant is the change of standards which converted a natural frailty into a resounding virtue. After all, it appears, a man can serve two masters, for — so happily is the world disposed — he may be paid by one, while he works for the other. Between the old-fashioned denunciation of uncharitable covetousness and the new-fashioned applause of economic enterprise, a bridge is thrown

by the argument which urges that enterprise itself is the discharge of a duty imposed by God. . . .

The transition from the anabaptist to the company promoter was less abrupt than might at first sight be supposed. It had been prepared, however unintentionally, by Puritan moralists. In their emphasis on the moral duty of untiring activity, on work as an end in itself, on the evils of luxury and extravagance, on foresight and thrift, on moderation and self-discipline and rational calculation, they had created an ideal of Christian conduct, which canonized as an ethical principle the efficiency which economic theorists were preaching as a specific for social disorders. It was as captivating as it was novel. To countless generations of religious thinkers, the fundamental maxim of Christian social ethics had seemed to be expressed in the words of St. Paul to Timothy: "Having food and raiment, let us be therewith content. For the love of money is the root of all evil." Now, while, as always, the world battered at the gate, a new standard was raised within the citadel by its own defenders. The garrison had discovered that the invading host of economic appetites was, not an enemy, but an ally. Not sufficiency to the needs of daily life, but limitless increase and expansion, became the goal of the Christian's efforts. Not consumption, on which the eyes of earlier sages had been turned, but production, became the pivot of his argument. Not an easy-going and open-handed charity, but a systematic and methodical accumulation, won the need of praise that belongs to the good and faithful servant. The shrewd, calculating commercialism which tries all human relations by pecuniary standards, the acquisitiveness which cannot rest while there are competitors to be conquered or profits to be won, the love of social power and hunger for economic gain — these irrepressible appetites had evoked from time immemorial the warnings and denunciations of saints and sages. Plunged in the cleansing waters of later Puritanism, the qualities which less enlightened ages had denounced as social vices emerged as economic virtues. They emerged as moral virtues as well. For the world exists not to be enjoyed, but to be conquered. Only its conqueror deserves the name of Christian. For such a philosophy, the question, "What shall it profit a man?" carries no sting. In winning the world, he wins the salvation of his own soul as well.

The idea of economic progress as an end to be consciously sought, while ever receding, had been unfamiliar to most earlier generations of Englishmen, in which the theme of moralists had been the danger of unbridled cupidity, and the main aim of public policy had been the stability of traditional relationships. It found a new sanction in the identification of labour and enterprise with the service of God. The magnificent energy which changed in a century the face of material civilization was to draw nourishment from that temper. The worship of production and ever greater production — the slavish drudgery of the millionaire and his unhappy servants — was to be hallowed by the precepts of the same compelling creed.

. . . In reality, though inherited dispositions may be constant from generation to generation, the system of valuations, preferences, and ideals — the social environment within which individual character functions — is in process of continuous change, and it is in the conception of the place to be assigned to economic interests in the life of society that change has in recent centuries been most comprehensive in its scope, and most sensational in its consequences. The isolation of economic aims as a specialized object of concentrated and systematic effort, the erection of economic criteria into an independent and authoritative standard of social expediency, are phenomena which, though familiar enough in classical antiquity, appear, at least on a grand scale, only at a comparatively recent date in the history of later civilizations. The conflict between the economic outlook of East and West, which impresses the traveller today, finds a parallel in the contrast between mediaeval and modern economic ideas, which strikes the historian.

The elements which combined to produce that revolution are too numerous to be summarized in any neat formula. But, side by side with the expansion of trade and the rise of new classes to political power, there was a further cause, which, if not the most conspicuous, was not the least fundamental. It was the contraction of the territory within which the writ of religion was conceived to run. The criticism which dismisses the concern of Churches with economic relations and social organization as a modern innovation finds little support in past history. What requires explanation is not the view that these matters are part of the province of religion, but the view that they are not. When the age of the Reformation begins, economics is still a branch of ethics, and ethics of theology; all human activities are treated as falling within a single scheme, whose character is determined by the spiritual destiny of mankind; the appeal of theorists is to natural law, not to utility; the legitimacy of economic transactions is tried by reference, less to the movements of the market, than to moral standards derived from the traditional teaching of the Christian Church; the Church itself is regarded as a society wielding theoretical, and sometimes practical, authority in social affairs.

The secularization of political thought, which was the work of the next two centuries, had profound reactions on social speculation, and by the Restoration the whole perspective, at least in England, has been revolutionized. Religion has been converted from the keystone which holds together the social edifice into one department within it, and the idea of a rule of right is replaced by economic expediency as the arbiter of policy and the criterion of conduct. From a spiritual being, who, in order to survive, must devote a reasonable attention to economic interests, man seems sometimes to have become an economic animal, who will be prudent, nevertheless, if he takes due precautions to assure his spiritual well-being.

The result is an attitude which forms so fundamental a part of modern political thought, that both its precarious philosophical basis, and the contrast which it offers with the conceptions of earlier generations, are commonly forgotten. Its essence is a dualism which regards the secular and the religious aspects of life, not as successive stages within a larger unity, but as parallel and independent provinces, governed by different laws, judged by different standards, and amenable to different authorities. To the most representative minds of the Reformation, as of the Middle Ages, a philosophy which treated the transactions of commerce and the institutions of society as indifferent to religion would have appeared, not merely morally reprehensible, but intellectually absurd. Holding as their first assumption that the ultimate social authority is the will of God, and that temporal interests are a transitory episode in the life of spirits which are eternal, they state the rules to which the social conduct of the Christian must conform, and, when circumstances allow, organize the discipline by which those rules may be enforced. By their successors in the eighteenth century the philosophy of Indifferentism, though rarely formulated as a matter of theory, is held in practice as a truism which it is irrational, if not actually immoral, to question, since it is in the heart of the individual that religion has its throne, and to externalize it in rules and institutions is to tarnish its purity and to degrade its appeal. Naturally, therefore, they formulate the ethical principles of Christianity in terms of a comfortable ambiguity, and rarely indicate with any precision their application to commerce, finance, and the ownership of property. Thus the conflict between religion and those natural economic ambitions, which the thought of an earlier age had regarded with suspicion, is suspended by a truce which divides the life of mankind between them. The former takes as its province the individual soul, the latter the intercourse of man with his fellows in the activities of business and the affairs of society. Provided that each keeps to its own territory, peace is assured. They cannot collide, for they can never meet. . . .

PURITANISM AND THE SPIRIT OF CAPITALISM

WINTHROP S. HUDSON

Winthrop S. Hudson is a Professor of Church History at the Colgate-Rochester Divinity School and the secretary and past president of the American Society of Church History. He holds a Ph.D. degree in history in addition to his Bachelor of Divinity and has written a number of articles on topics of church history in England and the United States.

CALVINISM as an historical movement was exceedingly complex. It was a phenomenon in which theology, economic theory, political philosophy, and a general cultural orientation were inextricably mixed and applied in an intense effort to refashion society into a Holy Commonwealth. In attempting to interpret this movement, as Sidney E. Mead has pointed out, "one is always in danger either of trying to do complete justice to the complexity and landing in a confusing incoherence and lack of clarity, or of seizing upon one interpretative theme in the interest of clarity and landing in over-simplification." Most of the discussions of Calvinism, in any or all of its various manifestations, have avoided the first alternative — falling into the morass of confusion and incoherence — but many have succumbed to the second — an over-simplification that is definitely misleading.

It is now generally acknowledged that Max Weber's attempt to explain the economic significance of Calvinism is a particularly conspicuous illustration of such over-simplification. It is not so generally recognized that R. H. Tawney, in his *Religion and the Rise of Capitalism*, has not entirely escaped the slanting of his material. This may be due partly to the fact that it was Tawney who exposed Weber's most glaring over-simplifications. A more fundamental reason for the failure to question some of Tawney's conclusions is that the distortion involved in his thesis is very subtle, and the thesis itself is carefully qualified, and on the whole quite sound. Nevertheless, the over-all impression as to the nature and character of the Puritan movement is somewhat misleading.

The problem to which both Weber and Tawney addressed themselves was the remarkable coincidence of a particular religious affiliation with a particular social status; specifically, the identification of Calvinism with the industrial and commercial classes of the new centers of capitalist activity. "By the middle of the seventeenth century," writes Tawney in his Foreword to the English translation of Weber's work, "the contrast between the social conservatism of Catholic Europe and the strenuous enterprise of Calvinist communities had become a commonplace." As a result of his examination of the evidence, Weber set forth the thesis that Calvinism was the parent of modern capitalism. Tawney, re-examining Weber's thesis some twenty years later, concluded that, while Calvinism was

From Winthrop S. Hudson, "Puritanism and the Spirit of Capitalism," *Church History*, vol. XVIII (March, 1949), pp. 3–16. By permission of the author.

not exactly the parent of capitalism, it was, in its seventeenth century English version, at least the handmaiden of capitalism. . . .

Tawney criticized Weber at several points, principally in terms of his over-simplifications. "It is the temptation of one who expounds a new and fruitful idea to use it as a key to unlock all doors, and to explain by reference to a single principle phenomena which are, in reality, the result of several converging causes." Tawney pointed out that Weber ignored or touched too lightly on other "intellectual movements, which were favorable to the growth of business enterprise and to an individualist attitude towards economic relations, but which had little to do with religion," and that he sought "to explain by reference to moral and intellectual influences developments which have their principal explanation in another region altogether." Tawney's major contribution to the discussion, however, was to emphasize that causation can work in two directions. "Is it not a little artificial," he asks, "to suggest that capitalist enterprise had to wait, as Weber appears to imply, till religious changes had produced a capitalist spirit?" It would be equally plausible "to argue that the religious changes were themselves merely the result of economic movements." Instead of Calvinism producing the capitalist spirit, both can with "equal plausibility be regarded as different effects of changes in economic organisation and social structure." Actually what occurred, Tawney maintained, was that, while Calvinism helped mould the social order, it was in turn moulded by it.

Weber's failure to give due weight to the reciprocal nature of causation led him into a further over-simplification — the equation of seventeenth century Puritanism with sixteenth century Calvinism. Tawney pointed out that "most of Weber's illustrations of his thesis are drawn from the writings of the English Puritans of the latter part of the seventeenth century," a fact which Weber readily admits. Weber proceeded on the assumption that, for his purposes, "ascetic Protestantism" can be treated "as a single

whole," which finds its clearest expression among the English Puritans of the late seventeenth century. This assumption, Tawney insisted, cannot be defended. Under the impact of new economic conditions, a profound change had taken place. The Calvinists of the sixteenth century believed in a rigorous discipline, and the economic individualism which both Tawney and Weber ascribe to the Puritan movement in its later phases would have "horrified" them.

Tawney's general conclusion is stated in these words:

"The capitalist spirit" is as old as history, and was not, as has sometimes been said, the offspring of Puritanism. But it found in certain aspects of later Puritanism a tonic which braced its energies and fortified its already vigorous temper. At first sight, no contrast could be more violent than that between the iron collectivism, the almost military discipline, the remorseless and violent rigors practiced in Calvin's Geneva, and preached elsewhere, if in a milder form, by his disciples, and the impatient rejection of all traditional restrictions on economic enterprise which was the temper of the English business world after the Civil War.

The explanation for such a radical shift in orientation, Tawney affirms, is to be found, not simply in the impact of large-scale economic change upon Calvinist thinking, but it stems from the very soul of Calvinism itself.

In reality, the same ingredients were present throughout, but they were mixed in changing proportions, and exposed to different temperatures at different times. Like traits of individual character which are suppressed till the approach of maturity releases them, the tendencies in Puritanism, which were to make it later a potent ally of the movement against the control of economic relations in the name either of social morality or of the public interest, did not reveal themselves till political and economic changes had prepared a congenial environment for their growth.

Like Weber, Tawney finds the key to the separation of economic from ethical interests in what they both considered "the very heart of Puritan theology" — the Calvinist conception of "the calling." Applied to commercial life, it meant that "poverty . . . was not a misfortune to be pitied and relieved, but a moral failing to be condemned," and that riches were "the blessing which rewards the triumph of energy and will." "By a kind of happy, preestablished harmony . . . success in business is in itself almost a sign of spiritual grace, for it is proof that a man has labored faithfully in his vocation, and that 'God has blessed his trade.'" Ethical distinctions in commercial life were thus obliterated, and the service of Mammon came to be identified with service to God.

Weber confessed that such a gross interpretation of "the calling" could not be found in the writings of John Calvin. Indeed, it was definitely rejected by him. But Weber felt that, if Calvin had not, then his followers, on the basis of psychological necessity, must have made such an interpretation, and Tawney, as we have seen, was convinced that such a conception revealed itself in the second half of the seventeenth century as the dominating feature of Puritan thought. Unfortunately, both men failed to realize that such an interpretation not only isolated the doctrine of the calling from its larger context in Calvinist thought, but it completely subverted the fundamental theological structure of Calvinism. Nor did they recognize that such an interpretation was not necessary as an explanation of the strenuous and energetic activity displayed by the Puritans in commercial life.

The failure to go to the root of Calvinism, even in its seventeenth-century English version, meant that its most characteristic feature was ignored and neglected — namely, a preoccupation with God as the supreme good, and the only worthy end, indeed, the necessary end — of all endeavor. "What is the chief end of man?" asks the *Westminster Shorter Catechism.* "Man's chief end is to glorify God and enjoy him forever." Incredible as it may seem to the modern mind, the Puritan held that God is more important than business, art, poetry, pleasure, or any of the other possible "goods" of life. It was almost an obsession, and the depth of this religious interest is reflected in even the most casual correspondence. God was, indeed, the be-all and end-all of existence, and the establishment of a right relationship to him was "the pearl of great price" without which all else was but dross. . . .

Post-Restoration Puritanism is the source from whence Weber drew most of his illustrations, and it is the particular phase of Calvinism on which Tawney rested his case. Of the post-Restoration Puritans both Weber and Tawney gave primary attention to Richard Baxter. Weber placed Baxter "at the center of the discussion," since he "stands out above many other writers on Puritan ethics, both because of his eminently practical and realistic attitude, and, at the same time, because of the universal recognition accorded to his works, which have gone through many new editions and translations." Tawney, following Weber's lead, gave equally prominent attention to Baxter as "the most learned, the most practical, and the most persuasive" of the champions of Puritanism in the last half of the seventeenth century. It would not seem unfair, therefore, to examine the Weber-Tawney thesis in the light of Richard Baxter's thought.

If any one thing is clear in the writings of Richard Baxter, it is his intensely anti-Mammon spirit. He constantly insists that God and Mammon are antithetical, and he lashes out against the hypocrisy of those who think they can be reconciled.

Take heed that you think not of reconciling God and mammon, and mixing heaven and earth to be your felicity, and of dreaming that you may keep heaven for a reserve at last, when the world hath been loved as your best so long as you could keep it.
If thy belly be thy god and the world be thy heaven, then serve and seek them (and pretend not to be a Christian). When seeming Christians are as worldly and ambitious as

others and make as great a matter of their gain and wealth and honor, it showeth that they do but cover the base and sordid spirit of worldliness with the visor of the Christian name to deceive themselves, and bring the faith of Christians into scorn, and dishonor the holy name which they usurp.

The person who seeks riches is

like a foolish traveler, who, having a day's journey to go, doth spend all the day in gathering together a load of meat and clothes and money, more than he can carry, for fear of wanting by the way; . . . You have all the while God's work to do and your souls to mind and judgment to prepare for, and you are tiring and vexing yourselves for unnecessary things, as if it were the top of your ambition to be able to say, in hell, that you died rich.

Prosperity, Baxter insists, is no sign of God's favor, nor is poverty evidence of his displeasure. . . . Indeed, far from being an indication of spiritual grace, one's own prosperity is frequently a temptation of the devil, for men thereby "think God, when he prospereth them, is not so angry with them as preachers tell them." It is the devil, not God, who "is exceeding diligent to get the wealth and prosperity of the world on his side that he may not seem to flatter his servants with empty promises but to reward them with real felicity and wealth."

In any vocation, the person who makes private gain his goal denies the end of his calling. One must constantly "take heed lest, under the pretense of diligence in your calling, you be drawn to earthly-mindedness, and excessive cares or covetous designs for rising in the world." Many a man deceives himself by thinking that "he is no worldling because he useth no unlawful means but the labor of his calling to grow rich." The lawyer is warned to

be sure that you make not the getting of money to be the principal end in the exercise of your function but the promoting of justice . . . and therein the pleasing of the most righteous God. . . . He is a lover of money more than justice that will sweat in the cause of the rich that pay him well and will slubber

over and starve the cause of the poor because he getteth little by them.

Physicians are admonished to

be sure that the saving of men's lives and health be first and chiefly your intention before any gain or honor of your own . . . Be ready to help the poor as well as the rich . . . Let not the health or lives of men be neglected because they have no money to give you.

Nor is the businessman exempt. In making a bargain or contract, the businessman must set his heart upon the true love of his neighbor and ask himself: "How would I be dealt with myself, if my case were the same with his?" Instead of thinking of his own gain, he must remember how much more he will lose by sin. He must consider his neighbor's situation, whether or not he can afford it, and he must not believe every common report of his neighbor's riches. He must regard the public good above his own commodity, for "it is not lawful to take up or keep up any oppressing monopoly or trade which tendeth to enrich you by the loss of the commonwealth or the many." He must give "special respect to the common estimate and to the market price." He must not quibble over prices, nor bargain more than necessary. In doubtful cases, he is told to "choose that side which is safest to the peace of your consciences hereafter, though it be against your commodity."

The one statement from the writings of Baxter which Weber and Tawney are able to use effectively in support of their thesis that Puritanism sanctified the pursuit of riches and thus led to the obliteration of ethical values in economic life is the much quoted sentence:

If God show you a way in which you may lawfully get more than in another way (without wrong to your soul, or to any other), if you refuse this, and choose the less gainful way, you cross one of the ends of your calling, and you refuse to be God's steward, and to accept his gifts, and use them for him when he requireth it. You may labor to be rich for God, though not for the flesh and sin.

This is a perfect illustration of the distortion involved in isolating the concept of "the calling" from its context. Tawney, ignoring even the qualification within the quotation itself, makes the blunt assertion that "so far from poverty being meritorious, it is a duty to choose the more profitable occupation." It is true, as Baxter says elsewhere, that "the largest stock must be accepted and used for God when he trusteth us with it," but this is a subordinate principle and cannot be generalized into a bald injunction to "get all you can."

The particular quotation from Baxter, cited by Weber and Tawney, concerning the choice of a vocation is actually only one of a series of directions devoted to this problem. In choosing a trade or calling, writes Baxter, the first consideration is "the service of God and the public good, and therefore that calling which most conduceth to the public good is to be preferred." Second, "when two callings equally conduce to the public good, and one of them hath the advantage of riches and the other is more advantageous to your souls, the latter must be preferred." For "next to the public good, the soul's advantage must guide your choice." One must also think of his physical and mental health, and if possible "choose a calling which so exerciseth the body as not to overwhelm you with cares and labor and deprive you of all leisure for the holy and noble employments of the mind, and which so exerciseth your mind as to allow you some exercise for the body also." . . .

It is only after carefully considering what one is "fittest for, both in mind and body" and finding that two possible vocations are equally conducive to the public good, the soul's advantage, and the health of mind and body, that it is lawful and meet to look at the commodity of your calling."

Though it is said, Prov. xxiii. 4, "Labor not to be rich," the meaning is that you make not riches your chief end: riches for our fleshly ends must not ultimately be intended or sought. But in subordination to higher things they may; that is, you may labor in that manner as tendeth most to your success and lawful gain: you are bound to improve all your Master's talents. But then your end must be that you may be the better provided to do God's service and may do the more good with what you have. If God show you a way in which you may lawfully get more than in another way (without wrong to your soul or any other), if you refuse this, and choose the less gainful way, you cross one of the ends of your calling, and you refuse to be God's steward, and to accept his gifts, and use them for him when he requireth it. You may labor to be rich for God, though not for the flesh and sin.

In the light of the prior considerations to be faced and the restrictions which surrounded commercial pursuits, and in the light of the fact that each individual was to be held personally accountable to God for the decisions he had reached, this direction "to improve all your Master's talents" does not represent a very significant concession to Mammon. Actually, as Baxter makes clear elsewhere, even under these circumstances, riches were not so much to be sought as to be regretfully accepted. The more profitable calling could not be pursued in any light-hearted manner or with a comfortable assurance that it constituted an easy and safe path to the narrow gate that openeth unto life. Always remember, Baxter counsels, that riches

are in themselves but dross, which will leave thee at the grave as poor as any. And as to their usefulness, they are but thy Master's talents, and the more thou hast the greater will be thine account. And very few rich men escape the snare and come to heaven.

Since riches are "the commonest cause of men's damnation" and "make it much harder for a man to be saved," they ought to be avoided if possible. When you realize, says Baxter, that you must make "a daily reckoning how you lay out all that God committeth to your trust," it will "quench your thirst after plenty and prosperity." You will become more concerned "to use well what you have than to get more."

"The first characteristic to strike the modern reader in all this teaching," confesses Tawney in discussing Baxter, "is its conservatism." But then he goes on to suggest that

these utterances came . . . from that part of the Puritan mind which looked backward. That which looked forward found in the rapidly growing spirit of economic enterprise something not uncongenial to its own temper, and went out to welcome it as an ally. What in Calvin had been a qualified concession to practical exigencies appeared in some of his later followers as a frank idealization of the life of the trader, as the service of God and the training ground of the soul.

Tawney, therefore, dismisses Baxter and his like-minded contemporaries as anachronisms, and finds the true Puritan spirit revealed in a man like Richard Steele who was adjusting himself to the ideas and ideals of the new Political Arithmetic. What Tawney fails to see is that when these new elements gained the upper hand, Puritanism ceased to be Puritanism. They represent the infiltration of a spirit which the convinced Puritan did not hesitate to label pagan and anti-Christian. Far from being the logical flowering of certain inherent tendencies in Puritanism, the economic ethics which increasingly dominated English commercial and business life toward the close of the seventeenth century were the very antithesis of those which were fundamental to the whole Puritan outlook. Their acceptance by nominal Puritans is an illustration of the attrition to which any idealistic movement is subject, and it marked the crumbling of the foundation upon which the Puritan structure rested. The victory of the spirit of capitalism in a very real sense meant the defeat of Puritanism.

Nor was the Puritan ethic mere pious verbiage. "The fundamental question," Tawney observes, ". . . is not what kind of rules a faith enjoins, but what type of character it esteems and cultivates." His contention, however, that "the rules of Christian morality elaborated by Baxter" found no response in souls awakened by Puritan preaching is patently absurd to anyone at all acquainted with Puritanism. It is not true that the Puritan character offered "but a polished surface on which these ghostly admonitions could find no enduring foothold." The few illustrations which Tawney gives of a sensitive and aggressive Puritan conscience were not exceptional and can be multiplied many times. To be sure, when the religious foundations crumbled and the spiritual vitality of the movement disappeared, the ethical injunctions, which derived their force from a vivid faith in God as a righteous judge, quite naturally lost their compelling power.

It should be apparent, as a result of this discussion, that the dynamic, which gave impetus to the tremendous Puritan drive in vocational activity, was not rooted in the Puritan conception of "the calling," but rather in the larger context of the Calvinist conception of God and of man's relationship to Him. God is the Lord — the "Owner," Baxter calls him — and man is his steward. As God's steward, man is accountable to God for two things — his time and his possessions. For the best possible use of every moment and every penny, he is personally responsible to God. Both time and money, therefore, must be redeemed in terms of being devoted to the highest possible good at any particular moment. Parasites, who live in idleness or in "unprofitable callings," are unfaithful stewards. In like manner, one stands in perpetual judgment with reference to the use he makes of his money. As a faithful steward he must shun needless luxury and ostentatious display, not because they are sinful in themselves, but because the money they require can be put to a better use, either in charitable activities or productive enterprises.

Emphasizing as they did the economic virtues of diligence and thrift as religious duties, it was inevitable that the Puritans should prosper and advance in economic status. It was also natural, since they were excluded by legislation from participating in public affairs and educational pursuits, that they should be found in disproportionate numbers among those engaged in commercial life. Nor is it surprising that Puritanism won its recruits mainly from among the merchants, lawyers, and small landholders. As Knappen had pointed out, Puritanism

was too cold and intellectually complicated for the lower classes, and a creed which might set a lord on the penitent stool before an entire congregation was no religion for a gentleman.

The middle class was less bound by tradition than the other classes of society and thus was more receptive to new religious ideas, and the virile character of Puritanism was the type of religious discipline that would appeal to any spiritually sensitive spirits who were engaged in the strenuous struggle of a rising class to make a place for itself in society. But this does not mean that Puritanism was primarily a middle class movement which rationalized and perpetuated middle class ideals. . . .

THE CONTRIBUTION OF THE PURITANS TO THE EVOLUTION OF MODERN CAPITALISM

HENRI SÉE

Although he was originally trained as a medievalist, Henri Sée devoted most of his efforts to economic problems and gained an international reputation as an economic historian. Most of his works are concerned with the economic development of Europe since the Middle Ages, and his studies of the evolution of capitalism naturally led him to consider the merits of the Weber thesis. Deeply devoted to the writing of objective history, he was careful and judicious in his assessment of the Weber thesis controversy, as the following selection indicates. Following a prolonged period of ill-health which forced his retirement from active teaching at the University of Rennes, he died in 1936.

THE THEORIES that we shall consider assume a role, in a way, as a counterpoise to the famous doctrine of historical materialism as it has been formulated by Karl Marx. Marx views economic phenomena as determining all other phenomena (political, intellectual, religious, etc.); economic factors are the foundation (*Unter-*

bau) which determines the form taken by the other phenomena. However, thinkers such as Max Weber, E. Troeltsch and W. Sombart, without making a direct criticism of historical materialism, attack it in its own stronghold by striving to show that these economic phenomena (at least capitalism, which is the most potent of them all) are,

From Henri Sée, "Dans quelle mesure puritains et juifs ont-ils contribué aux progrès du capitalisme moderne?" *Revue Historique*, vol. 155 (1927), pp. 57–59, 61–64. Translated by the Editor. By permission of the Presses Universitaires de France.

in very great measure, the product of a religious spirit such as Puritanism or Judaism. For Max Weber and, above all for Sombart, economic and social life are determined to a decisive degree by psychological elements in historical development.

Moreover these two writers, to approach the problem in question, begin by defining what they call the capitalist "spirit" (*der Geist des Kapitalismus*). This spirit would necessarily have had to exist before the triumph of capitalism, or, to state it more clearly, it would have been the unique, or at least the principal initial cause of capitalism. One is astounded by the importance and all the implications of this doctrine.

Of what does this capitalist spirit consist? Max Weber was the first to attempt to define it. One of its most characteristic traits is the search for profit, not just to provide for the needs of life, as profit was conceived of during the Middle Ages, nor to gratify any special joys of life, but simply to seek profit for its own sake. Moreover, the capitalist spirit particularly prizes the intensity of work; the love of work is considered as a "vocation" or "calling" (*Beruf*), in a way religious itself. Max Weber points out that this conception of "calling" is truly anti-traditional and rational. What proves this is that the man imbued with the capitalist spirit attributes great importance to planning in all its forms, to exact accounting, to evidence of precision and honesty in affairs; he condemns equally the waste of money and time. Max Weber cites very significant passages in this respect from the writings of Benjamin Franklin. . . .

The excessive importance attributed to money, to the earning of interest, to credit, to sobriety and rectitude in affairs for the purpose of realizing a profit, the equal horror of the waste of time or money — all these are so many attitudes which clearly would have been incomprehensible to men of the Middle Ages and repugnant to the doctrine of the Church. But are these traits truly basic to the capitalist spirit?

Sombart, in this regard, has a broader view of the capitalist spirit, precisely because his knowledge of economic history gave him a more general, more profound, and more justifiable concept of modern capitalism. Undoubtedly, he assigns great importance to the "bourgeois virtues" (temperance, self-discipline, rectitude in affairs, etc.), to the use of calculation; the capitalist spirit seems to him, as to Max Weber, rationalist and anti-traditional. But, at the same time, he gives an important role to the spirit of enterprise, to speculation and to mental subtlety and ingenuity; this is why the somewhat inflexible Puritan merchant seems to him less an actual example of the capitalist spirit than the subtle and supple Jewish man of affairs. . . .

To what degree does [Max Weber's] description of [the capitalist spirit] correspond to reality?

Let us concede that the conception of economic life among the Puritans was as it has been described to us. Is its source purely religious? Cannot the capitalist aptitudes of the members of the Puritan sects be attributed, in part at least, to the whole combination of political and social circumstances? Let us observe, first of all, that Calvinism spread chiefly in France, in the Low Countries, and in England, in the urban environments among the bourgeois and merchant classes who were naturally apt to become imbued with the capitalist spirit even without submitting to the influence of the reformers' doctrines. Thus, the new ideas, whatever they might have been, spread chiefly in the cities. Besides, everywhere except in Holland the Calvinists and the Puritan sects were in a religious minority and thus were barred from government positions and the liberal professions; naturally, they devoted themselves to business. Persecuted, treated as outcasts, almost everywhere they were considered as foreigners (resident foreigners, like the Jews, but in less marked degree). Scattered and dispersed across the world, of necessity they established relations with each other, and they developed a sort of international character. Their religious bonds predisposed them to form economic relationships which contrasted with the economic nationalism of the different countries where they lived. Thus, it seems clear when one studies the problem, that one should not ignore the political and social circumstances in which Calvinism spread. Max Weber, it may be noted, refers rarely enough to general history.

Now here is an objection of another sort which has been skilfully developed by R. H. Tawney in his recent and very interesting work, *Religion and the Rise of Capitalism* (London, 1926). The objection is that Max Weber has been too inclined to consider the Puritan movement as a single, unchanging entity although it is very complex and constantly modified itself with the passage of time. The Puritans had followers in all the classes of society, including the small masters, who were still very numerous in the sixteenth and seventeenth centuries, and whose work was organized and carried on as it had been in the Middle Ages. They recruited many followers among the country yeomen who formed the bulk of Cromwell's armies. In the left wing of the Puritan movement during the seventeenth century were the radical democrats, the Levellers, who protested so vigorously against the exploitation which the people suffered.

The capitalistic tendencies were fortified among the Puritans only after the Revolution of 1688; but this was precisely the time when economic ideas were being stripped of their religious content, when economic life strove to secularize itself. This was also the period when the concept of Christian charity was finally abandoned; poverty was considered shameful, as "the product of idleness and vice"; "new medicine for poverty" was applied by the pitiless repression of begging and vagrancy. This was the time when Defoe's *Giving alms no charity* (1704) and Petty's *Political arithmetic* appeared. Nevertheless, this Puritan harshness did not manifest itself among all the non-conformists; again, as Tawney indicates, the Quakers, although very active from an economic point of view, considered it a duty to aid their unfortunate brothers and liberally practiced charity. . . .

It is certain, as Tawney has indicated in very strong terms (and this is the most substantial portion of the Weber thesis), that Calvinism and the sects which were derived from it stimulated the energies and the individualism of its adherents. But it is also possible that precisely those individuals who were the most energetic and independent embraced the Calvinist cause. It is possible to have action and reaction, or convergence, among these diverse phenomena; for individualism has been able to express itself by religious reform or by the development of capitalism or by both at once. The entanglement is difficult to unravel. At all events, we can admit with Tawney that "the spirit of capitalism was not the offspring of Puritanism, but the latter was a tonic for it."

A CRITICISM OF MAX WEBER
AND HIS SCHOOL

H. M. ROBERTSON

The first version of *Aspects of the Rise of Economic Individualism* was written in 1928–29 as a dissertation for the Ph.D. degree at Cambridge University. Mr. Robertson had collected most of the material for the study while a research student at Emmanuel College, Cambridge, and actually wrote the greatest part of it while he was a Lecturer at the University of Leeds. When the book appeared in 1933, Dr. Robertson was the Senior Lecturer in Economics at the University of Cape Town. His study was welcomed by many historians as an historical, rather than psychological or sociological, study of an historical problem. Robertson was sharply criticized for his assertion that the Roman Catholic Church and the Protestant churches stressed the same economic precepts in the sixteenth and seventeenth centuries, but his work remains one of the most impressive to emerge from the Weber thesis controversy.

MAX WEBER is responsible for the opinion, widely held today, that Protestantism, especially in its Puritan form, has had a very great influence in forming the "spirit of capitalism," and, therefore, in forming capitalism itself. In 1904–5 he published two articles under the title of "Die protestantische Ethik und der Geist der Kapitalismus" in which this thesis was maintained. They not only inaugurated a whole literature, they gave a new direction to the whole of modern thought on a fundamental problem of economic history. I claim that they directed it on to the wrong lines.

It is not hard to understand why these theories should have been adopted so widely. They are the type of generalisation that would obviously have a popular appeal; and they can be made to form a convenient and serviceable weapon in religious controversy. They have been accepted in many cases because of their utility to the propagandist. Many writers have taken advantage of an unpopularity of capitalism in the twentieth century to employ them in attacks on Calvinism, or on other branches of religion. But the theories have also been accepted in other and less likely quarters.

It is remarkable that historians should have been so ready to accept the arguments of this piece of dialectic. For the reasoning employed is not that of the historian. Despite a wealth of references, its foundations have not been laid on a sound historical analysis. A philosophy of historical development which has been fashioned in the "constructional"[1] method of the sociologist might have been expected to have met with more opposition.

Weber attempted to establish a reverse chain of causation from that advanced by

[1] "Constructional" because it constructs abstract ideal types instead of accurately describing facts.

From H. M. Robertson, *Aspects of the Rise of Economic Individualism* (Cambridge, 1933), pp. xi–xvi, 1–8, 10–12, 14–18, 21–38, 44–45, 52–56, 159–167, 207–213. By permission of the Cambridge University Press.

Marx in the economic interpretation of history. He sought a psychological determination of economic events. In particular he saw the rise of "capitalism" as the result of the rise of a "capitalist spirit." What was this capitalist spirit?

To Weber it was hardly more than bilateral. It consisted first in a rationalist as opposed to a traditionalist outlook. It consisted also in the desire to seek profit continuously (by means of the rational organisation of free labour) for its own sake — even as a duty — and not for the purpose of enjoying the fruits. It cannot be denied that the ideal capitalist mentality is rational, if the spirit of capitalism is to mean anything more than that of acquisitiveness. It is probable, also, that Calvinism, created by a man whose favourite idea was considering "things in themselves, not words," has led to the expansion of a rational methodising of life. It may be admitted at once that to this extent Calvinism has been favourable to the growth of a spirit of capitalism. But Weber's second criterion of the capitalist spirit is too narrow. It leads inevitably to the defect which I feel vitiates his whole argument; he hardly considers any capitalist other than the Puritan capitalist who seeks wealth for the fulfilment of his "calling."

This added refinement is quite superfluous. A realist like Marx, who originated the discussions on capitalism, would no doubt have been greatly astonished if he had been asked to consider only those whose money-making activities were promoted by religious or quasi-religious ends to be possessed of the true capitalistic spirit. This is what we are asked to do. The great renaissance financier, Jakob Fugger, a good Catholic, was urged by his nephew, Georg Thurzo, to retire from business on account of the involved state of the family affairs. He rebuked his nephew for his faint-heartedness and said that he "had quite another disposition, he would make money as long as he could." This is disregarded as an expression of the capitalistic spirit, as it had no ethical tinge. Yet it was an example of

precisely the type of "worldly asceticism," making earning an end in itself, which is put forward as the great contribution of the Calvinists and the Puritan sects to the rise of the spirit of capitalism.

To most people today the typical "capitalist" is a purely secular creature who, far from regarding his daily occupation as a religious calling, sees no reason for religion to meddle with business affairs at all. He was the same in previous ages. Perhaps he resented the claims of religion to act as a moral witness in the affairs of everyday life, like the merchant Gromelgayner in Dr. Wilson's *Discourse of Usury*:

Merchants doings must not thus be over-thwarted by preachers and others, that can not skill of their dealings. And thys over great curiositie of some to meddle in other mens matter, I muste tel you plaine, it is even the verie right waye to undoe al in the ende.

Or perhaps he behaved like the typical capitalist whom Milton described in *Areopagitica*:

A wealthy man addicted to his pleasure and to his profits, finds Religion to be a traffic so entangled, and of so many piddling accounts, that of all mysteries he cannot skill to keep a stock going upon that trade. What should he do? fain would he have the name to be religious, fain would he bear up with his neighbours in that. What does he therefore, but resolves to give over toiling, and to find himself out some Factor, to whose care and credit he may commit the whole managing of his religious affairs; some Divine of note and estimation that must be. To him he adheres, resigns the whole Warehouse of his Religion, with all the Locks and Keys into his custody; and indeed makes the very person of that man his Religion; esteems his associating with him a sufficient evidence and commendatory of his own Piety. So that a man may say his Religion is now no more within himself, but is become a dividual moveable, and goes and comes near him, according as the good man frequents the house. He entertains him, gives him gifts, feasts him, lodges him; his Religion comes home at night, prays, is liberally supt, and sumptuously laid to sleepe; rises, is saluted, and after the malmsey or some well-spic't bruage, and better breakfasted, than He whose morning appetite would have gladly fed on green figs between *Bethany* and *Jerusalem;* his Religion walks abroad at eight, and leaves his kind entertainer in the shop trading all day without his religion.

Nothing could be further from the Puritan than either of these two types. In neither case was the conception of the "calling" of any influence; in neither case did it stir the merchant to activity. Neither fits in with a Puritan setting. The second, indeed, would be much more at home among the Jesuits with their system of expert casuistry. Yet Milton described him as a typical possessor of the commercial spirit — a man who was not interested in religion, but was in business. And Wilson's Gromelgayner was intended to be the typical merchant of 1569.

A quite unnecessary element has, then, been introduced into the definition of the capitalist spirit. Men do not need to be "called" to riches to devote themselves whole-heartedly to their pursuit without stopping to enjoy them. When King Pippin asked Alcuin, "Of what have men never enough?", he received the reply, "Of gain." If men have the appetite for riches without a "call," they require no "calling" to organise a continuous striving after them.

The survey of the capitalist spirit inaugurated by Max Weber has also been unduly limited by a definition which excludes "Jewish pariah-capitalism" as something entirely alien to the real, respectable "bourgeois-capitalism." This narrowness of definition, which dismisses every manifestation of the speculative or entrepreneur spirit from consideration, seems hardly suitable as a method of approach to the understanding of that frequently very eclectic person, the capitalist.

I do not, however, propose to press this line of criticism very far. To do so would involve me in a wider discussion of the growth of capitalism and the capitalist mentality than I am prepared to undertake. Though I criticise the theories connecting Protestantism with capitalism on account of the narrowness of their scope, I cannot do more than indicate alternative ways of approach to the subject of the rise of the spirit of capitalism. In the main, my criticisms will touch these theories on their own grounds.

My criticism must concern itself very largely with Max Weber's celebrated essay on "Die protestantische Ethik und der Geist des Kapitalismus". It is a topic which he made peculiarly his own; and as I am concerned with the repercussions of his theories I must often refer to their origin. I hope to show that owing to Weber's adoption of a sociological, and not a historical, approach to the subject, his main argument, which deals with the Puritan doctrine of the "calling," cannot be sustained. I hope to show also that secondary considerations make it impossible to accept the argument that the capitalist spirit is a product of the Protestant Ethic. I hope briefly to indicate, therefore, another approach to the problem of the rise of the "spirit of capitalism," which takes into account factors which religious sociologists have ignored, and gives a truer explanation of the formation of the psychological elements in the historical development of economic forms, which I believe have been rightly (though over-) emphasised, but wrongly explained. I wish to show that the spirit of capitalism has arisen rather from the material conditions of civilisation than from some religious impulse.

According to Weber, the influence of Protestantism was not merely negative, in permitting the exercise of practices forbidden by the Catholic Church, but also positive, turning religion to capitalistic ends. The chief instrument of this he considered to be the doctrine of the "calling" which came in with Luther and introduced the ideal of an asceticism incumbent upon the laity as well as the religious; an asceticism not of the cloister, but practised in the affairs of everyday life, by the utter sacrifice of any self-indulgence, by unremitting industry in one's "calling," which was thus promoted to the quality of a religious exer cise. He asserted, moreover, that on the Calvinists taking over this doctrine they made success in one's "calling" an outward and visible sign of the acquisition of spiritual grace.

He employed philological arguments to bring out the importance of the doctrine of the "calling." He pointed out that there are no equivalents in the Romance (and Catholic) languages to the Protestant-German *Beruf*, the Protestant-Dutch *beroep*, the Protestant-English "calling," in the sense of "a life-task," "a definite field in which to work." He contended that Luther's reformation introduced both the word and the concept.

Luther is said to have written *Beruf* quite gratuitously in two places in his translation of Ecclesiasticus where the Septuagint gave in the one case *ergon* and in the other *ponos*, and where the Vulgate gave *opus* and *locus*.

This contention was strongly denied by Brentano, who pointed out that the Vulgate has not merely *work* but *work of the calling* (or *thy commissions*) — "et in opere *mandatorum tuorum* veterasce." He also asserted that "calling" *Beruf* had its exact equivalent in the Latin of the Vulgate version of the passages of I Corinthians vii, 20–24, from which the Puritan use of the word "calling" was derived.

Unusquisque in qua vocatione vocatus, in ea permaneat. Servus vocatus es? non sit tibi curae; sed et si potes fieri liber, magis utere. . . .
Unusquisque in quo vocatus est, fratres, in hoc permaneat apud Deum.[2]

There seems to be little doubt that Brentano's criticisms have value. It is not proved that Luther introduced both word and concept. It is true that the Vulgate versions do not express the modern conception of the "calling." But, on the other hand, it is also true that the early Protestant

[2] "Let every man abide in the same calling wherein he was called. Art thou called being a servant? care not for it: but if thou mayest be made free, use it rather. . . . Brethren, let every man wherein he is called, therein abide with God." See Brentano, *Die Anfaenge des modernen Kapitalismus*, pp. 136 ff.

conceptions of the "calling" were different from those of the present day and nearer those of the Vulgate.

There is one noteworthy feature of Weber's philological argument. Apart from this discussion of Luther's *Berufskonzeption*, Weber has made practically no use of Lutheran Protestantism in advancing his views, as he found himself unable to trace the spirit of capitalism in Lutheranism, but only in Calvinism, and among the Baptists and some Puritan sects. But Genevan Calvinism shared the use of a Romance tongue with French Catholicism, and therefore there is no contrast between Catholic and Calvinist phraseology.

To destroy the philological argument it is only necessary to quote the Calvinist version of the passage in Ecclesiasticus:

Demeure en ton rang et t'exercise en celui, et veille en faisant ton *office*. Ne t'émerveille point des oeuvres du meschant; fie toi au Seigneur, et continue en ton *labeur*.

Here we find *office* taking the place of *Beruf*, and are reminded that it very often did so. The French *office*, the Spanish *oficio*, the Italian *officio* all of them bring to mind a similar identification of the worldly and the religious (for instance the French *office* means both "employment" and "worship") and are frequently used by Catholics in a way not radically different from the Protestant-English use of "calling" or German use of *Beruf*.

Weber's case for asserting, on philological grounds, that Luther had introduced a novel conception of the "calling," bringing with it a new ideal of worldly asceticism, is not established. It seems on other grounds to have been an unnecessary innovation. The doctrine of Work has at any rate as old a history in the Christian *mores* as St. Paul's — "we commanded you, that if any would not work, neither should he eat." Medieval Catholicism had recognised that the deadly sin of Accidia must be combated with work as well as watchfulness. This recognition had taken form in the Augustinian and Benedictine rules, the foundations of all monastic disciplines. The asceticism of which an essential element was a divinely ordained worldly toil was not, then, foreign to medieval Catholicism. And Luther had been an Augustinian monk.

But it is argued, this asceticism was in the Middle Ages confined to the cloister. It had no part in the lives of any of the laity. To say that is to ignore the part which the friars were sent out to play — to take religion from the cloister into everyday life. It is to ignore the motives which led to the foundation of third orders. (It is not sufficient excuse for ignoring them to say that it was not considered to be as meritorious to be a member of a third order as to be a full religious; Calvinists do not consider the butcher's "calling," even if the butcher is an elder of the Kirk, to be as honourable as the minister's.) The Franciscan Order of Penitents, as befitted an order founded in the thirteenth century, was in some ways very similar to a religious gild. But it was more than this. It called for an asceticism exercised in the world not in the cloister, and it cultivated some of the bourgeois virtues — the same virtues which Weber stressed so much when he indicated the importance of Benjamin Franklin's worldly creed, his insistence that time is money and not to be wasted, his love of detail and exact reckoning. To the members of the Franciscan third order extravagance was forbidden; also, as with the Puritans, wasting one's time at feasts or masques or dances. It was recognised that the Brethren and Sisters of Penitence had worldly matters to which they had to attend. They had, for instance, to go to Mass during the Lent of St. Martin and the Greater Lent "nisi personarum vel rerum incommoditas immineret" — their worldly duties had, in some measure, precedence over their duties of church attendance, which might perhaps have proved to be a greater concession to the commercial spirit than was allowed to the Puritans. Yet nobody has thought of pointing to Franciscan Puritanism as a breeding ground for the spirit of capitalism. Weber has indeed confessed that the preaching of the friars, and especially of the Franciscans, had anticipated very markedly the teaching of the Baptists (a sect in which he affirms the encouragement of capitalism through worldly asceticism was very strong) in attempts to impose an ascetic rule on the laity. But this, he said, can be accounted for first by the fact that all asceticism based on Biblical commands would tend to be similar, and secondly by the general tendency to reach the same results in all systems of mortifying the flesh. This is probably very true; yet the fact remains that if the teaching of the Baptists and of the friars was so similar one should only guardedly employ the teaching of the Baptists as a means of proving that the spirit of capitalism was a product of the Protestant sects.

The great objection to all the arguments based on the Puritan doctrine of the "calling" is, however, that it has not always had the content so constantly ascribed to it. Even if Weber is correct in his interpretation of the doctrine in its eighteenth-century manifestations, he is incorrect in projecting this back into the sixteenth century, when the doctrine wore an entirely different aspect.

At the beginning it was nothing but a new expression of the old belief in the existence of divine and natural distributive justice, a belief that different men were "called" to their several occupations and estates by a divine providence — as a result of which it was flouting providence to exhibit capitalistic enterprise!

There seems to be no essential difference between the doctrine of the Catholics and the Puritans on this point. St. Thomas Aquinas' teaching on distributive justice was that:

This . . . division of men in different occupations occurs in the first place through divine providence, which distributes the condition of men in such a way . . . and also in the second place from natural causes, as a result of which it happens that there are different aptitudes for different occupations amongst different men.

Despite the assertion that Aquinas has

set his conception on an entirely different plan from the Puritans' by the stress laid upon natural causes in determining the choice of an occupation, this seems to contain much the same idea as the doctrine of the "calling" in the sixteenth and seventeenth centuries The practical lessons which the Puritans derived from their doctrine were also on the whole merely the same as those taught to the Catholics who were brought up to avoid the deadly sin of ambition.

Nothing expressed the early doctrine of the "calling" more succinctly than Robert Crowley's verse:

Fyrste walke in thy vocation
 And do not seke thy lotte to chaunge;
For through wycked ambition,
 Many mens fortune hath ben straynge.

Yet nothing could be further from the truth than to suggest that this verse introduced a new doctrine favourable to the rise of a "spirit of capitalism," or that the "calling" was an invitation to amass and continue to amass great riches.

When we remember the great use Max Weber has made of the doctrine of the "calling," it seems important that evidence should be accumulated to demonstrate what the earlier Puritan conception of the "calling" really was.

. . . In the sixth of Hugh Latimer's sermons preached before King Edward VI he reminded his congregation that:

Our Saviour Christ before he began his preaching, lived of his occupation, he was a carpenter, and got his living with great labour.

He did not say this with any intention of encouraging the capitalistic spirit. It was with the intention of condemning idleness indeed; but to Latimer as to many another reformer, the capitalists were the idle rich, battening on surplus value. He was concerned with the dignity of labour, not with gain and ambition.

"Therefore let no man disdain," he continued, "or think scorn to follow him in a mean living, a mean vocation, or a common calling and occupation. For as he blessed our nature with taking upon him the shape of man, so in his doing he blessed all occupations and arts. . . .

"It is lucre enough, it is advantage enough to be content with that, that God sends. The faithful cannot lack, the unfaithful is ever lacking, though he has never so much."

Once more we find the "calling" employed to combat capitalistic ambition.

The "calling" was man's earthly state, allotted to him by God, and his opportunity for Grace. As a gift from God, it was a gift with obligations. Weber has stressed the point that the doctrine of the "calling" caused the Puritans to be diligent in their application to business, to the greater glory of God. But it was not only in a sober application to worldly toil, it was in every department of life that their acts were designed *ad majorem Dei gloriam*. It was from this broader conception of the "calling" that Latimer derived his saying:

For God gave never a gift, but he sent occasion at one time or another to show it to God's glory. As if he sent riches, he sendeth pore men to be helped with it.

and it was with disregarding one's "calling" that such an opportunity was missed:

But now must men occupy their goods other ways. They will not look on the poor, they must help their children, and purchase them more land than ever their grandfather had before them.

Nothing could be further from the truth than to suppose that the "calling" was an invitation to amass and continue to amass great riches. It was an invitation to live the orderly and settled life ordained for one by God, and to perform all the duties pertaining to it.

Robert Crowley was a militant Puritan, and one whose rhymes did much to further the adoption of the idea of the "calling." His writings are filled with this conception. Yet nobody could accuse this fearless champion of the poor, this fervent opponent of the active new social order, of any bias in favour of capitalism. In 1550 he published his *Voyce of the laste trumpet . . . callyng al estats of men to the ryght path of theyr vocation.* In this he set out to advise the reader as to the correct pursuit of his "calling." The general advice has been quoted above, and the particular advice given to the various classes of men was in the same strain. . . .

It would be easy to multiply instances of the use of the conception of the "calling" as a basis for pronouncements of this sort. Weber very rightly stressed the importance of the vocation or "calling" as a fundamental part of the Puritan ethical system, but he painted a very misleading picture of what it meant. If it encouraged industry, it did so to a much smaller degree than it discouraged covetousness and ambition — the ambition which made men break out of their "calling," which would not let them be content with one "calling" but made them try to engross the livelihoods of many into their hands. It was by the doctrine of the "calling," the doctrine that every one should have *one* settled life-task, that Crowley condemned the enclosing landlords, the graziers, the leasemongers of his day:

Of good maisters, what should I cal you? You that have no name, you that have so many occupations & trades that there is no name mete for you! You ungentle gentlemen! You churles chikens, I say!

He had little good to say of those whose enterprise overstepped the bounds of a "calling" in so shameless a way.

The "calling" did not embody a progressive ideal. The demand for an ordered life, for an innerworldly asceticism, which Puritanism made and expressed in the conception of the "calling" had no message of a capitalistic nature to give the world. It placed in the forefront the age-long static ideal of content with the decrees of providence; as the author of a typical seventeenth-century theological treatise put it:

Then ye Common-wealth is blessed, and all ye Citizens therof happie; when every one knoweth his own vocation and diligentlie doth ye Duties therunto belonginge; and gives others their place, & breake not out of ye bounds of their owne Callinge.

Yet Weber has not misconceived the Puritan "calling." His description of the doctrine is exact — but not for all time. A mistake lies in the assumption that the "calling," as a guide to the conduct of life, has meant the same thing throughout its history. He has only studied the later phases of the doctrine. In the latter part of the seventeenth century and in the eighteenth he has found numerous examples of Puritan literature counselling a course of worldy prudence as a religious exercise, as the fulfilment of a "calling." He has projected the prudential character of this doctrine backward as having always been an essential element. Owing to his unhistorical treatment he has not noticed the change in the conception of the "calling" from an antidote against covetous ambition to a comfortable doctrine suitable for a commercial people. He has treated the doctrine as having been the same for all time; and the adherent of the school of "economic determinism" may be excused if he criticises Weber for neglecting the converse study of the influence of capitalism on the Protestant Ethic.

The development of the new prudential conception of the "calling" (which did not become general until the eighteenth century) may be traced quite easily in the three most influential manuals of Christian conduct of their respective ages — *The Whole Duty of Man* of 1657, Baxter's *Christian Directory* of 1673, and the *New Whole Duty of Man* which appeared first in the reign of George II and retained its popularity for over a century.

The first of these manuals was produced as an antidote against solifidianism. It affirmed strongly, therefore, the necessity for good works and reasserted the need for a strict application of the customary ethical system.

Baxter occupies a much less decided position. His work stands half-way between the wholly traditional morality of the first *Whole Duty of Man* and the freer mode of the second. Weber quotes it largely in support of his thesis; yet the real conservatism of its position is very apparent.

Every one, it is true, was under the necessity of living in a "calling" in which he might redeem his time. But the spirit of gain was not to be allowed as a guide to choosing one's "calling":

Choose that employment or calling, (so far as you have your choice) in which you may be most serviceable to God. Choose not that in which you may be most Rich or Honourable in the world; but that in which you may do most good, and best escape sinning.

One was exhorted to choose the "calling" which most conduced to the public good; only in cases where there were two "callings" equal in this respect might there be any doubts as to which must be chosen, and in this case it was important to choose the one which might be followed with the greater advantage to one's soul, not the more gainful.

Baxter was at pains to point out that:

If you have a necessity of labouring in your callings, you have no necessity of loving the world or caring inordinately, or of being discontented with your estate.

He also seems to have been very far from the belief that to grow rich in a "calling" was a sign of grace:

Another thinks he is no worldling because he useth no unlawful means, but the labour of his calling, to grow rich. The same answer serves to this. The love of wealth for the satisfying of the flesh is unlawful whatever the means be.

It must be allowed, then, that even Richard Baxter's conception of the "calling" was not a very whole-hearted influence in favour of capitalism. He accepted the purposive philosophy of the social idealist rather than the mechanistic one of the individualist, and so he insisted on giving moral advice as to the conduct of business affairs:

The public welfare, or the good of many is to be valued above our own.

Regard the public good above your own commodity. It is not lawful to take or keep up an oppressing monopoly or trade; which tendeth to enrich you by the loss of the Common-wealth or of many.

As a result Baxter retained many of the older canons of business dealings. He disapproved of the maxim *Caveat Emptor* and he tended to advise a modified doctrine of *Just Price* being maintained. He said that in buying and selling one should

. . . have special respect to the common estimate, and to the market price. Though it be not alwayes to be our Rule, yet ordinarily it must be a considerable part of it; and of great regard.

Further, he stood wholeheartedly on the side of the objective determination of the *just* value, quite in the medieval manner:

But if that which you have to sell, be extraordinarily desirable, or worth to some other person, more than to you or another man, you must not take too great an advantage of his convenience or desire.

It is true that in this matter he showed himself ready to make some compromise — he would allow a greater price to be exacted of the rich than of the poor, and he believed that some latitude must be allowed in determining the just price, as "to be alwayes just at a word is not convenient." But the general tenor of his advice was in favour of fixing rules for trade which were inconsistent with a simple search for gain; the contention that his influence lay in promoting the rise of a spirit of capitalism must be accepted with considerable reserve. . . .

It must remain open to dispute whether the most characteristic feature of Baxter's writings was his respect for the traditional morals which the Churches had agreed in applying to the conduct of business, or his practical feeling that the good business man was not necessarily a bad Christian, and his readers are likely to decide the matter according to their own predilections. But of one thing we can be certain — that his favour shown to the business man was not the result of his Puritanism. It was the result of being, through his exceptional relations with his congregation, bound up with the practical life. It is impossible to regard Baxter as lending a wholehearted support, either to the capitalistic or the old traditionalist side. He was not a leader; he was trying to reconcile the Christian and the commercial life, as St. Thomas had tried in the thirteenth century. But he had to make greater concessions to the commercial spirit than Aquinas, and, being a man of his age, he probably made them more easily.

When we come to the book of Christian conduct which succeeded Baxter's in popular esteem, we find that the movement towards looking through business spectacles has made rapid progress. *The New Whole Duty of Man, containing the Faith as well as Practice of a Christian: Made Easy for the Practice of the Present Age* . . . was also undecided in the guidance it offered with regard to some of the economic duties. But on the whole it made greater and more numerous compromises with Mammon. The work bore still evident traces of the old traditional morality — how long it lasted! — such as are exemplified in these "Rules of Traffick":

. . . Neither ask far beyond, nor bid much below, what reason must inform you to be the real worth. . . . Do not impose upon any man's unskilfulness or ignorance. So long as you keep within the latitude of lawful gain, you may use your skill against another man in driving a bargain: for in an ordinary plenty of commodities there is an ordinary price, which those that deal in them know and understand; and when the contractors equally understand the price, there can be no deception or injustice in the contract, be it made ever so hard. On the contrary, if he whom I contract with be ignorant or unskilful, I must not rate his want of understanding, or set a tax on his ignorance, but use him justly, as one that reposes a trust in me, and casts himself upon my equity; for if I do not do this, I am guilty of injustice. . . .

In spite of this surface conservatism, however, the *New Whole Duty* bears the mark of being, as the title says, "made easy for the practice of the present age." It is recognised that with time's changes new codes of moral guidance were called for, and that the first *Whole Duty of Man* was not "(by any means) suited to the present times; for how can it be? it having been written near one hundred years since."

When the *New Whole Duty* discoursed on honesty, it dealt quite literally with nothing else than the advantages of honest dealing to a nation of shopkeepers. It delivered a long homily on "Honesty is the Best Policy." . . .

By the time of the *New Whole Duty of Man* the doctrine of the "calling" had lost its early character of an antidote against ambition. The author did not see in it any ban on enterprise. In his discussion of the duty of servants he wrote that:

The state of servitude is necessary by the appointment of the wise Creator; the world cannot be governed and maintained without it; and it is their lot to be instrumental to the publick good in that state of life. Yet this is no token of God's displeasure: for, he in no wise forbids them to use honest means to make themselves free as soon as they can. . . .

It was a different outlook from Crowley's "And do not seke thy lotte to chaunge."

The author of the *New Whole Duty* was amongst the first of the English moral writers to consider that worldly success was of great moment, and of paramount importance in deciding in what esteem a man should be held:

. . . As titular dignities intitle men to an outward respect and observance, so also doth wealth and large possessions; for, when God bestows upon one man a larger fortune and possession than on another, he doth thereby prefer and advance him into an higher sphere and condition; and when God hath set him above us, it is just and fit that we should rise and give that place to him which is of God's appointment. Though, it may be, a wise or virtuous poor man hath more right to our esteem than a fortunate knave or fool; yet, forasmuch as in outward rank or condition God hath preferred the latter, he hath the rights of precedency, and of outward respect and observance; and ought to be treated with greater regard and obeisance.

A very typical and significant illustration of the part which religion had come to play in the mind of the author of the *New Whole Duty* may be found in his attitude to those who leave their "calling" "under a pretence of purer religion":

. . . hereby they are not only rendered useless to the commonwealth, but they do oftentimes a great deal of mischief to it, by unsettling and subverting other men, and filling their heads with abundance of foolish notions and scruples in religion, which are dangerous to government, and the publick peace and happiness . . . the man that serves God by continual application to the duty of his calling and state of life, besides the comfort of a good conscience, which is of all others the greatest happiness, such an honest and industrious labourer may entirely depend upon the goodness of God, that he will always take care of him: God will bless and prosper him in the work of his hands. . . .

It is evident that the influence of this book was in favour of the rise of a spirit of capitalism, and it is on evidence such as this that the assertions have been made that Puritan doctrine has resulted in the growth of the capitalistic spirit. There has been a complete lack of historical method.

It was not till the eighteenth century that the commercial ethics of English Puritanism reached this point. Even then the old conservative views were not entirely lost. They were found still scattered on the pages of the *New Whole Duty*. They were found even more strongly expressed in the writings of Defoe, a Nonconformist as well as an author of books on commercial practice. . . .

It was only in a long progress of time that English Puritanism came to be favourable to the claims of commercial men — that the doctrine of the "calling" ceased to be a Puritan antidote against the temptations of ambition. This fact is insufficiently recognised; and it shows the dangers of trying to explain historical developments without having recourse to historical methods. The shopkeepers' morality of the eighteenth-century *New Whole Duty of Man* is, properly understood, an argument against the thesis which connects the Protestant ethic with the spirit of capitalism; an argument for seeking in social changes the reasons for alterations in religious outlook. In the argument that Calvinist and Puritan Protestantism has provided the religio-sociological background for the rise of the capitalistic spirit too much has been made of those numerous passages in the *Works of the Puritan Divines* and the writings of later Americans which condemn idleness by virtue of the doctrine of the "calling." There are many passages to be found in the same *Works of the Puritan Divines* which condemn covetousness and ambition in accordance with the same doctrine; and many more among the works of these writers' forerunners. The doctrine of the "calling" did not breed a spirit of capitalism. The spirit of capitalism was responsible for a gradual modification and attrition of the Puritan doctrine; and this attrition had barely begun in England before the Restoration.

When one glances at the state of affairs on the continent of Europe, the conviction is deepened, that serious misconceptions of the nature of the relations between religious ethics and the spirit of capitalism have arisen. Generalisations have been too hasty.

One finds amongst the Catholics, both Jesuit and Jansenist, doctrines favourable to the emergence of the steady type of business man who was in favour with the later Puritans. The Catholics employed doctrines cognate with that of the "calling" with the same practical effect. "One must rise, for example," said the Jansenist Nicole, "to obey God, Who only allows us sleep for the body's needs and commands us, when these needs are satisfied, *to busy ourselves with the work which He prescribes for us according to our state.*"

The Jansenist preachers in particular reminded their flocks that the Christian life was "a serious life, a life of toil and not of diversion, play or pleasure" so that one ought never to forget that it "should be filled with some useful and sober occupation suitable for one's state of existence."

The Jesuits stressed almost the same beliefs. Little could have been more favourable to a rational methodising of life than Father Crasset's panegyric on Order:

Order and virtue are two words which mean almost the same thing. It is order which makes Paradise, and disorder, Hell. . . . Everything which God makes, He makes orderly, and everything that is not made in an orderly manner is not of God. Order leads us to God.

In France the Church went out of its way to welcome the honest bourgeois — the self-made man — on the ground that he was the only type of man who followed God's commands and lived in a "calling." It is true that the phrase was not employed, but the idea was:

Do not seek true piety among the great, the noble, the rich, whose life is only amusement and luxury; and do not expect to find purity of behaviour amongst them. Where then may one find it? In the huts of a donothing poverty, which has no occupation but begging? No, Christians: they as well as the rich are lost through idleness, and this class of the poor, whom Jesus Christ does not recognize, are also given to disorder. To whom then is purity reduced? I have told you — to these middle states of life who subsist by work, to these less noticeable conditions of men, who are however more assured of salvation, merchants engaged in the cares of lawful business, workmen who measure the days by the labour of their hands, servants who fulfil to the letter this divine command: as ye work so shall ye eat.

The Catholic Church was forward to reduce all the duties of a Christian to the due performance of his earthly tasks. The Catholics also tried to consecrate the world of labour, even to make it the only world that mattered:

All your piety is included in your station[3] and duties. I say: in your tasks faithfully observed. Do not neglect anything that is required by your employment, your bidding, the different relations you enjoy most directly, whether with God, as ministers of altars, or with the public as judges, or with servants in virtue of being masters, or with children as fathers and mothers; it does not matter with whom or how — include everything, accomplish everything, neglect nothing.

It was easy to serve God in this indirect way by performing all one's worldly responsibilities with a sober sense of duty:

One serves God by faithfully serving one's Prince; one serves God by employing one's capital (*en faisant valoir son bien*) according to all the rules of probity and justice. There are duties to be performed in all conditions of life, and it is in acquitting oneself of these duties that one is sanctified.

The French Jesuits even claimed that there was no incompatibility between self interest and the service of God:

God deigns to be grateful to us for what is done on our own behalf, if it is for the love of Him that one does it. So there is no incompatibility of service and business. One is soldier, lawyer, business man, but one is also a Christian. One can serve the same master in all these different states, and one can work fruitfully for God, for men and for oneself.

It might just as easily be claimed for Catholicism as for Puritanism that it made a demand for a worldly asceticism of rational toil. The spirit of Christianity, said the Abbé Réguis, "is a spirit of order and activity, of prudence and precaution, of

[3] If it were not for the risk of being accused of trying to support my argument by inserting in the translation words which are not in the original I should be tempted to translate *condition* here as "calling," not as "station." It would be the only satisfactory translation. It would also suit *charge* a little lower down, which I have translated as "bidding."

fear and trepidation, because of the temptations of every sort to which we are exposed, and against which it is impossible to defend oneself if one lives an idle and unproductive life."

And so the ordered life which would be recommended by a Puritan by virtue of the doctrine of the "calling" was also recommended by the Catholics. By them also it was stressed as a religious exercise, and the due performance of its discipline was recognised as a mark of grace:

When all is ordered, and one does everything in due time, one acts as a Christian, and it is by this means that many become sanctified and perfect. . . . Often they can only be distinguished from others of the same occupation by the application and the nicety with which they perform their tasks; they only do the same as all the others, but do it with an exactitude which takes the place for them of greater and more beautiful actions.

The necessity of worldly labour was incumbent upon the Catholic as well as the Protestant rich, in the days of the eighteenth century:

Since we are all sinners by birth, we are all included without exception in the decree which condemned Adam to work, sickness and death. As neither rank nor riches, then, discharge anyone from the necessity of death, no one ought to believe himself to be relieved of the obligation to work under pretext of being of distinguished rank or of not requiring to work in order to live.

After a time, also, the belief that labour is a curse fell out of fashion, and it was stated instead that:

The necessity of working is not a penalty; it is the decree of a Father Who makes all creation tributary to our needs.

It was not only recognised by the French Church that it was favourable for business to have these doctrines; it was stressed that this was so, in an attempt to secure the goodwill and support of the commercial classes. "Religion, in making a sacred duty of work and a sin of idleness, is the soul and the nourishment of useful industry," was the actual claim of a Catholic preacher, de Boulogne.

Thus there was nothing exceptional in the Church doctrines of the later seventeenth- and eighteenth-century Puritans. They were shared by the Catholics, and the encouragement given by them to the capitalist spirit was not the contribution solely of the Puritan and Calvinist sects. They did not develop until the end of the seventeenth century, when they spread both amongst Protestants and Catholics. It would appear that this is in itself enough to prove that the problem has been viewed through the wrong end of the telescope — to show that the chief relation between the rise of the capitalistic spirit and the Protestant Ethic is the reverse of what Weber has indicated. The Protestant Ethic changed as the result of the influence of a rising capitalistically-minded middle class. The Churches of the Calvinists and the Puritans did not always bear the same witness as regards the duties of the man of business. A changing emphasis, reflecting a changing spirit of the age, transformed a doctrine outwardly uniform. From being a hindrance to enterprise it became a spur.

The same change of emphasis took place among the Catholics. Was this due in some obscure way to the influence of the Protestant Ethic? We must think so, if we believe that the Protestant Ethic was the efficient cause of the rise of the spirit of capitalism. Or did both transformations take place under the same influence — the growing strength of an independent spirit of enterprise. The choice of hypothesis can hardly be in doubt.

If it is true that modern capitalism is the product of a new spirit of capitalism introduced with the Reformation, it must necessarily follow that there was no capitalism before that time.

In so far as we can think of the Middle Ages as a unity, we tend to think of them as a period from which capitalism was largely absent, and if we were to indulge in the habit of dividing history into hard and fast stages, we should be tempted to speak of the Middle Ages as being characterised by a pre-capitalistic stage of economic development. But it is only by concentrating on the static general view that such a conception is possible. If one looks at the changing elements of medieval life one receives a different impression.

The typical medieval conception of social relations was that the life and activities of the individual should be regulated according to certain pre-conceptions of a Divine ordering of society — a graded society. The principles of medieval life were quite in accordance with this doctrine. In the country there was the authoritarian feudal system, with its clearly marked ranks and well-known customary duties. The general principles of town life (though they were of necessity a little more individualistic) were found chiefly in monopoly — or exclusive rights of buying and selling — and in the regulation of trade by authority. Both in town and country a sort of egalitarianism was mixed with the principle of well-marked class distinctions. Men were regarded as members of functional groups within each of which there was a rough equality of material conditions. All this is saying very little more than that one inevitably thinks of manor and gild when one thinks of medieval economic life.

It was opposed completely to the individualism which is the basis of all that is best in capitalism. It is not true, as too many writers nowadays suggest, that the difference between the individualist scheme of life and the typical medieval or the typical socialist scheme of life is that the individualist has no social ideals while the others have. What is true is that the individualist has different ideals. Individualism, as a doctrine, sees in the individual and his psychological aptitudes the necessary basis of society's economic organisation, believes that the actions of individuals will suffice to provide the principles of society's economic organisation, seeks to realise social progress through the individual by allowing

him all the scope for his free self-development which is possible. It believes that for this two institutions are necessary: economic freedom (that is, freedom of enterprise) and private property. It believes that different individuals have different aptitudes and that each should be allowed to develop them in competition with others to the best of his ability. Therefore, as a system, individualism is the system of free trade, of competition, of private property. As doctrine and system it is entirely opposed to the typical medieval scheme of life. Only the regime of private property is common, and the medieval attitude to property was not the same as that of the modern world.

Nevertheless, the Middle Ages were never completely medieval in this sense. The medieval scene and the medieval mind had each of them elements of change, which grew and became more important, until finally they transformed medieval life. These are the elements which are of greatest moment to the historian, who is interested more in the physiology than in the anatomy of society. However flat and uniform the Middle Ages may have been, they contained currents flowing straight into modern times. Capitalism, even if not generalised, was not uncommon in the Middle Ages. It will be difficult, then, to look on it as the product of the Reformation.

Sombart, like Weber, believes that modern capitalism is the product of a specific "capitalistic spirit," which found no place in the Middle Ages. He affirms that the principle of economic life in the Middle Ages was the provision for one's needs (the *Bedarfsdeckungprinzip*) which he contrasts with the pursuit of gain (the *Erwerbsprinzip*) that is the principle of modern capitalistic life. He defines capitalism as "a definite economic system which may be recognised by the following characteristics: it is organised on the basis of exchange, and in it two different classes cooperate; the owners of the means of production, who direct operations, as subjects of the system, and propertyless labourers pure and simple as objects. It is ruled by the principle of gain and economic rationalism." The definition seems very just; but it does not show why the whole of the Middle Ages should be considered pre-capitalistic. All these characteristics can be found there.

The *Erwerbsprinzip* is not a modern invention. We have lived in an acquisitive society for some thousands of years. Modern capitalism is not distinguished by exclusive possession of this principle. Aristotle had indeed long ago brought it into light, and traced the ways in which it was satisfied, whether by speculation, labour or usury. That is to say, he had discussed it as a rational pursuit, or rather, as Sombart himself also regards it, as an irrational pursuit rationally pursued. Thus the two criteria of rationality and the striving for gain, which Sombart is prone to suggest are confined to the modern age, were both known in ancient Greece.

Nor were they unknown in the Middle Ages. It may be wrong to follow Brentano in thinking that the exploitation-capitalism of Rome throughout the duration of the Pax Romana, and the fact that the Punic Wars were first and foremost trade wars, have any direct connexion with the capitalism of modern times. But it is difficult not to admit that modern capitalism was emerging in Ravenna (which, under Roman Emperors or Gothic Kings was the chief entrepôt for the lucrative trade of the West with Byzantium) as early as the fifth century. Commercial enterprise on a large scale, a whole-hearted and rational organisation of the pursuit of gain, and the rise to importance of fluid capital capable of being applied wherever the chances of profit were most tempting, were phenomena of very early occurrence in the eastern Mediterranean. The rise of the Saracen power in the Mediterranean acted as a check on this capitalistic development. But it was a check caused by external circumstances, not by a psychological change. There was no loss of the capitalist spirit in Italy; it was not from lack of will but from lack of power that commerce declined in the Mediterranean, just as it was not from love of a self-sufficing economy that the agrarian estates of the greater part of Europe came to adopt the policy of subsistence farming, but because of decline of town life and the dislocation of trade caused by the destructive invasions of the barbarians, and later of the Saracens and Norsemen. As soon as conditions began to be in any way favourable, the commercial spirit emerged in the operations of the merchants of the Italian towns such as Amalfi, Venice, Genoa, Pisa and, later, Florence. It was the same further north, where in Flanders, Artois and Brabant a long-distance trade grew up, at first chiefly in fish and salt and Baltic products, and later in the cloth and metal goods of the Belgian industrial hinterland. Of course, trade between these two centres soon sprang up, raising to prosperity convenient centres along the chief trade routes — in Champagne, at Geneva and Lyons; at Frankfurt, Strassburg, Ulm, Nuremberg, Cologne and Aix-la-Chapelle — and peopling them with capitalistic merchants.

Sombart has been tempted to deny that the activities of these centers were capitalistic. But to do so, he appears to have introduced another criterion of capitalistic development: the amount of trade carried on as compared with the present day. He has collected a great deal of information with the object of proving that no large-scale economic activity was carried on in the Middle Ages, that even commerce was only conducted on a scale comparable with small handicraft industry. He has controverted very strongly Ehrenberg's dictum that commerce must of its very nature be carried on capitalistically. He has based his arguments on these grounds: firstly, on the large number of merchants who were engaged in carrying on a very limited trade; secondly, on the small size of the capital subscribed by merchants going into partnership (of the first fifty partnerships registered in Genoa in 1156 the average capital subscribed was only about 150 lire); thirdly, on the small amounts of property owned by the inhabitants of cities like Basel and Augsburg in the fifteenth century as revealed by their tax returns; and, fourthly, on the small size of the ships generally employed and the small value of their cargoes. He has pointed out, for instance, that seven Spanish ships carrying iron, fruit, and wool, which were captured by English warships in 1470, varied from 40 to 120 tons and were worth, cargo included, from £70 to £180 in sterling money of the time.

He suggests that with regard to commerce, "everywhere the same picture is offered us: apart from a few greater and often not professional merchants, only a swarm of small and insignificant traders." And so the merchant was entirely of a piece with the petty town workman; his whole outlook on life was the same; he was without capitalistic motives, he was content to receive as the reward of his labours what would ensure him the common sort of existence of his social class; he was without the desire to strive after greater and greater gain which distinguishes the modern entrepreneur.

Sombart is right on many points. It does not do to pretend that medieval commerce was on a scale comparable with that of the present day. Conditions of transport and the comparative smallness of the population alone would have prevented it. But this means only that technical conditions were not suitable for such a capitalist expansion as we have known in recent times, and on the same grounds one must deny the existence of capitalistic activity before the railway age. The total amount of merchandise carried over the St. Gotthard each year at the end of the Middle Ages would only fill two goods trains passing through the tunnel today, and the tonnage compared with what passes today would be in the proportion of about 1:237. But the rise in the amount of traffic carried over the St. Gotthard by 1831–3 was only in the proportion of 1:3.2, which is no very enormous growth. And to argue in this manner is, as Pirenne said, like arguing that the Middle Ages knew no urban life, because they knew no large cities like those of the present day. . . .

Should the concept of capitalism, however, be confined to this? Does not capitalism consist in a fusion of a romantic and a rationalist tendency as well as in the purely rational pursuit of gain through industrial organisation? Sombart expressed this feeling very well when he wrote in the first edition of his *Der moderne Kapitalismus* that if he were pressed to give a definite birth-date for modern capitalism, he would choose A.D. 1202 — the year in which Leonardo Pisano's *Liber Abbaci* (the arithmetical treatise which first rendered exact calculation possible) appeared, and in which Venice began the attack on Constantinople which marked the beginning of the exploitation of the East by Western Europeans — especially by the Italian communes — and through which the large-scale accumulation of money began.

Sombart has indicated here what seem to be very valuable considerations. The warfare of the period of the Crusades deserves some prominence in the history of capitalism. It is doubtful if one should dignify much of it with the name of warfare — piracy and brigandage would be more appropriate — but it is important in at least two respects. It was carried on as a commercial undertaking for plunder (Sombart's "one-sided trade"), and the equipment of a warlike band called for a large capital, larger than for any ordinary commercial or industrial undertaking of the time. Also the booty secured was one of the great sources of the early hoards of capital. Thus the pillaging of the Levant was of importance in the early history of capitalism.

The second consideration called forth by Sombart's statement is even more enlightening. The rise of financial science was a necessary condition of the growth of capitalism. It enlarged the institution of private property by mobilising all forms of capital and removing the obstacles which differences of time and place might set in the way of its profitable employment. It allowed capital to become impersonal and abstract, a mere counter of general purchasing power, of general productive capacity.

Trading was not great in middle Ages

It enabled one to invest capital in an under-taking and withdraw and dispose of one's holding at will without withdrawing any of the equipment of the undertaking or interfering with the business in any way — the transfer being made in paper which represents a share in the undertaking. It is by attaining to impersonality and so to mo-bility that capital has gained in strength and security, and it has been the mathe-matician, the accountant, who has provided the rational basis for giving all forms of capital mobility. The great cause of the rise of rational capitalism was not Christian at all — it was a secular scientific development, taken over by Western Europeans from Muslim Arabs and Syrians. . . .

It would take too long to follow out the actual history of these various medieval capitalistic developments. It should be noted that the Catholic Church was itself largely responsible for some of them. The industrial and agricultural activities of the Cistercians in the end necessitated com-plex capitalistic arrangements for the sale of wool. The abbeys used to act as mortgage banks. And the Roman curia was an enor-mous financial organisation collecting taxa-tion from all parts of the Christian world, served by a galaxy of important banks and money-changers. These *campsores Romanam curiam sequentes* must not be forgotten as weighty influences on the his-tory of capitalism.

One other influence on the rise of capi-talism already in existence in the Middle Ages deserves some comment. Reference has already been made to the suggestion that the appearance of Pisano's *Liber Abbaci* might be considered a landmark in the history of capitalism. It is to scientific book-keeping much more than to the ethic of any religious system that we owe the ra-tional methodising of business life. Sys-tematic organisation is one of the most powerful agents of economic progress, and this holds good perhaps more of systematic book-keeping than of any other form. As Sombart has said:

Organization and clearness increases the desire to save and to acquire. A man who manages badly finds himself in a fog; he does not like to correlate the entries to see what he owes. On the other hand, nothing can be more acceptable to a good manager, than to examine every day the amounts of his growing fortune. Even a loss, if it annoys and surprises him, does not perturb him, for he knows at once what profits he has gained to set on the other side.

Is it not likely that this has had a greater effect than the doctrine of the "calling," which must always remain a little alien to business thoughts?

The organisation of business on the basis of double-entry book-keeping must have had an overwhelming importance in the development of a capitalistic order of society:

Capitalism without double-entry book-keep-ing is simply inconceivable. They hold together as form and matter. And one may indeed doubt whether capitalism has procured in double-entry book-keeping a tool which acti-vates its forces, or whether double-entry book-keeping has first given rise to capitalism out of its own (i.e. rational and systematic) spirit.

Until the emergence of systematic book-keeping there naturally remained some-thing of the old "subsistence" ideal of life of the canonists, the ideal of all business activity being carried on primarily to pro-vide subsistence for the merchant and for those with whom he dealt — what might be called a "commodity" conception of busi-ness. But the man who devotes himself to transactions on a book-keeping basis has only one aim — the increase of values com-prehended only quantitatively. He does not consider mainly corn or wool or cotton or cloth or the cargoes of ships, or tea or pepper. These (the true realities of com-merce) become mere shadows, they become unreal and the apparent reality seems to lie in book-keeping ciphers. All that the mer-chant who employs systematic book-keep-ing sees are money values which increase or grow less. . . .

It is so difficult to conceive of economic activity today not carried on with a book-keeping basis that we take its existence for granted, and it is hard to imagine what a revolution the introduction of scientific book-keeping methods must have caused. Yet nowhere has the rational element entered more strongly into economic activity than through accountancy — it is a necessary condition of the separation of the firm from the individuals of which it consists and therefore of the growth of large joint-stock businesses — and the slow spread of scientific book-keeping was one of the chief causes of the persistence of traditional and unbusinesslike methods of ordering affairs throughout the Middle Ages. An adequate book-keeping system is one of the cultural conditions necessary for the emergence of capitalism. It is a purely secular influence, and it was not absent from the Middle Ages. Double-entry was practised in Italy from the second half of the fourteenth century, though the yearly balance did not come in before the seventeenth century. Its rapid extension throughout Europe after the middle of the sixteenth century — following its introduction into Flanders by Ympym in 1543 — was no doubt of great moment in the spread of economic activity and the spirit of capitalism. That the countries in which the science of book-keeping made the most progress were always those in which most economic progress was being made can no doubt best be explained as a mixture of cause and effect. But working on the same lines as Weber, it would be very easy to substitute systematic books for the Protestant Ethic as the origin of the capitalist spirit. There is no doubt that reliance on good books meant more than reliance on the Good Book. And there is still less doubt that the rise of the capitalist spirit is the same as the rise of economic rationalism — something which took place independently of Church teaching, on the basis of commercial experience. The great cause of the rise of the spirit of capitalism has been capitalism itself; and it has been

conditioned by general cultural conditions, more particularly by developments in business technique, and by governmental and legal institutions affecting commerce. . . .

Is there any justification, then, for suggesting that Calvinism introduced a new outlook on the investment of money? The Jesuit doctrine of the direction of the intention, by which one and the same contract might be lawful or usurious according to the intentions of the parties, made it impossible to distinguish unlawful usury, and in that way justified all payments for a loan. The Jesuits accepted the arguments of Calvin against the sterility of money. They went so far as to justify payment of interest on the individualistic grounds that a free contract was in itself just. And the fact that the chief motive for entering a contract was the desire for gain did not make the intention bad. The fact that the Jesuits did not take the step of denouncing or casting aside all usury restrictions does not prove that they were less advanced than the Protestants. It only proves that the Jesuits were satisfied that the contracts which had been evolved to evade the usury prohibition met all reasonable needs. As Pirot said, the rent charge and the triple contract were all that was necessary, for in practice nobody would lend to those who could not offer sufficient security — and if the security offered was a hereditament or property of some sort a rent could be settled on it, while if the security offered was the ownership of some profitable business, a triple contract of partnership and insurance would suffice.

Our studies so far have not shown that the encouragement of the spirit of capitalism has been the exclusive work of any one section of Christians. The development of Protestant thought on usury was certainly no more significant than the development of Catholic thought on rent charges and threefold contracts, and on implicit contracts of which the legitimacy was secured by good intentions. The attempts at strict regulation of the economic life made by the Calvinist churches were definite hin

drances to capitalistic development and the
spread of capitalistic ideas which formed a
strong contrast to the comfortable and
accommodating religion of the Jesuits.

These are matters with which the sociological school has not dealt. But a comparative study of Protestant and Catholic
thought also disposes of many of the chief
arguments which this school does employ.
It reduces considerably, for instance, the
importance which can be given exclusively
to the Puritan doctrine of the "calling" — a
doctrine which studied by itself, however,
proves to have been by no means always
an encouragement to capitalism.

It makes some very favourite arguments
drawn from the writings of Benjamin
Franklin of small account. Weber had
drawn much of his inspiration from reading
Franklin. He believed that Franklin's insistence that *Time is Money* and not to be
wasted, that *Honesty is the Best Policy,* his
love of detail and exact reckoning, were the
apotheosis of Puritan doctrines of worldly
prudence. He said that Franklin's strict
avoidance of time- and money-wasting vani-
ties were typical fruits of his Puritan up-
bringing. But are they characteristic of any
one religious creed? Werner Sombart has
suggested that these writings are only an
echo of fourteenth- and fifteenth-century
Florentines, such as Leon Battista Alberti,
Agnolo Pandolfini, Antonio and Lorenzo da
Vinci, and that the wealth of the burghers
of Florence was built up with parsimony
and industry on just such a scheme of life
as Franklin's. Nobody could build up a
theory to connect Puritanism and capitalism
on a basis of studying these Florentine writings, or not dissimilar ones produced by the
Roman moralists. Weber had denied the
validity of this criticism. He asserts that
Sombart has been guilty of mistranslating
or misunderstanding the Florentine authors.
Whether he has or not — a controversial
matter into which there is no present need
to enquire — it may be noted that the ordering of one's life for the pursuit of gain,
which was not enjoyed, through the exercise of parsimony, was sufficiently estab-

lished before Luther's doctrine of the "calling" was evolved for Erasmus to lampoon
it in his colloquy *Opulentia sordida.* The
victim of this attack is supposed to have
been one of Erasmus's Italian hosts. It is,
moreover, certain that Franklin's advice
about the careful ordering of one's daily life
and avoidance of unnecessary indulgence
were also commonplaces in the writings of
seventeenth- and eighteenth-century Catholics. The Christian, said Father Tronson,
"does not pluck flowers, or wear any, simply
for the pleasure of flaunting them" — "he
does not waste his time at a door or window
looking at the passers-by."

Father Crasset believed that it was following divine precept to conduct one's
everyday life with a rigorous adhesion to
plan:

Prescribe for yourself an order in the day's
routine, which you keep inviolable, unless you
are hindered by a higher command which
forces you to depart from it. Regulate the
time of your resting, your eating, your study
and diversion! In Heaven one's whole life is
orderly; begin a life which you will continue
in eternity; it will be more acceptable to
God, more agreeable for your family, if you
have one, and more advantageous for your
salvation.

Father Croiset's advice was also not very
dissimilar from Franklin's:

Have a fixed hour for rising and going to
bed; and, as far as you may, fix it so that you
may be early to bed and up betimes. Nothing
is more opposed to a regular and Christian life
than late rising.

Above all, one had to eschew "laziness,"
and never forget that "all your devotions
should be subordinated to the necessary
duties of your estate, of your employment."
Even Franklin's plan for ordering his life
was the same as that recommended by
French Catholics as a religious exercise.
Father Réguis said:

One of the greatest advantages which one
enjoys in religious houses and in all those
where one lives in community, is following a

definite rule which accounts for all the hours of the day, prescribing, so to say, the task for every minute. . . . Now, my dear parishioner, why should you not make yourself a rule which sets down in detail what you ought to do from morning till evening?

*   *   *

Weber has collected a number of Protestant writings which seem to favour capitalism; but he has also mentioned that there was a strong current in Puritan teaching which stressed the dangers of riches, and the Christian's duty of not striving after them. Is he right in saying that this was overshadowed by advice, pro-capitalistic in tendency, to work hard in an orderly way, especially when both elements were also prominent in Catholic teaching? He has not proved that the Puritans introduced a new economic ethic. The Protestants as well as the Catholics spoke with an ambiguous voice. But as a rule the Calvinistic contribution to the capitalist spirit was the same as that of the Jansenists or stricter school of Catholics, consisting of the encouragement of industry, thrift, order and honesty; while the Jesuits went further and favoured enterprise, freedom of speculation and the expansion of trade as a social benefit. It would not be difficult to claim that the religion which favoured the spirit of capitalism was Jesuitry, not Calvinism.

But there is an explanation of the relations between the Churches and the spirit of capitalism which is "more probable" than any other. A historical method of analysis may be introduced into the discussion.

Such a method has here been attempted. It has been shown how English Protestantism underwent a great deal of change between Lever and Richard Baxter, and between Baxter and the second *Whole Duty of Man*, "made easy for this present age." It has been shown how there was a progression from Luther to Gerhard, from Calvin to Saumaise, on the question of interest. It has been shown how there was a gradual relaxation of the economic casuistry of the Jesuits, and a rebuilding on a basis more in favour of capitalistic beliefs. All has gone to prove one point: that the Churches, one and all, have had to accommodate themselves to an extraneous development of a busy commercial spirit; that capitalism has created, or found already existent, its own spirit, and set the Churches the task of assimilating it.

The Church of the Middle Ages had easily known its duty towards the different classes of men, for there were only two important classes — the rich and great and the poor and miserable. As this simple class division became obsolete the Church was faced with new problems. They were beginning to become urgent when Aquinas wrote his famous half-hearted justification of the merchant's activities. St. Antonino met them more insistent in fourteenth-century Florence. In the sixteenth century they had to be faced for the first time almost throughout Europe. The same problems affected all the Churches, and none had any previous experience to call to its aid. . . .

It was a problem which all the Churches had to face. A new hard-working, hardheaded type had sprung into prime importance. It was a type predisposed to regard itself as self-sufficient. It basked in the knowledge that it had done no man harm; that it fully deserved the honest portion which it had secured by its trade and industry. Even as sinners the new type sinned less palpably, less full-bloodedly than the other types, and, as we have seen from the reports of some of their confessors in Upper Germany, these "bourgeois" were unwilling to accept a burden of sin thrust upon them by a Church which was unsympathetic because ignorant of their ways, on account of actions in which they could see no wrong.

It was left for the Churches to find a place for this newly important class. What we are told to believe is the Reformed Churches' formation of a capitalistic spirit is in reality only their attempt to find a place for the commercial classes, newly important and freshly aware of their importance. But the Catholics also attempted to fit the middle-classes into the ecclesiastical scheme; in some way to sanctify and find an other-worldly significance in their solidity, diligence and honest respectability — characteristics which were really virtues despite their worldly origin — and to justify the aims and methods of their trade. . . .

It is noteworthy that the writings of the religio-sociological school on the origins of the capitalist spirit are infected with a deep hatred of capitalism. The essay on "Die Protestantische Ethik und der Geist des Kapitalismus" ushered in as heavy an attack on the capitalist position as the materialist writings of Karl Marx. This is not immediately apparent; but even a cursory second glance shows that its general tendency is to undermine the basis of a capitalist society. It attempts to show that modern capitalism is a massive and imposing superstructure on a foundation of shifting and out-of-date religious ideas, a Moloch of Calvinist selfishness. Its great pre-occupation has been to show that, as a form of social organisation, capitalism was not a natural growth, but a crass construction of the Calvinist mind, and therefore as easily assailed as that which made it in its own image. It tried to demonstrate that capitalism is no mere piece of social mechanism which should be judged only on its own merits, but a creation of evil import and unreasonable origin.

This seems to be the natural corollary of the arguments of all who accept this line of thought. Even Professor Tawney, who, in his *Religion and the Rise of Capitalism*, has admitted that the capitalist spirit was not the offspring of Puritanism, has yet affirmed that it "found in certain aspects of later Puritanism a tonic which braced its energies and fortified its already vigorous temper." He accepted the theory that "Puritanism had its own standards of social conduct, derived partly from the obvious interests of the commercial classes, partly from its conception of the nature of God and the destiny of man," and "became a potent force in preparing the way for the commercial civilisation which finally triumphed at the Revolution." He believed that two elements in Calvinism

were responsible for this. One was the doctrine of the "calling." The other lay in the fact that though Calvin had given approval to the life of business enterprise whilst subjecting it to an iron discipline, the demand for discipline later dropped into the background, leaving Calvinism as a religion which demanded free play for all forms of enterprise. Mr. Aldous Huxley has stated the position still more clearly:

The Reformers read their Old Testament and, trying to imitate the Jews, became those detestable Puritans to whom we owe, not merely Grundyism and Podsnappery, but also (as Weber and Tawney have shown) all that was and still is vilest, cruellest, most antihuman in the modern capitalist system.

Yet to follow this modern way of connecting capitalism with the religion founded by Calvin is to follow a mere will-o'-the-wisp. Too much attention has been paid to certain aspects of Puritanism, and too little to what was happening outside the Puritan world. Bunyan's *Pilgrim's Progress* (which is very anti-capitalistic in attitude) has been used to show the singularly antisocial nature of the Calvinist creed which is supposed to have fashioned modern capitalism:

In the description of Christian's attitude after he had realized that he was living in the City of Destruction and he had received the call to take up his pilgrimage to the celestial city, wife and children cling to him, but stopping his ears with his fingers and crying, 'life, eternal life,' he staggers forth across the fields. No refinement could surpass the naive feeling of the tinker who, writing in his prison cell, earned the applause of a believing world, in expressing the emotions of the faithful Puritan, thinking only of his own salvation. It is expressed in the unctuous conversation which he holds with fellow-seekers on the way, in a manner somewhat reminiscent of Gottfried Keller's *Gerechte Kammacher*. Only when he himself is safe does it occur to him that it would be nice to have his family with him.

But this fear of earthly ties, even of earthly love, was also strong amongst the

Catholics and especially amongst the Jansenists. "Love of God's creatures always diminishing our love of God, deprives us of a part of our true life, which consists entirely in the love of God," said Nicole. "The soul which pauses over His creatures retards the course of the journey by which it reaches to God; and in wishing to enjoy them it deprives itself in proportion of the enjoyment of God." "God having given me a heart to love Him," said Arnauld, "He must be the sole object of our love." As usual, Puritan opinions had their Catholic counterparts.

There were Catholic counterparts for most of the Puritan beliefs which are supposed to demonstrate capitalism's Puritan origins. The special mission of the doctrine of the "calling" in preparing the way for a commercial civilisation cannot be determined by reference only to Puritans. The significance of Baxter or Perkins, Steele or Flavell emphasizing the necessity of living an ordered life and serving God by diligence in one's wordly occupation seems much less when one remembers that across the channel priests like Crasset, Croiset, Houdry, Réguis, Bourdaloue were teaching exactly the same thing. The Puritan bourgeois morality of England loses some of its significance when it is considered how similar was the Catholic peasant morality of the Continent. And the relaxation of Calvin's strict discipline of the economic appetites in English nonconformity (on which Professor Tawney lays some stress) seems to be a less important factor in establishing a connexion between Puritanism and capitalism when one takes into account the tolerance of the Jesuits.

It was only to be expected that Calvinist discipline should have become less strict. Apart from the fact that a Church's practical beliefs in any age are always to some extent unconsciously the product of other influences — the prevailing political, scientific and philosophical temper, material conditions and so on — a Church must often be prepared to make concessions to the spirit of an age if it is to retain any influence at all. The concessions which the later Calvinism made to the commercial spirit were in large part the sacrifice of some part of the Churches' claims in order to be able to retain others. The English had shown themselves unwilling to tolerate Presbyterian discipline; if the Calvinist Churches had refused to temper their claims to control men's everyday actions they would have been rejected as tyrants and reactionaries. Calvinism was not betrayed from within. It lost the power before it lost the will to bind business within the discipline of Christian justice and Christian charity. Catholicism exhibited no greater power over its adherents.

The chief factor in the triumph of bourgeois liberalism was the factor of economic development which made the bourgeoisie important. It came into its own as a secular force. The rise of bourgeois morality in England as a substitute for religion was not the product of Puritanism. In Catholic France one found preachers complaining in the eighteenth century that a "gospel of worldly probity, in which is comprised all the duties of reason and religion" had arisen "on the ruins of the gospel of Jesus Christ"; and that the bourgeois preferred to be known as *honnête homme* rather than as a good Christian. The Churches in each country had been unable in the end, in spite of all their efforts, to assimilate the class of self-made men. The decline of the Churches in England as witnesses to a Christian code of social ethics was not due to a Puritan belief that "the Lorde was with Joseph, and he was a luckie felowe." It was due to the unwillingness of a rising bourgeoisie to be bound by what it considered to be antiquated rules.

Even so, there is no reason to decry too violently the new bourgeois individualism with its profane, not Puritan, origins. It was not a mere product of greed. It inculcated a belief in honour and justice, it believed firmly in justice, thought that independently of all religion there was implanted in man a love of justice, and on this it built. It did not ask for liberty for men to indulge their anti-social greed. It asked liberty for them to look after themselves in accordance with the rules which life and business both require to be respected and the observance of which was thought to be innate to man's nature; the rules of respecting contracts and of not doing to others what one would not have done to oneself. It did not ask for economic freedom because it believed that man's spirit of emulation raised an antithesis between the common and the private good, but because it disbelieved it.

It believed that man was rational enough to prefer justice to injustice, and that free competition would be more efficacious in promoting just dealing (on the assumption that, in general, men had a preference for justice whilst any who had not would find it bad policy to indulge their love of cheating) than restrictions based on the assumption that all men were rogues.

It was not from greed that the new individualism attacked the restrictions on forestalling and regrating. It was because it believed that free competition would see the market better and more cheaply supplied. It was not greed that silently broke down the restrictions on usury; it was a recognition that the usury restrictions did not work as they were intended. It was not mere greed that protested against the restrictions on foreign trade formed by the existence of the chartered companies. It was a just protest against injurious monopolies. It was a demand that regard should be had for the realities of things, not words; that sentimentalism should not be allowed to mask the grasping selfishness of the corporations which were impairing the well-being of the country they were supposed to serve. Self-interest played a part in promoting the rise of economic individualism, but not the only part — even when it is recognised that much apparently disinterested reasoning may be merely the rationalisation of selfish motives. The problem must not be simplified too far. . . .

CATHOLICISM, PROTESTANTISM
AND CAPITALISM

A M I N T O R E   F A N F A N I

Although Amintore Fanfani is quite well known as an Italian economist, he is even better known as a politician since he is at present (August,
1958) the Premier of Italy. Born in 1908, he began his teaching career
at the Catholic University of Milan in 1932 and later became a Titular
Professor in Economic History there. Shortly after that, he was appointed
a professor at the University of Rome, and, after World War II, carried
on an energetic and successful political career, having been a member
of the Chamber of Deputies and of several De Gasperi cabinets before
he became Premier. Fanfani has been termed an apologist for Catholicism and Fascism, but his writings on economic history seem to be based
on sound scholarly research.

OUR INVESTIGATIONS have led us to the
conclusion — which is now shared
even by those historians whose conceptions
of capitalism differ from our own — that
Europe was acquainted with capitalism before the Protestant revolt. For at least a
century capitalism had been an ever growing collective force. Not only isolated individuals, but whole social groups, inspired
with the new spirit, struggled with a society
that was not yet permeated with it.

Once we have ruled out that Protestantism could have produced a phenomenon
that already existed, it still remains for us
to enquire whether capitalism was encouraged or opposed by Protestantism. Such
encouragement or opposition could result
either from events to which the Protestant
movement gave rise, or from doctrines implicit in Protestant ideology.

The Reformation led to so many events,
which had such far-reaching consequences,
that it is not hard to pick out at least a few
that encouraged capitalistic progress. This
naturally did not come about in Italy or

Spain, or in the countries that raised bar-
riers to the spread of the new doctrine,
though even these ended by feeling the
effects of the revolution in thought. But it
came about in the lands where Protestantism was able to establish itself, and especially in those where prevailing conditions
were propitious to an expansion of economic life in a capitalistic direction.

Leaving out of account the anti-slavery
movement and the economic effects of the
Wars of Religion, we may say that the
religious revolution was able to produce
results of most universal consequence where
it first took possession of the State. In no
European country did this come about more
swiftly than in Catholic England, where
the revolt against Rome, at first merely
schismatic, was the work of the King. In
England, more completely than in any
other country, the revolutionary changes
entailed by heresy following on schism led
to confiscation of church property, sale of
lands, speculation, a reshifting of classes,
an influx from lower to higher strata of

society, and the advent of new plutocrats, new land-owners, new rulers. The very vagueness of the official form of the heresy led to doctrinal confusion which had its effects on practical life. . . .

It has been said by various authors that Protestantism encouraged the spread of capitalism by the migrations of its persecuted followers. In support of this thesis, it has been pointed out that the Flemish Reformers and Huguenots introduced the art of fine weaving into England, and the religious exiles from Locarno and Bergamo established new branches of the textile industry in Zurich and Bâle. According to Voltaire, the Huguenots in Germany peopled the towns, introduced the cloth and hat industry, and reclaimed the Mark of Brandenburg. Others have noted how the Protestant colonies, by their thrifty spirit and untiring industry, speedily accumulated capital, which assuredly encouraged the expansion of economic life in their new country. These facts are perfectly true, but are in no way connected with the religion of the social groups concerned. For even if it were true that their particular religious ethos encouraged such exiles in industry and thrift, it is also true that such virtues are characteristic of all foreign groups in new countries. This has been shown by various researches into the effect of foreigners on the economic life of countries receiving them. It may be objected that nonetheless these exiles were such on account of their religion, but this argument, if it led anywhere, would lead to the absurdity of attributing the effects of such enforced exile, not indeed to the religion of the persecuted, but to the measures taken by their persecutors.

On these lines there is therefore little to say of the influence of Protestantism, as a religion, on capitalism. We should rather ask whether these exiles, by their economic virtues and their technical knowledge, did not increase competition in their new countries, and thus expose themselves and their hosts to an increased risk, for to our mind risk is a most important factor in determining a capitalistic mode of action. It might also be said that any emigration, but especially that produced by religious persecution, means a spiritual cleavage from the persecuting fatherland, and hence fosters in the emigrants an internationalism that is no small element in capitalist mentality. And, again, we might ask whether these exiles, persecuted in their own countries, viewed with suspicion in their new ones — as Levy has shown in respect of England — as a result of their misfortunes did not become the most fervent apostles of religious toleration and freedom — a fact of immense importance for the expansion of business, and highly prized by the capitalist. It is indisputable that Protestantism, by immigration and otherwise, destroyed the unity of the State in the religious sphere and made its restoration impossible, so that King and subjects were faced with the problem of shelving the religious question in order to obtain such unity. Protestantism thus obliged the States to face the problem of freedom of conscience, which, advocated by authoritative Protestants, once solved, meant the removal of an obstacle to economic life and encouraged the tendency to count the religious question among problems that could be left out of reckoning. From that time forth the State became more favourably disposed towards capitalism; it had no longer a creed to defend, but only interests, and in this sphere it was not hard to reach an understanding.

Protestantism, where it was represented by a minority or wherever it had the sovereign against it, encouraged the rise of a sentiment that is wholly modern, even if it was not unknown to some or other mediaeval politician. It presented subjects with the problem of whether they were the State or whether the Sovereign was the State; of whether their policy, interests, and will should prevail, or that of their sovereign. It does not take much reflection to see the immense importance of even the raising of such a problem in regard to capitalistic aims. The moment it was raised, in view of the struggle to obtain possession of the State, efforts would be made by the capitalistically minded to make the interests defended by the State coincide with their own, which they idealized to appear as the interests of civilization. The final victories in this struggle would be provided by parliamentary régimes and democratic systems, which, as Weber has shown, found full justification in the idea, peculiar to the Calvinistic groups, that creatures must not be glorified or accorded any differential treatment. . . .

That Protestantism in the ways we have mentioned exercised a positive influence in paving the way for the establishment of capitalism seems indisputable. Nevertheless, such action would have been of small moment had it not encouraged the capitalistic spirit for other reasons. We must hasten to add that such encouragement was unconscious on the part of the reformers. Of this we find proof in the fact that the theologians and moralists of the various sects opposed the manifestations of capitalism, in which they saw acts of Mammon. Bearing this in mind, we may extend to the whole of primitive Protestantism what Tawney wrote of its English forms: "If it is true that the Reformation released forces which were to act as a solvent of the traditional attitude of religious thought to social and economic issues, it did so without design, and against the intention of most reformers." "We ought" — writes Weber — "to realize that the effects of the Reformation on civilization were in great part" — we ourselves should say for the most part — "consequences that the Reformers did not foresee, and indeed definitely did not desire, and which often differed from or conflicted with all that they hoped to obtain by their ideals."

Luther's conservatism in economic matters, to which his patriarchal ideas on trade and his decided aversion to interest bear witness, has been proved beyond all question. Not only this, but there are writers who definitely rule out that he could have brought "an urge to enter the mighty progressive moment of modern economic life." Even Calvin, who when he seeks social

justification for commerce recalls St. Thomas, has violent attacks on Venice and Antwerp, which he considers as centres of the Mammon of Catholicism. With less precision than the Scholastics, but with an equally anti-capitalistic bias, Calvin condemns as unlawful all gain obtained at a neighbour's expense, and the amassing of wealth *"pour remplir nostre avarice, ou despendre en superfluité."*[1] Nor does the Genevan Reformer say anything that is new for Catholics when, speaking of the use of goods, he remarks that they must be used with moderation, since all that we possess is a deposit for which we shall have to render account. If in regard to usury, for reasons that we shall see later, Calvin adopts a non-Catholic attitude, through the sixteenth and seventeenth centuries we find a continual repetition of the prohibitions of usury issued by the synods of the Huguenots and by those of the Dutch Reformers, whose ethical code also condemned even excessive labour, as robbing time and energy from the service of God, and held action born of desire for gain to be a sign of madness.

Nor did the Scottish Church show itself any more favourable to the first manifestations of capitalism. The economic ethical code of the English Reformers and schismatics, in its most characteristic form, tends to agree with the most rigid Catholic view, and often goes even further. The ideas on property of the theologians of the Anglican Church in its early days derive from Scholastic doctrines. We also find many echoes of these doctrines in the views of American Protestants of the eighteenth century. The famous Bucer, in his *De Regno Christi*, starting from the gloomy statement that all traders are thieves, demands that only pious persons, more devoted to the State than to their own interests, should engage in commerce. Hipler goes further still, and in his *Divine Evangelical Reformation* demands the suppression of all merchant companies. Wilson, in *A Discourse upon Usury* (1572),

1 "to satisfy our greed, or to spend on superfluity." [Editor's note]

and Jewel, in his *Exposition upon the Epistle to the Thessalonians* (1583), support the English Protestant authorities who at the end of the eighteenth century still continue to forbid loans at interest. On the other hand, Bullinger, author of the famous *Decadi*, follows Calvin in declaring such loans to be lawful. Anyone wishing to gain an idea of how a sixteenth-century Puritan regarded business has only to read Robert Crowley's verses on the merchant's behaviour in his *Voyce of the laste trumpet ... calling al estats of men to the ryght path of their vocation*, published in 1550.

The later-formed branches of the reformed religion showed themselves no less uncompromising. Various American Protestant sects pronounced in favour of a limitation of capitalistic industrialism. ...

Thus, on the whole . . . the letter of Protestant moral teaching maintains a constantly critical attitude towards capitalism. This has led some to say that here Protestantism does not differ from Catholicism. That Catholic teaching is reiterated by Protestants is indisputable; we find that this is the case even in those expressions in Baxter, in which Weber has sought to find a departure from the Catholic attitude. The demonstrable errors of this writer should make us very cautious in accepting views on the favour shown to capitalism by Protestantism, when they are based on a few moral maxims. Not seldom such convictions spring from the authors' ignorance of Catholic moral teaching. They take for original sentiments what are often merely translations of Latin expressions of Catholic doctrine.

Calvin, when he allows the lending of money at interest, is not reiterating Catholic social doctrine. But this concession — which is an argument for the thesis of our next sub-section — by the very fact of the motives inspiring it, is contrary to Protestant praxis, which seeks a return to the doctrine of the Gospels. For its justification it depends on an idea of fundamental importance for our investigations — the uselessness of works as a means of salvation.

Calvin no longer forbids usury, because he sees it as corresponding to the natural order of events, and in this sixteenth-century Calvinism is truly logical. If in judging other facts the Protestants adopted an attitude more akin to traditional teaching, it was because they did not draw the necessary consequences of their new basic principle, or else because they did not perceive the real nature of economic phenomena. Where it had this perception, and drew the logical conclusion, Protestantism was faithful to its "discovery" and showed itself in opposition to Catholic social ethics. A typical case is that of the Protestants of America, who at the beginning of the eighteenth century still observed rigid economico-ethical ideals, not unlike those of Catholicism, and who, as they became aware of the realities involved, ended by a practical indulgence, which, however, entailed no conflict with the fundamentals of their religion.

Thus, when Robertson writes that Protestantism did not influence capitalism, but capitalism influenced the social ethics of Protestantism, he is not saying anything new nor anything absurd, though he should not find in this any cause for astonishment. For, once the idea was admitted that salvation was independent of works, with the idea of free enquiry, a Protestant was only acting in a logical manner if he accepted the rational order of the world as it resulted from the free operation of man. While the Protestant who still envisaged a "should-be" state was illogical. The fundamental principles of Protestantism lead inevitably to the sanctification of the real; the obstinate attempt to prescribe other-worldly limits to the world is a remnant of doctrines that Protestantism seeks to overthrow.

Weber's far-reaching hypothesis, with which he concludes his well-known study, on the possibility of the influence of social conditions on the development of Protestant ethics, is ill-formulated inasmuch as it gives the idea of a deviating influence, whereas the course of events influenced Protestant ethics by making them ever more

Protestant, hence more logically consequent on the two fundamental principles of Protestantism than they were at first, when, though works were to receive no reward, they were still subject to an extrinsic law as though by that law they would be judged. It seemed at first as if the glory of God, not salvation, demanded an action in conformity with certain ideals. But as the idea of predestination developed, it was not hard to extend it to the circumstances, to the most trivial facts of life, and this meant to free all action from any bonds not implied by its intrinsic rationality.

In final analysis, it is not on Protestant anti-capitalistic action that we must base our estimation of the relationship between Protestantism and capitalism. It is the fundamental principle of Protestantism that counts; the limits set to economic life disappear as soon as a more penetrating logic deduces the full consequences of this principle. The fabric of precepts is broken by contact with life, which shows itself more orthodox than the moralists, and in the end leads even these to issue curious ordinances — like that of the Quakers, who expelled bankrupts from their sect — through which religious motives became a spur to shrewd dealing; men were led to fear failure more as likely to entail excommunication than poverty.

According to Max Weber, Protestantism encouraged the development of capitalism by introducing into the world the idea of vocation, by which each individual was bound to devote all his powers to the field of work to which he was called, in the conviction that this was his sole duty towards God. In this we do not agree with Weber, although he is far more correct than those who declare that "compared with Catholicism, Protestantism in general perhaps gives greater encouragement to the spirit of individual initiative, since it confers on the individual direct and complete responsibility in the sight of God, and does not admit any intercession, neither that of the Saints, nor that provided by the prayers of others." Leaving aside this utterly erroneous opinion, we venture to say that Weber's solution is inacceptable for various reasons, above all because it does not admit that the capitalist spirit existed before the Protestant idea of vocation. It is true that Weber tries to anticipate the objection, that there were capitalistic manifestations prior to Protestantism, by attributing a different spirit to their authors and distinguishing between capitalism and the capitalist spirit, but though his evasion of the objection is skilful, it altogether fails to satisfy. Is it possible for the essence of a thing — and for Weber the capitalist spirit constitutes the essence of capitalism — to come into existence long after the thing itself? We must none the less take Weber's theory into consideration if we are to understand the gravity of the true problem, which is quite other. And it is this: there were capitalistic "facts" before Protestantism, and if we admit that they could not be capitalistic unless they were produced by the capitalist spirit, we must conclude that the capitalist spirit existed before Protestantism. If we reason logically from the data with which Weber supplies us, we cannot fail to reach this conclusion. Therefore we cannot accept the idea of vocation as the origin of the capitalist spirit, or else we must say that it existed at an earlier date.

On the other hand, we cannot grant that man never sought for gain in a rationalized manner before the idea of vocation. It is true that the idea of the rational is relative, but it is also true that the idea of the economically rational, the idea of the minimum means, though affected by later knowledge, was known before Protestantism. So much so, that at bottom those theorists are right who hold that, from the point of view of pure gain, and from the point of view of an economic rationality confined to scattered manifestations on the part of isolated individuals, capitalism has always existed. As against these, and against Weber, we would point out that man has an inborn instinct for gain; that he strives always to attain the minimum means as far as his state of knowledge allows; that external factors either check this instinct or encourage it. It is this instinct, this tendency, that is the germ of the capitalist spirit. Therefore, *in nuce,* the capitalist spirit has always been and always will be. But the capitalist spirit as a social force has not always been, nor will it always be. It is of this capitalist spirit that we speak and ought to speak. It is this that is the essence of capitalism as a social phenomenon; capitalism, so understood, has relations with the various religions, because these, in seeking to discipline the spiritual powers of man, can, in combination with other social phenomena, destroy it, check it, or stimulate it. They cannot bring it to birth, because it has been born already, or, rather, it is inborn in man.

But Weber's text lends itself to further criticism. A few months ago Robertson proved that the idea of vocation, to which Weber attributes so great significance in determining the origin of the capitalist spirit, has not always implied what the German sociologist supposed. The Protestants of the sixteenth century, Latimer and Lever, for example, make use of the idea of vocation to combat those manifestations that Weber considers characteristic of the capitalist spirit. Even in the seventeenth century the very Baxter whom Weber believes to supply so many proofs in support of his thesis attributes an ambiguous significance to the idea of vocation, and only in the eighteenth century do we find among the Puritans a pro-capitalistic content to the idea of vocation. The exhaustive proofs brought forward by Robertson, and which gain an added value from the conclusions of a work by Beins, perhaps give him too great assurance, and he goes so far as to write that Weber's theory should be reversed and that the time has now come to ask whether it was not the predominance of a capitalist mentality in the middle classes that led to a slow but sure evolution of the social ethical code of Protestantism in a capitalistic sense. Robertson adds that no historian can be unaware that if the idea of vocation was the origin of capitalism,

since this idea is identical in the Protestantism of the seventeenth century and the Catholicism of the fourteenth century, and in the Protestantism and in certain Catholic currents of the eighteenth century, we should have to conclude that Protestantism and Catholicism had an equal importance, in this respect, for the development of the capitalist spirit. Nor does Robertson's observation appear ill-founded, once we realize that the idea of vocation, attributed by Weber to the Protestants, was a living idea before the Reformation, and remained alive in the Catholic camp even after. . . . This most decidedly Catholic idea does not even lend itself to Groethuysen's recent reproach that Catholic teaching condemned men's efforts to better their position, for, since Gaetano's sixteenth-century interpretation of St. Thomas' doctrine, it is plain that a man who seeks to obtain that position in life for which he is qualified by his gifts and capacities is not rebelling against God, but striving to reach the post that God has potentially assigned to him.

Weber's explanation is therefore inadequate, and we must ask whether there were not other ways in which Protestantism either encouraged or restrained the capitalist spirit — which has always existed in man in an embryonic state; which, opposed and held in check by Catholicism, became a social force when, in the fifteenth century, Catholicism declined; and which was encouraged by humanism inasmuch as humanism weakened Catholic ties.

Protestantism encouraged capitalism inasmuch as it denied the relation between earthly action and eternal recompense. From this point of view there is no real difference between the Lutheran and Calvinistic currents, for while it is true that Calvin linked salvation to arbitrary divine predestination, Luther made it depend on faith alone. Neither of the two connected it with works. Nevertheless, Calvin's statement was the more vigorous, and therefore better able to bear practical fruit in a capitalistic sense.

Such an assertion invalidates any supernatural morality, hence also the economic ethics of Catholicism, and opens the way to a thousand moral systems, all natural, all earthly, all based on principles inherent in human affairs. Protestantism by this principle did not act in a positive sense, as Weber believes, but in a negative sense, paving the way for the positive action of innumerable impulses, which — like the risks entailed by distant markets, in the pre-Reformation period, the price revolution at the time of the Reformation, and the industrial revolution in the period following — led man to direct his action by purely economic criteria. Catholicism acts in opposition to capitalism by seeking to restrain these impulses and to bring the various spheres of life into harmony on an ideal plane. Protestantism acted in favour of capitalism, for its religious teaching paved the way for it. Thus the effects of Protestantism combined with those of natural agencies, and Tawney's criticism of Weber does not apply.

In the last chapter we saw how the capitalist spirit began by showing itself in the single act of a man who felt, momentarily, that he need not confine his activity within the limits prescribed by revealed morality. We saw, too, how a continuous series of such acts lessened the possibility that they would be checked by remorse. The possibility of remorse only disappears with the weakening of the conviction from which it springs. It is a case of separating the world from God, of unifying the duality of heaven and earth, so dear to the Christian; of detaching earthly happiness from any higher destiny. This means to banish Saints and moralists, agonies and ecstacies. Such was the work that humanistic scepticism began, and the positive teaching of Protestantism completed. "The creation of a new mentality in the economic field cannot therefore be considered as the work of Protestantism, or rather of any one of the Protestant sects, but it is a manifestation of that general revolution of thought that characterizes the period of the Renaissance and the Reformation, by which in art, philosophy, reli-

gion, morals, and economy, the individual emancipates or tends to emancipate himself from the bonds imposed on him during the Middle Ages." In this evolution Protestantism represents the stage at which religion perceives that business morality has legitimate foundations in the earth. If an action is to have no reward but its results, the rationalizing principle of action will remain that of the maximum result. This is the profound revolution brought about by Protestantism, purely through the doctrines we have mentioned, and which acquire an immense significance inasmuch as they represent the religious beliefs of vast multitudes, for whom they become norms of life. Once human actions, including economic actions, must no longer be measured by the yard-stick of salvation, but by the yard-stick of success, man's struggle between his own instincts, his own needs, and divine commandment, finds a human solution. If God Himself allows intrinsic success to be the measure of order, and Himself guides man along this path, does not the economic rationalization of economic actions become the realization of a divine plan. And does not the labour of the man who seeks to perform his task in the best manner possible — estimating the best manner solely from the point of view of results — become a tranquil labour, free from doubts, unhampered by uncertainty, unmarred by remorse.

By instilling this conviction into man, by basing human endeavours on this new rock, Protestantism favoured the dominance of the capitalist spirit, or, rather, it legitimized it and sanctified it. It transformed capitalistic efforts into religious efforts which, although not meritorious, for otherwise God would be rewarding man, were the sole way in which man could burn a grain of incense to the terrible Lord of Heaven and Earth. Truly Hauser is right when he declares: "Calvin, by boldly separating that which is God's from that which is man's, teaches that the Christian may attain salvation in his profession if he follows it as best he can and fully utilizes the gifts of God. . . . Calvin could not foresee a Rockefeller or a Carnegie. But nearer to Erasmus and Rabelais than he supposed, he helped to restore merely human virtue to its rights." Thus Protestantism appeared as the religious sanction of the free efforts of man to attain wealth. The capitalist spirit was justified and no opposition could be made to the action of those natural circumstances that urged man to arm himself to defend his economic interests to the last ditch.

In conclusion, Protestantism, as far as we are concerned, only marked a further stage in the emancipation of human action from supernatural limits. Working in this sense, it produced no new effects, but facilitated the manifestation of a movement that had shown perceptible signs of vitality before the Reformation, and which would continue its course after the Reformation, beyond what the Reformers intended, for, dreaming of a return to the Gospels, they never suspected what would be the fruits of their action.

THE ECONOMIC VIEWS OF THE PROTESTANT REFORMERS

ALBERT HYMA

At present Professor of History at the University of Michigan, Albert Hyma was born in the Netherlands and came to the United States before World War I. He received his A.B., A.M., and Ph.D. degrees from the University of Michigan and taught at Knox College and the University of North Dakota before returning in 1924 to a position at the University of Michigan, where he has since remained. Professor Hyma has written extensively, concentrating upon the Reformation, the Christian humanists, and Dutch economic and colonial activity in the sixteenth and seventeenth centuries.

JOHN CALVIN, as is well known, differed from Luther in that he was of Latin stock, belonged to the upper class, spent much of his life in large and prosperous cities, and was twenty-six years younger. This difference in heredity and environment is commonly utilized as a well-nigh infallible criterion for establishing a definite line of demarcation between the two reformers. Luther the "peasant" could not help but be reactionary and opposed to capitalism, while Calvin the bourgeois was friendly to the modern spirit.

Max Weber's thesis on the relation between Calvinism and capitalism was modified by E. Troeltsch, who reasoned thus: "It was just because the economic conditions at Geneva were so bourgeois, and on such a small scale, that Capitalism was able to steal into the Calvinistic ethic, while it

From Albert Hyma, *Renaissance to Reformation* (Grand Rapids, 1955), pp. 440–443, 455–457, 466–468, 472–475, 480–481, 484–486, 488–489, 494, 497–503, 565–570. By permission of Wm. B. Eerdmans Publishing Co.

was rejected by the Catholic and the Lutheran ethic. That is officially expressed, properly speaking, in the important fact that Calvin and the Calvinistic ethic rejected the canonical veto on usury and the scholastic theory of money, and on the contrary supported a doctrine of money, credit, and usury which were nearer to the modern economic idea, with limitations, certainly, with which we shall have to deal presently. . . .

"The exhortation to continual industry in labour, combined with the limitation of consumption and of luxury, produced a tendency to pile up capital, which for its part — in the necessity of its further utilization in work and not in enjoyment — necessitated an ever-increasing turnover. The duty of labour, coupled with the ban on luxury, worked out 'economically as the impulse to save,' and the impulse to save had the effect of building up capital."

Those who have carefully studied Luther's remarks about money and interest, as well as those about the necessity of hard work and of thrift, will wonder why Calvin's views, which are almost identical, assisted the swift growth of capitalism, while those of Luther had much less effect. Is it perhaps because Calvin devoted more attention than did Luther to economic questions? It must be so, for Troeltsch remarks that Calvin's letters "deal constantly with the interests of finance, trade, and industry (from the point of view of the manual labour)." Nevertheless, Luther filled one hundred folio pages with his comments on the various aspects of capitalism over against fewer than fifty written by Calvin, who certainly was as voluminous a writer as was Luther.

"The practical situation in Geneva," so continues Troeltsch, "was the decisive turning-point: Calvin was convinced that this 'anti-Mammon' Christian spirit could express itself and maintain its existence within the sphere of a society which was based essentially upon a money economy, upon trade and industry." Troeltsch also alleges that Calvin regarded "profit as a

sign of Divine approval." He makes this remarkable conclusion: "This conception of the 'calling' and of labour, with its taboo on idleness of every kind, with its utilization of every chance of gain, and its confidence in the blessing of God, now, however, to a great extent approached the commercial professions and the business of making money. It laid the foundation of a world of specialized labour, which taught men to work for work's sake, and in so doing it produced our present-day bourgeois way of life, the fundamental psychological principles which gave it birth."

Attention has been drawn to these words of the famous German writer, because they have exerted a tremendous influence in Great Britain and this country, although neither Max Weber nor his celebrated follower had ever thoroughly studied the life and thought of John Calvin. Consequently, it has been inevitable that very strange opinions about the Lutheran and Calvinistic conceptions of capitalism were produced in this country, including the extraordinary theories on this subject concocted by so well-known a writer and lecturer as Reinhold Niebuhr, as quoted in the *Calvin Forum* of August, 1937: "Lutheranism is called a *Weltfeindlich* [hostile to this world], quietistic religion, which emphasized 'the kingdom within' and paid little attention to the social situation. Calvinism is *Weltfreundlich* [friendly to this world]. It influenced politics and economics, made 'a valuable contribution to social progress' and became 'the spiritual foundation upon which the whole structure of modern civilization has been built.' . . . 'The love and reverence for personality which is the basis of the ethics of Jesus,' Niebuhr claims to be totally lacking in Calvinism."

Let us also briefly note what Max Weber himself had said about Calvinism and capitalism, for Niebuhr has obviously copied some of Weber's ideas on the subject: "In Calvin's theology the Father in heaven of the New Testament, so human and understanding . . . is gone . . . Though the sacraments had been ordained by God for the increase of His glory, and must hence be scrupulously observed, they are not a means to the attainment of grace." And Weber even goes so far as to aver that in the Calvinist religion no priest was required, "because the chosen one can understand the Word of God only in his own heart." This means that the elect of God must spend his time building up capital for the glory of God, work chiefly for work's sake, save all he can, and look around for signs of his election in the amount of profit he can make with his business. The Lutherans and the Catholics, on the other hand, who did not believe in predestination, did not work nearly so hard nor try to save so much money. Hence the poverty of Germany and Italy in the seventeenth century as contrasted with the prosperity in the Netherlands and England. (Scotland, however, is carefully omitted as a rule, for good reasons.)

Now it is one of the most remarkable facts in the career of John Calvin that, after he had spent fifteen years in succession in Geneva (1541–56), he still said nothing of the slightest importance about economic theories or capitalism in general, in his most famous work, *The Institutes of the Christian Religion.* Luther's most widely discussed treatise, the *Address to the German Nobility,* on the other hand, contains startling comments about the wickedness of the rich bankers, the evil results of usury, the need of hard work, and the necessity of frugal living. . . .

The following points of agreement may be noted between Luther's views in the years 1520, 1524, and 1525, and Calvin's opinion as expressed in the letter on usury, dated 1545. First, the Mosaic law and all other passages in the Old Testament are intended for Jews, and not necessarily for the gentiles. Secondly, no statement to be found anywhere in the Bible can be construed as condemning every form of lending money on interest. Thirdly, a Christian (for Luther and Calvin have only Christians in mind) is to be subject to the laws and regulations of the country or city in which he is residing. Fourthly, no matter what those laws say, it is prohibited to charge interest of a poor person. Fifthly, one must constantly bear in mind the injunction of Christ, not to do unto others what one does not want done to himself. Sixthly, the proper rate of interest is five per cent, but in special cases it is permissible to charge up to eight per cent. Seventhly, the ideal way is to loan money on security, in the form of real estate. Eighthly, Aristotle's dictum, "Money is sterile," is to be interpreted to mean that money buried in a box is indeed sterile, and nobody would be [so] foolish as to pay interest on such money. Ninthly, it were well if all manner of usury were abolished from the face of the earth, for the name *usury* has rightly earned for itself a very bad reputation. However, the word *interest* newly introduced describes a practice which has been generally accepted since the first of the fifteenth century. Consequently, the Christian will do well to abide by this well-established custom. Tenthly, the desire for personal gain must always remain subordinate to that Christian spirit of brotherly love which seeks to aid the poor and the outcasts, for they are to receive all the property and profit which exceed one's moderate needs.

Emile Doumergue says in the fifth volume of his admirable biography of John Calvin that he cannot understand how a scholar like Max Weber, highly revered as he is in every country of western Europe, could have distorted the Calvinist spirit so amazingly as he did in playing havoc with the doctrine of predestination and its social consequences. As we have indicated above, it is sheer folly to infer that all the Calvinists were interested in was to work directly for the glory of God. A careful study of Calvin's works shows plainly that concern for one's neighbor's welfare was the guiding factor in the whole problem of usury, and of business in general. In this respect there is no fundamental difference between Calvin and Luther, or between Calvin and the Catholics. Weber's followers, in their anxiety to prove his main thesis, have set up an artificial group of differences between the two leading reformers which does not improve the reputation of the thesis. . . .

"The school of Heidelberg," says Doumergue, "knows much about neo-Calvinism in England and America, but about the Calvinism of Calvin they know almost nothing more than what they have gleaned from second-hand sources." This is very true, and it applies especially to Troeltsch, the best mind in that school. One might wonder, continues Doumergue, whether Calvin was a Calvinist. Again, very true, for both John Wesley and Benjamin Franklin are quoted to show what Calvinism was, or at least what it had done to make modern capitalism possible. . . .

Calvin, instead of having been the first to distinguish between interest and usury, showed so little desire to understand this difference, that, . . . he thought the word *interest* signifies something that is of interest to us. He knew so little about the history of money and of interest that not until 1555 did he voluntarily discuss usury, and as late as that year, he apparently did not know that it was Aristotle who had invented the celebrated maxim, "Money does not beget money." Calvin's discussion of the word *interest* comes much later than that by Luther, and it must have sounded very naive to those jurists who knew that more than one hundred years before Calvin wrote on the subject, it had been analyzed by capable scholars.

During the past fifty years it has been the almost universal belief among the leading authorities on economic, social, and religious history that the canonical prohibition of lending money on interest, supported by the opinions of the Church Fathers, and fortified by the authority of Thomas Aquinas, restricted the flow of capital during the fourteenth centur[y]. Luther with his "peasant" mind, as even Sombart thought, made little or no progress in freeing capital from the shackles of ecclesiastical hostility. But Calvin, the Bourgeois, helped to make the Dutch Republic and the English commonwealth the two first successful capitalistic powers.

In this connection we must consider first the remarkable view of Sombart, who holds that the scholastic philosophers proved their friendship for capitalism by refusing to oppose the canonical teaching about usury: "Capitalism appealed to them. It was on that account that they clung to the teaching of the Canon Law concerning usury. For what did the prohibition of usury mean to the Catholic moralists of the 15th and 16th centuries? Expressed in modern terms it denoted: Don't prevent money from becoming capital." Sombart wonders why "no one has noticed this before." He believed that "possibly one reason is that the specialists who have hitherto devoted themselves to scholastic philosophy were not economists and lacking that knowledge of affairs which Bernard of Siena and Antonine of Florence possessed."

It would seem to the present writer, however, that both Max Weber and Werner Sombart, who in this respect have presented theories which are exactly the opposite of each other, were lacking in a proper understanding of the religious factors involved in the rise of capitalism. That two scholastic writers of the fifteenth century who were declared saints by the Church, should have favored capitalism through their support of the Canon Law, is indeed a preposterous assertion. On the other hand, the canonical prohibition just mentioned probably did less harm to the attempted expansion of commerce and industry than is commonly believed. If this conclusion of ours is correct, it follows that the defiance of the prohibition by the Calvinists did not materially assist the growth of modern capitalism.

Nevertheless, we shall open this chapter with a discussion of theories relating to the lending of money on interest, in order to determine whether there is really any truth at all in the vaunted thesis of Weber and Troeltsch. The first two Protestant writers whose opinions rivaled those of Thomas Aquinas, and of both Luther and Calvin, were Philip Melanchthon and Martin Bucer. Their views have been neglected by recent commentators, although it has often been claimed that Calvin and his immediate followers were strongly affected by them. . . .

Now the question arises, Was Melanchthon really so "far ahead of his contemporaries" as is often surmised? Did he seem so anxious to break with Aristotle and the Canon Law? He certainly does not say so himself in any of the passages where he discusses lending of money on interest, for which he is often praised as an advanced thinker. Not only is he more vague and obscure than Luther, but he is farther removed from actual practice. It would not be difficult to prove that the Roman Catholic clergy in Melanchthon's time were more in favor of what he still called *usury* than he was, for they openly practised what he deemed an evil. Their connections with the banking house of the Fuggers in Rome and Augsburg gave a decided impetus to the rapid spread of so-called usury. It is all very well to say that the Catholic church has always been opposed to capitalism, but theory and practice have not coincided with each other in certain critical periods, which is particularly true of the very age in which modern capitalism was born.

Another Protestant writer who was closely associated with Luther's career in Germany, and whose views on capitalism will prove nearly as reactionary as those of Melanchthon, was Martin Butzer (French spelling is Bucer). This scholar is known to have exerted great influence upon Calvin's theological development, and one writer has suggested that Calvin derived his views on usury from Butzer, but he has been refuted successfully by E. Doumergue.

Butzer simply taught that not all forms of usury ought to be condemned, which had to be done by the "foolish scholastics." Certainly, he reasoned in 1527, the lending of money to others on interest is laudatory, in case both parties derive from it a fair and

just profit. In 1539 he suggested that the interest charged by the Jews should not exceed the rate of five per cent. Finally, in 1550 he wrote a treatise of considerable interest, entitled *On Usury,* in which he expressed views which were almost identical with those of Calvin. There can be no doubt that when he was professor of theology at Cambridge in the reign of Edward VI, he must have sowed there the seeds of opposition to the old régime. But we shall see presently that about this time the English government passed a regulation requiring that all interest on loans was to be illegal. Butzer's influence was great in the field of religion, but his support of the lending of money on interest cannot have weighed heavily with the English. . . .

Although Huldreich Zwingli preceded Calvin and Melanchthon in a chronological sense, he is mentioned here last, because his opinions on capital and interest are confused and naive. Zwingli claimed that every form of interest should be condemned, for one should give alms outright to those who needed money. He made scarcely any distinction between the problem of private property and that of lending money on interest. . . .

Zwingli condemns rates above five per cent and all lending of money on interest where no security is offered. He advises that henceforth no new loans be made on property, for there will be enough old ones left for those wealthy unbelievers who feel they must keep up the old practice. The poor must adjust themselves to their lot. Far better for him to sell his home and land than to sell himself. "For what else does he do when he borrows money on his property than to sell his own labor to some one else; he will work, and what he gains with his labor, he will donate to the other person." . . .

It appears that Zwingli recognized how far the Catholic clergy had wandered from the biblical injunctions against the lending of money on interest. Protestant criticism in the sixteenth century was directed against the Catholic clergy, wherever the latter had, in the eyes of the reformers, deviated from the path prescribed by Christ and His disciples and apostles. Whereas some modernistic interpreters with practically no knowledge of either church history or theology weave fantastic theories about the relation between Protestantism and capitalism, it behooves the conscientious historian to return to the original sources of early Protestantism. Here he will find that the Protestants, far from encouraging what is called the "capitalistic spirit," put innumerable stumbling blocks in its way. Instead of looking upon Zwingli as more advanced than Luther in his attitude toward usury, it would be more nearly correct to conclude that Luther was more advanced than Zwingli. Moreover, it would be equally correct to surmise that early Protestantism was less advanced than was Catholicism, either modern or medieval.

There is no sense in the way the majority of the Catholics and the orthodox Protestants seek to overemphasize the alleged differences in their respective attitude toward the political, economic, and social problems which have always confronted mankind. Those contributions to the spirit of modern capitalism which were supposedly made by orthodox Protestantism, the rejection of the canonical prohibition on the lending of money on interest, the duty of working hard, the desire to save, the hallowing of one's vocation, the friendly attitude displayed to the expansion of commerce and industry, and the justification of private property beyond one's personal needs — all these, as the great Italian authority, A. Fanfani, has aptly demonstrated, were present in Italy during the fourteenth and fifteenth centuries, when modern capitalism was born. But not all of these are symptoms of Catholicism. Only the following factors were and still are the proper symptoms, namely, the duty of working hard, as a form of penance and not as a means of making money; the desire to live frugally, and to save, in order to give alms to the poor or do anything else to better social conditions generally; the hallowing

of one's vocation; and the belief that a Christian may acquire more of the world's goods than he needs for his own family. . . .

That Luther, Zwingli, Butzer, Melanchthon, and hundreds of other orthodox Protestants recognized what had been going on in the world about them, and that they recalled what Peter had said about the duty of the Christians to obey civil authorities, is not surprising. The Catholics likewise had made the same observations, for they did not differ in this respect from the Protestants. If Calvin had been so favorably inclined toward the lending of money on interest, and if he had had no scruples (which we know he exhibited in great number) about this form of "usury," it cannot be explained easily why the French, English, and Dutch followers of his were so severe in their condemnation of what they considered usury. As late as the year 1646, the outstanding Calvinist professors of theology in the Dutch Republic stated in a printed treatise that no interest ought to be charged on any loans granted to the poor, and less than two or three per cent on moderately large loans. The decisions of the French, German, and Dutch Calvinistic churches from 1559 to 1656 show that those members of the church who charged interest on loans to the poor, or who charged high rates of anybody, were not permitted to participate in the sacrament of Communion. And when, shortly after the demise of King Henry VIII, Calvinist members of the English nobility gained control of the government under young Edward VI, they repealed the act of Henry VIII which had permitted the lending of money on interest at the rate of ten per cent. The men who were responsible for such steps were sincerely of the opinion that they conformed faithfully to the wishes of Calvin and Luther. Could it be said of them that they did not know what Calvin's views on the subject were? That would be very strange indeed, since they scrupulously adhered to the political and religious and ecclesiastical doctrines of the churches at Geneva. It seems much more likely that certain modern writers, who were not industrious enough to read what Calvin, Luther, and the leading Catholic scholars from 1400 to 1600 had said themselves, concocted what was thought a brilliant theory, and bent their energy toward the task of proving this theory. . . .

If the orthodox Protestants differed from the Catholics in this respect [their attitudes toward usury and interest], they were more anticapitalistic than were the Catholics. When all the extreme views on both sides are thrown together with all the moderate views into a great mixing machine, we shall find the average view of the orthodox Protestants and the Catholics respectively to be almost identical. [But] quoting from ten or twenty writers and preachers will not help us a great deal, for individual opinions varied considerably, and theory and practice did not always coincide. It is to be hoped that in the near future a large amount of pertinent opinions will be collected and properly analyzed by competent critics. In the meantime it is possible to draw some general conclusions about the relation between orthodox Protestantism and capitalism which will not be altered afterward by any quantity of quotations from the writings of individual Protestants. At present we have already available the official confessions of faith, the records of the synods or assemblies of clergymen, the pronouncements of theological faculties, and the words of Luther, Calvin, Zwingli, Melanchthon, and Butzer, besides the writings of numerous Puritans which have been searched by R. H. Tawney and others. Finally, the biographies of a large number of eminent continental Protestants of the sixteenth century help to complete a picture which we admit remains fragmentary in parts but will nevertheless enable us to make a fairly comprehensive comparison between the attitude displayed respectively by the Roman Catholics and the leading Protestants of the sixteenth century toward the rising tide of capitalism.

In the first place, it will no longer do to deny that capitalism and the spirit of capitalism were expanding rapidly before there were any Protestants. A reference to the works of A. Doren and A. Fanfani and W. Sombart . . . will suffice here.

In the second place, the more is said about the problem of usury in the sixteenth century, the more certain it appears that Protestantism either was more conservative than Catholicism or else it merely accepted as proper what the civil governments had enacted. This point has been fully demonstrated by now.

In the third place, the duty of the Christian to labor as hard and as well as he can was recognized by the great Church Fathers and the medieval doctors. Luther and Calvin read with approbation what St. Augustine had said about the subject. It is a matter of common knowledge that early Protestantism drew heavily upon this Father. Unfortunately, many Protestants in recent times have made the erroneous conclusion that modern Catholicism is farther removed from Augustinianism than is early Protestantism. Even medieval Catholicism rested firmly upon the views held by the learned bishop, as may be gathered most convincingly by looking through the tables of contents of the Latin manuscripts preserved today in the European and American libraries. Such an examination will reveal that Augustine rather than Gregory the Great was the most influential among the Church Fathers.

The duty to work is strongly emphasized by Augustine, who argues that it ennobles man. He regards with admiration the various handicrafts and the products of manual labor: industrial establishments, agriculture, the building of cities, architecture, inventions, as well as poetry, music, and mathematics. "All of this is grand and fully deserved by mankind." Although he felt that mental and spiritual work was higher than physical, he added that "those who want to be spiritual only and not labor with the body, reveal their indolence." He was rather afraid of commerce, realizing that though it was fully permitted, it carried with it the dangers which antiquity had always dreaded. And the lending of money on interest he naturally abhorred.

Following two centuries of neglect by some of the leaders in the Church, the study of Augustine reached greater heights than ever in the sixteenth century and the first half of the seventeenth century. This renewed interest in the leading Church Father was shared by Catholics and Protestants alike, with the result that his theory of predestination as slightly modified by Luther and Calvin, was adopted by many in the Roman Catholic Church. For nearly a quarter of a century (*ca.* 1585–1610) a tremendous controversy raged in the ranks of the clergy, both in Spain and in Rome itself, but after eighty-five sessions the problem of predestination was left unsettled.

We may conclude, therefore, that during the sixteenth century both Protestants and Catholics gladly sought justification for their beliefs and actions in the writings of Augustine. Moreover, we may bring up in our comparison between Protestantism and Catholicism, where they were in accord, the need to save and to build up a surplus for the support of the poor and for the glory of God. Much has been made of this point by Weber and Troeltsch as far as the early Protestants were concerned, and there is no need of repeating what is well known about the Calvinists in particular. That the Catholics both before and after 1500 were no different has been debated. But it would be hard to find any Protestants who spent so little for their own needs as did the Franciscans and the Dominicans. They, much more than the Protestants, took to heart the saying of Jesus, "If you will be perfect, sell what you have and give the proceeds to the poor, and you will possess a treasure in heaven, and come and follow me." The imitation of Christ was nowhere more nearly accomplished than among the friars of the thirteenth century, and it is to be doubted that the spirit of their founders ever left them completely. Today it is very powerful still. . . .

We now turn to . . . the problem about the vocation of the Christian in this world.

Several Protestant authorities have gone to strange extremes in their belief that the Catholic ideal of the vocation is identical with monasticism. Weber, Tawney, and many others have argued that in the early Church this was not yet the case, and that Protestants, in their return to the primitive church, brought the vocation back to the place it has held in the minds of the orthodox Protestants ever since. How erroneous this viewpoint has been may be seen in the chapter on the *Beruf,* the German word for vocation, of a book by H. M. Robertson, entitled, *The Rise of Economic Individualism* (Cambridge, 1933). Robertson has devoted much attention to this question. He has shown that not until the eighteenth century did the typical Puritans exhibit the attitude toward their individual vocations which might be considered favorable to the development of capitalism.

Mr. Robertson brings up a viewpoint with which we are in hearty sympathy. He claims that the thesis of Weber should be reversed, for then it can be proved to be correct. In his opinion capitalism altered Protestantism, and not the reverse. Gradually the spirit of capitalism, which is hostile to the fundamental essence of Catholicism and of orthodox Protestantism, affected the Dutch, and afterward the English, in such measure that many of them ceased to be interested in spiritual values. It would hardly be fair to Calvinism to call them Calvinists, or even Neo-Calvinists, as Troeltsch does, for they had become so deeply engrossed in the quest after material riches that they ignored the injunctions of their spiritual fathers.

A. Fanfani adds much weight to the contention of Robertson when he points out that the "idea of vocation, attributed by Weber to the Protestants, was a living idea before the Reformation, and remained alive in the Catholic camp ever after." He adds that Bourdaloue, Houdry, Feugère, Griffet, Massillon, and others have repeatedly reminded the faithful Catholics of modern France that in accordance with God's will each person has his place in the social order, and that he must perform his daily tasks with religious zeal, as if they were a part of his religion. . . .

Another curious error indulged in by various European and American writers is the discussion of the alleged Calvinist doctrine about the relation between financial success and eternal salvation. According to the early Calvinists, so we are told, capitalistic efforts were transformed into religious efforts, "which were the sole way in which man could burn a grain of incense to the terrible Lord of Heaven and of earth." It must give Catholic and liberal Protestant scholars a feeling of great satisfaction to pass such a verdict upon the Calvinists of the sixteenth and seventeenth centuries. They have even constructed a bridge leading from Calvin to Carnegie and Rockefeller, disregarding the fact that a twentieth century Baptist like John D. Rockefeller entertained views deviating fundamentally from Calvin's basic principles.

For example, it matters little what Henri Hauser says about Rockefeller and Carnegie. He and Fanfani, and a host of others can easily conclude that "thus Protestantism appeared as the religious sanction of the free efforts of man to attain wealth." They will make bold and go a bit farther still by saying, "The capitalist spirit was justified and no opposition could be made to the action of those natural circumstances that urged man to arm himself to defend his economic interests to the last ditch." Again we would ask this question, Where do these writers find proof for supporting their idle fancies? Have they studied the confessions of faith, the records of the synods, and the commentaries on the Bible which were produced in the sixteenth century by the Calvinists? If so, will they be kind enough to quote from them? . . .

John Calvin would have been amazed, had he been told that in the twentieth century a wealthy business man would be cited as exemplifying his attitude toward the art of money-making. John D. Rockefeller was indeed an adept in this art. He also believed that he knew how to spend his money to the best interests of society as a whole. He may well have found the perfect way to glorify God, but if he did, his way was far removed from that which Calvin would have pointed out to him when a boy in his catechism. The stern reformer reasoned that man needed much time for sanctification, which would have to be preceded by penitence. One should fear God, it is true, because one could make no progress until he fully realized the nature of sin. This is exactly what the Catholics also taught, for the Christian religion demanded much concentration on the process of sanctification. . . .

A study of the relation between Calvinism and capitalism in the German section of the Rhine valley (Rhineland) will throw welcome light on the practical results of the creeds and decisions of the local synods during the sixteenth century. Such a study was made by a competent German scholar,[1] who published his treatise on the subject in one of the best economic journals in Europe. He observed that both Weber and Troeltsch had based their theories upon an inadequate study of the original sources, and proceeds to repair some of the damage done by these two writers. He argues that it is a queer way to write an account about Calvinism in the Rhineland by paying no attention to the original sources and to individual facts, and by quoting from Anglo-Saxon writers, as if they, living across the sea, could be relied upon to show how capitalism was affected in the Rhineland by German and Dutch Calvinists.

Another serious error committed by Weber at least, so continues the author, is the failure to study the social and economic views of Calvin himself, which remarkable folly is not yet sufficiently abhorred by several writers today. Weber quotes primarily from the latter generations of Calvinists, and so distorts his own structure of reasoning. Calvin showed a decidedly anticapitalistic attitude in frowning upon all at-

[1] J. Hashagen, "Kalvinismus und Kapitalismus am Rhein," *Schmoller's Jahrbuch*, XLVII (1924), 49–72.

tempts to secure a superabundance of temporal riches, and by condemning the consumption of luxuries. Moreover, too much emphasis has been placed upon the significance of the "calling" in the development of Calvinism, but the repeated references to the duty of hard work and saving are the sound feature of the Weber thesis. . . .

The influence exerted by Calvinism in the Rhineland exemplifies the ethical phase of Calvinism which closely resembles socialism, and which must be described as decidedly hostile to capitalism. A quotation is then given by the author [Hashagen] from the writer[2] who devoted, as we saw above, a whole book to the influence exerted by Butzer upon the economic views of Calvin: "Many a thought uttered by Calvin about the relation between employer and employee, between labor and capital, would fit perfectly into the program of a socialist. If this emphasis upon the duty of both parties had been perpetuated, capitalism would have assumed a very different form from that which it eventually adopted." The chief error in the Weber-Troeltsch thesis and in the researches which produced the thesis, according to the author, is therefore the failure to recognize the spiritual and moral antithesis between Calvinism and capitalism. . . .

In examining the general aspect of Protestantism in the sixteenth century, and in comparing it with Catholicism, it begins to look very much as if either has been generally studied altogether too much without considering the principal features of the other. The emphasis on the duty of hard work and saving, on almsgiving and simplicity is so typically medieval, and so typically Christian, and so typically European, that thus far the whole problem which we have been discussing has been rather badly treated because of prejudice in favor of a certain theory or a certain religious system. Denifle and Grisar [prominent Catholic

scholars], in depicting the life and character of Luther, have marred a magnificent piece of scholarship by ridiculous exhibitions of personal bias, thus often undermining their own workmanship. Many of the Protestants, on the other hand, are so deeply impressed by the superiority of Protestantism, that they cannot adjust their minds sufficiently to see that in many cases the good qualities in certain Protestant leaders are merely there because all virtuous Christians have possessed them. What we need particularly at the present time is more extensive study and a more unbiased interpretation of the original sources.

The spread of Calvinism in Hungary, its subsequent decline, and its recent revival will furnish as excellent illustrations of how little Calvinism aided the growth of capitalism. The Reformed Church in 1935 counted 1,813,000 members in Hungary, and nearly one million more members belonged to the Hungarian Reformed Church outside the boundaries of what now constitutes Hungary. Although Calvinism is said to have aided the Hungarians in the past when fighting for national independence, even so enthusiastic a disciple of Calvin as Professor Emeric Révész of the University of Debreczen has to admit that Calvinism could not help the economic life of Hungary. In an excellent study of the history of Calvinism, based on numerous original sources, he reports that "we cannot find in the lives of the Hungarians of the sixteenth and seventeenth centuries a trace of the political and economic ideas of Calvinism." He thinks that is largely owing to the fact that there are so few documents left of the period. However, he notes a little farther that "in the field of economics, Calvinism could not operate very well, because Hungarian commerce, which flourished in the sixteenth century, was largely destroyed by the Turks and the Hapsburgs in the seventeenth century. The relations between Hungary and western Europe were broken up just as Calvinist ideas were ready to influence the economic life." Nevertheless, so continues the author, "the most flourish-

[2] G. Klingenburg, *Das Verhältnis Calvins zu Butzer, Untersucht auf Grund der wirtschaftethischen Bedeutung beider Reformatoren* (Bonn, 1912).

ing period of Calvinist theology in Hungary was the first half of the seventeenth century." Does this not indicate clearly that secular forces must be closely followed in determining how commerce and industry expanded or declined? These secular forces must be seen in this relationship with the religious ideas.

The history of Calvinism in Scotland is so destructive to the Weberian thesis that the supporters of this thesis scrupulously avoid this subject as a rule. Professor G. D. Henderson writes: "The Scottish theological and ecclesiastical system was traditionally Calvinistic from the time of John Knox and of the 'Scots Confession' and 'First Book of Discipline' which so largely expressed his thought and will. The influence of Geneva continued, Beza in particular being well known and highly esteemed; but it was the development of Presbyterianism which took place in France that came to be the basis for the organization of the Scots Kirk. . . . As soon, however, as Holland secured its political independence, and showed signs of the wonderful commercial, intellectual, and cultural advance which characterized it in the 17th century, there commenced very definite inter-relations with Scotland which were not without real importance for the country. . . . Calvinistic Europe was indeed one in those days as it has never since been. . . . The situation in Scotland made it inevitable that Scotland should take theological guidance from without, and in Holland it found a principal source of instruction and edification.

Scotland in the seventeenth century became much more thoroughly Calvinistic than either England or Holland. But, as in the case of Hungary, the rapid spread of Calvinist ideas and theology did not by any means correspond to the development in commerce and industry. In Hungary, trade declined as Calvinism spread, while in Scotland trade lagged far behind the growth of Calvinism. And as for the relation between the expansion of industry and commerce in France and the growth of Calvinism, it can easily be demonstrated that during the second half of the sixteenth century and the first half of the seventeenth century, when Calvinism was at the height of its power in France, economic expansion, growth of sea power and colonial expansion was in abeyance. Only with the coming to power of the great minister Colbert, after the Huguenots had been greatly weakened by Richelieu, that is, after 1660, did France finally return to its status of leadership attained previously in the thirteenth century. Three times the French tried to establish an East India Company, in imitation of the English and the Dutch, and each time their attempt was an ignominious failure. Nearly all the foreign trade of France was controlled by the Dutch for a time, just when Calvinism was very powerful politically. And we are sure that a careful study of the French sources will demonstrate the true character of Calvinism as the arch-enemy of capitalism. . . .

Having sketched the rise of Puritanism in England, we are now in a position to investigate more fully the relation between Puritanism and capitalism. We may start with the recently adopted assumption that Lutheranism, Catholicism, and Anglicanism were too conservative to yield to the demands of the growing trade and industry, but that Calvin and his followers were progressive, thus explaining the great success attained by the English in the field of economic expansion. That this assumption is not supported by the history of Dutch capitalism need not disturb us at this point. We did note, however, that at the very moment when the friends and disciples of Calvin were in control of the ecclesiastical policies of the English government under Edward VI, the statute was passed permitting no more lending of money at interest. It also seems remarkable that Henry VIII, who was by no means a Calvinist, had been so liberal as to permit interest charges up to ten per cent, which was twice as high as Calvin thought proper, and also much higher than seemed just or fair to Luther. When in 1571 his statute was resurrected under Queen Elizabeth, England was a Protestant country, and Henry Sée, the best-known authority on economic history in France, has suggested that possibly the Puritans might have had something to do with this.

Professor Sée reasons that the Anglican Church was resolutely opposed to loans at interest and to speculations of all sorts, but somehow it was obliged to recognize usury as legitimate as long as the rates of interest did not exceed ten per cent. This line of reasoning is perfectly in accord with that of Professor Hauser, as seen above, and also with a former pronouncement by Sée himself in a charming book dealing with the origins of modern capitalism, where he draws this conclusion: "The religious revolution, especially Calvinism, powerfully contributed to the modern conception of capitalism, as has been admirably indicated by two German scholars, Max Weber and, later, Troeltsch. The doctrine of Calvin, as far as the taking of interest is concerned, was diametrically opposed to that of the Roman Catholic Church. . . . This viewpoint of Calvin approaches closely that of the Jews. . . . We shall see later that the Puritans were precisely the people who were among the most active supporters of modern capitalism."

It would seem that Professor Sée did not study the circumstances under which the statute of 1552 was passed. Calvinism was much in evidence there, and also in the making of the Forty-Two Articles of the Anglican Church, especially when the doctrines of transsubstantiation and predestination were discussed. But in 1571 the monarch upon the throne was Elizabeth, whose attachment to the altar and the candles was such that the Calvinists in England were sorely vexed. When the Puritans objected to the elaborate ceremonies in the state church she turned to them a cold shoulder. Furthermore, when the change in church government was discussed by the Puritans, she grew angry. We have seen that some of the Puritans were actually imprisoned, and presently we shall hear of a number of English congregations which were forced to worship on Dutch soil before the end of the sixteenth century.

Calvin, so argues Professor Sée, was not opposed to manual labor, nor to the emphasis placed by certain persons upon their vocation, nor to the acquisition of great wealth. Consequently, the Calvinists in Holland were responsible for the great expansion experienced by Dutch trade and banking. The same may be said of the Puritans. Here we are face to face again with the old legend. That the Calvinists and Puritans whom we have met thus far would also have considered it a legend, is certain. In their separation from the Lutherans and the Catholics, and later, from the Anglicans as well, they did not pay any attention to the question of hard work, the importance of one's calling, and the right to acquire great material wealth. On the contrary, their attention was concentrated upon doctrinal and ecclesiastical differences, as we have noted above. There were certain points of difference between the Catholics and the Lutherans, between the Lutherans and the Calvinists, and between the Anglicans and the Puritans. When these points were discussed, the problems of usury, almsgiving, relief of the poor, and manual labor, were generally ignored, since all the great leaders were agreed upon the measures that should be taken to solve these problems. No Puritan dreamed of leaving the Church of England, or of letting himself be imprisoned because the policy of relief of the poor, or the attitude displayed by the bishops toward the importance of hard work, did not please him. Nobody left for Switzerland or Germany in the reign of Queen Mary, because she and her Catholic advisers showed a reactionary trend of thought in trying to solve economic problems. Nobody came to America because Archbishop Laud did not want the Puritans to work so hard as they were doing. Inasmuch as Calvin could find time to fill only fifty pages out of more than thirty thousand to devote to economic problems, it must not surprise anyone that his "advanced" followers also were sadly lacking in this respect. . . .

Mr. H. M. Robertson has won the gratitude of many readers by making a careful study of the Puritan doctrine of the "calling," and he has seen fit, with much justice, to reserve for it a whole chapter in his interesting book on Weber's thesis. He reproduces numerous passages from the works of Robert Crowley, Thomas Lever, and Hugh Latimer, not to mention Richard Baxter, who unwittingly served to illustrate for the German and French schools of economics what his brethren in the faith believed one hundred years before he ever wrote a line. Robertson indicates, for example, that when Latimer referred to the manual labor performed by Christ, in which respect He acted as our example, the writer merely expressed a viewpoint that was common to all good Christians. He mentions the work published in 1550 by Crowley, entitled *Voice of the Last Trumpet . . . Calling All Estates of Men to the Right Path of Their Vocation*, and in this connection he explains that the Puritans of the sixteenth century, when they discussed their calling (vocation), were vastly more interested in being honest and virtuous than in trying to make a lot of money. Certainly, they were of the opinion that virtue pleased God far more than the making of money. But after the middle of the seventeenth century, so admits Robertson, when Puritanism had been diluted and weakened by the enormous expansion of capitalism, the typical Puritan writer or preacher showed exactly how this weakening of Puritan qualities was reflected in their own viewpoints.

Even so, we may conclude that Robertson, like E. Beins and Professor K. Holl, . . . made a greater concession to the Weberian school than was at all necessary. When W. Sombart is attacked by Weber for allegedly having mistranslated the pronouncements of scholastic writers like Antonine of Florence, Robertson does not know whether Sombart is guilty or not. And when Beins, in preparing his summary of an excellent treatise for which he deserves much credit, concludes that Weber's thesis is refuted by the history of Dutch capitalism, he grants that perhaps R. H. Tawney in his treatment of seventeenth century Puritanism is justified in supporting Weber. More than that, he feels that Calvinism in the Dutch Republic assisted capitalism in about the same degree as, according to Tawney, Puritanism supported capitalism in England, namely, after 1650. Similarly, Professor Holl, after having smashed the Weber thesis in important sections with reference to events in the sixteenth and the first half of the seventeenth century, graciously admits that Weber may be right in his analysis of the subsequent period. In England and America, says Holl, Calvinism strongly assisted the growth of capitalism. Holl probably made this concession simply because he had never studied the history of Calvinism in England and America.

It is likely, however, that when a theory does not fit a religion in a certain century, being exactly the reverse of the truth, its application to the same religion in the following century will probably reflect the fundamental weakness of the theory once more, though perhaps to a lesser extent than was the case before. The reader will surmise that, since Calvinism was strongly opposed to the spirit of capitalism in the sixteenth century, a seeming change in that religion must mean simply that many persons who professed that religion had become untrue to its fundamental principles. If we can now pass on to the following period with an open mind, we shall probably find that capitalism caused many Calvinists and many Puritans to surrender the old antagonism to Mammonworship. These pseudo-Calvinists will no doubt look for and find excuses for their behavior, and they will create a demand for treatises and books to be written by eminent scholars and virtuous preachers, who will still parade under the name of Calvinists, even after they have rejected Calvin's doctrine of predestination; yes, in many cases after they have ceased to be Christians.

THE HISTORY OF A CONTROVERSY

EPHRAIM FISCHOFF

A New Yorker by birth and schooling, Fischoff received his doctoral degree in sociology from the New School for Social Research in 1942. He was a Lecturer at Hunter College and later a Professor and Head of the Department of Sociology at American International College. He is at present a member of the faculty at Yale University and is especially interested in the sociology of religion and in social legislation.

WEBER's original intention in *The Protestant Ethic* must be seen against the background of his time. An heir of the historical school (he regarded himself as one of the epigoni of Schmoller) and of the Marxist tradition, both of which had combatted the isolative treatment of the economic process and the *homo economicus* by abstract classical economics, he probed the history of culture to determine the decisive interconnections of economics with the totality of culture. The whole historical work of Weber has ultimately one primary object, the understanding of contemporary European culture, especially modern capitalism. It presses forward to the underlying morale (*Geist*) of capitalism and its pervasive attitudes to life; and beyond this to modern Occidental rationalism as such, which he came to regard as the crucial characteristic of the modern world.

The discussion of problems raised by Marx, who gave the subject of capitalism its large importance in modern social theory, resulted in a great literature on this theme. Certain German scholars had already begun to assimilate Marx's theoretical work into the conceptual framework developed by the German historical school, among them some of the *Kathedersozialisten*, principally Toennies and Sombart.

These bourgeois economists and social theorists were much concerned with the problem of the psychological foundations of capitalism, and suggested certain corrections of the Marxist hypotheses under the general rubric of "the spirit of capitalism." Weber paid the highest tribute to Marx's genius and recognized the enormous usefulness of the materialistic method as a heuristic device, but he resisted all efforts to absolutize it into the sole method of social science, much less into a *Weltanschauung*. The truth value of this method, as indeed of all intellectual schemata, he regarded as only "ideal-typical." As against the Marxian doctrine of the economic determinism of social change, Weber propounded a pluralistic interactional theory.

It is necessary to be clear as to the limited character of Weber's goal and the cautious manner of his procedure in this essay. In this first work inquiring into the influence of religious doctrine on economic behavior, he had not the slightest intention of producing a complete theory of capitalism, a social theory of religion, or even a complete treatment of the relation between religion and the rise of capitalism. The essay was intended as a tentative effort at understanding one of the basic and distinctive aspects of the modern ethos, its pro-

From Ephraim Fischoff, "The Protestant Ethic and the Spirit of Capitalism: the History of a Controversy," *Social Research*, XI, (1944), 61–77. By permission of the author.

fessional, specialized character and its sense of calling or vocation. Already he was impressed by the dominantly rational character of modern life; and he was concerned to demonstrate that there were various types of rationalization, a fact generally overlooked by technological theories of history.

Defining capitalism from his historistic view as a unique system characterized by the general trends of antitraditionalism, dynamism, rationalism and calculated long-range industrial production, he was principally concerned to analyze and trace the genesis of the character-structure adequate to and congruent with it. In his view, modern capitalism was not the automatic product of technological development but of many objective factors, including climate — which influences the conduct of life and labor costs — and many social-political factors, such as the character of the mediaeval inland city and its citizenry. But he insisted that there was one factor which could not be ignored: the emergence of a rational, antitraditional spirit in the human agents involved. The two main aspects of this are the evolution of modern science and its comparatively modern relationship to economics, and the growth of the modern organization of individual life (*Lebensführung*), particularly in its practical consequences for economic activity. Weber's limited thesis was merely that in the formation of this pattern of rationally ordered life, with its energetic and unremitting pursuit of a goal and eschewal of all magical escapes, the religious component must be considered as an important factor. How important he was unable to say, and indeed he felt that in historical imputation such quantification is impossible. Consequently his view was that no one can tell how the capitalist economic system would have evolved had the specifically modern elements of the capitalistic spirit been lacking.

In tracing the affinity between the bourgeois life pattern and certain components of the religious stylization of life, as shown most consistently by ascetic Protestantism,

Weber emphasized the gradual genesis of a psychological habit which enabled men to meet the requirements of early modern capitalism. That is, instead of the entrepreneur feeling that his gaining of wealth was at best tolerated by God, or that his *usuraria pravitas* had to be atoned for (as did the native Hindu trader), he went about his business with sturdy confidence that Providence purposely enabled him to prosper for God's glory, that this success was construable as a visible sign of God and, when achieved by legal means, as a measure of his value before God as well as man. On the other hand, the handworker or laborer, with his willingness to work, derived his sense of a religious state of grace from his conscientiousness in his calling. Finally, because of the abomination of the generic sin of idolatry or apotheosis of created things (*Kreaturvergötterung*), as manifested in hoarding possessions, indulgence and frivolous consumption, the money accumulated in the exercise of a calling was turned back into the business enterprise, or saved.

Weber strongly emphasized the importance to bourgeois accumulation of planned this-worldly asceticism (*innerweltliche Askese*), as distinguished from otherworldly asceticism, and of the emotional type of pietism. He insisted that Protestant sects, especially the Quakers and Baptists, engendered a methodical regulation of life, in striking contrast to Catholicism, Lutheranism and Anglicanism. His crucial point was that ascetic Protestantism created for capitalism the appropriate spirit, so that the vocational man (*Berufsmenschen*) in his acquisition of wealth no longer suffered from the deep inner lesions characteristic of the more earnest individuals of an earlier day, no matter what their apparent solidity and exemplary power. One example of this inner uncertainty regarding economic activity was the practice of restoring at death goods obtained by usury; another was the establishment of religious institutions to atone for financial success. There were innumerable theoretical and practical compromises between conscience and economic activity, between the ideal of *Deo placere non potest,* accepted even by Luther, and the acquisitive careers entered into by many earnest Catholics. In Weber's view the noteworthy degree of congruence or affinity between the modern capitalistic system and the set of attitudes toward it made for a high inner integration, which was of great importance for the subsequent development of capitalism. It was this integration which was the central concern of his essay (*Archiv,* vol. 30, p. 200).

Weber made it clear that it was his intention to analyze just one component of the generic *Lebensstil* of our rationalized civilization, among the many which stood at the cradle of modern capitalism, and to trace its changes and its ultimate disappearance. He warned against exclusive concentration on the religious factor, as exerted through the inner psychological motivations and the powerful educational force and discipline provided by the Protestant sects. It was, he insisted, only one factor, and he rejected all attempts to identify it with the spirit of capitalism, or to derive capitalism from it. Taking the religious ethic of Protestantism as a constant, and assuming temporarily that it was predominantly a religious product, he proposed to trace the congruence between it and the characterological type requisite for capitalism. It was his intention, however, to return to the problem and investigate the nonreligious components of the religious ethic.

As to the insistence by some of his critics, such as Fischer and Rachfahl, that the problem required a statistical-historical approach, Weber recognized the need of research on the development of particular areas in order to determine the numbers and strength of the various religious groups involved, and the importance of the vocational ethics in comparison with other factors. But he insisted that his was a study in the sociology of cultures, investigating the convergence of religious and economic factors in the production of modern "rational" man, and that for his type of study the statistical method was not indicated. His concern was to as-

certain the specific direction in which a given religion might operate, the diverse effects of a specific system of religious ethics on the style of life. This problem, he felt, could be approached only by the "understanding" method of motivational analysis which he employed. In this first essay, therefore, he concentrated on tracing the complex ramifications leading from articles of faith to practical conduct, in an acute and learned examination of the psychological motivations issuing out of Reformed Protestantism and leading to methodical rationalization of activity and the consequent encouragement of capitalist behavior and attitudes. This thesis is carried through all the varieties of Reformed Christianity with a subtle and insightful *dogmengeschichtliche* analysis.

The Protestant essay was not regarded by Weber as a final or dogmatic formulation of a theory of the genesis or evolution of the Reformation, but as a preliminary investigation of the influence of certain religious ideas on the development of an economic spirit or the ethos of an economic system. He was not producing an idealistic (or as he preferred to term it, a spiritual) interpretation of capitalism, deriving it from religious factors. Much nonsense has been written on this point because of his alleged rejection of Marxism. Actually, he was an admirer of the Marxian hypothesis, only objecting that it should not be made absolute and universal, a summary philosophy; but then he rejected all absolutes and all monisms. Hence he rejected at least as forcibly any idealistic monism, and in the essay and its supplements he explicitly disavowed the foolish attribution to him of any spiritualistic hypothesis.

He sought no "psychological determination of economic events," but rather emphasized the "fundamental importance of the economic factor." He recognized clearly that economic changes arise in response to economic needs, and are conditioned by a wide variety of factors, including the demagogic, geographic, technological and monetary. He recognized that capitalism would have arisen without Protestantism, in fact that it had done so in many culture complexes; and that it would not and did not come about where the objective conditions were not ripe for it. He admitted that several other systems of religious ethics had developed approaches to the religious ethic of Reformed Protestantism, but he insisted that the psychological motivations involved were necessarily different; what was decisive was the ethos engendered, not preachments or theological compendia, and this, he argued, was unique in Reformed Protestanism for a variety of reasons. He recognized that there are constant functional interactions between the realms of religion and economics, but in this study he concentrated on the influences emanating from the side of religion. He not only indicated his awareness of the other side, but demonstrated how by an irony of fate the very fulfilment of religious injunctions had induced changes in the economic structure, which in turn engendered the massive irreligion of a capitalist order. He admitted that the religious ethic itself is not determined exclusively by religion, and he clearly urged the necessity of investigating the influence of the social milieu, especially economic conditions, upon the character and development of religious attitudes.

Yet he held that the religious revelation of the founder of a sect is an autonomous experience and not a mere reflection of accommodation to economic or other needs. It was his feeling that it is no solution to the problem of the distinctiveness of the Calvinist religious form to say that it is an adjustment to capitalistic practices already in existence; the question then arises as to why Catholicism did not show the same results after making the accommodation. But when a religious revelation has become a social phenomenon and has given rise to a community, a process of social selection sets in and class stratification supervenes in the originally homogeneous religious group, causing the formation of distinctive, socially determined differences within the religion. Weber was going to study this side of the

problem, but he never returned to the task. In *The Protestant Ethic* he concentrated on the religious factor alone, considering it as though it were exclusively a religious entity. He was, however, well aware of the tentative nature of his contribution, and he sketched the mammoth and indeed unrealizable program of studies necessary before the project could be regarded as complete.

By no means all the criticisms leveled against Weber were due to bias or failure to heed his cautions regarding the intention of his essay. First, there is the indubitable fact that as the essay stands it has certain elementary defects of structure, particularly because of the incompleteness which exposes it to misunderstandings by a careless reader, although Weber protested that an academic critic should never be guilty of such malfeasance. Writing in the *Archiv* in 1908, Weber explained again the reasons for the noncompletion of the essay — partly personal factors, partly the pressure of other work and partly the fact that Troeltsch had begun to treat in the "most felicitous manner a whole series of problems that lay on Weber's route," which the latter was loath to duplicate; and he expressed the hope that in the coming year he might work on the essay and issue it separately. He admitted that critics had a right to charge that the original essay was incomplete, and he recognized the danger that the hasty reader might overlook this fact, but he insisted that it could scarcely be construed as an idealistic construction of history.

Replying to Fischer's criticism, Weber insisted that in the Protestant essay he had expressed himself with utter clarity on the relationship between religion and economics generally, but he none the less admitted that misunderstanding might possibly have arisen from certain turns of phrase. Accordingly he promised to remove in a future reissue all expressions which seemed to suggest the derivation of institutions from religious motives; and he expressed his intention of clarifying the fact that it was the spirit of a "methodical" *Lebensführung* which he was deriving from Protestant asceticism, and which is related to economic forms only through congruence (*Adäquanz*). In a later anticritical article, adverting with regret to the incompleteness of the essay, Weber suggests ironically that had he completed it as promised by tracing the influence of economic conditions on the formation of reformed Protestantism, he would probably have been accused of having capitulated to historical materialism, even as he was now charged with an overemphasis on the religious or ideological factor. Hence, he insisted, his essay should properly be regarded only as a fraction of an investigation into the history of the development of the idea of vocation and its infusion into certain callings.

Apart from its incompleteness this essay betrays the other faults so characteristic of most of Weber's writing — a great carelessness of the reader's requirements, evinced in the plethora of detail in the text and above all in the ocean of footnotes, inundating the reader and frequently sweeping him far from the mainland. His wife speaks of "die montströse Form dieser Abhandlung," which was aggravated in the second edition when the "Fussnotengeschwulst" increased enormously. She sought, however, to justify this flood by pointing out that since Weber was using "careful causal imputation of intuitively apprehended connections," he wished to provide all possible proof in this extensive scholarly apparatus, and "to guard himself against any misunderstanding of his cautious relativizations."

The essay may be justly criticized for various errors of fact and interpretation. Weber himself later corrected some erroneous statements appearing in the original essay, as by indicating that when he had said that Calvinism shows the juxtaposition of intensive piety and capitalism, wherever found, he had meant only Diaspora Calvinism.

Another justifiable line of attack on Weber's thesis is based on concrete researches into the economic history of the continent, principally Holland and the Rhineland. Both Weber and Troeltsch had based their work on inadequate study of sources, and had quoted Anglo-Saxon writers to demonstrate the effect of German and Netherland Calvinists on the economic development of the Rhineland. On the basis of investigations into the history of Holland — and it must be recalled that this republic was probably the first country in which capitalism developed on a large scale — recent Netherland historians like DeJong, Knappert and de Pater find no proof to sustain such a theory of a connection between Calvinism and capitalism among the Netherlanders. Further, Beins' researches into the economic ethic of the Calvinist church in the Netherlands between 1565 and 1650 lead him to raise serious objections to Weber's thesis. A similar view is expressed in the important economic history of the Netherlands by Baasch, who stresses the secular factors in the evolution of capitalism in Holland which made the Netherlanders the chief bankers of the seventeenth century and by the end of the eighteenth made the colony of Jews in Amsterdam the largest in Europe. The same adverse conclusion is reached by Koch's investigation of the economic development of the lower Rhine area and Andrew Sayous' study of the Genevans; Hashagen's essay on the relation between Calvinism and capitalism in the German Rhineland comes to similar conclusions. Evidence has also accumulated that Calvinism did not have any necessary effect on the rise of capitalism in Hungary, Scotland or France.

These researches militate against Weber's hypothesis that the Calvinist belief buttressed capitalism or even favored its emergence. But this line of criticism readily degenerates into the oversimplification referred to above, that Weber was intent on establishing the causal primacy of the Protestant ethic in the genesis of capitalism and the necessary determination of the latter by the former wherever it appeared. The tendency toward such an oversimplification vitiates most of the arguments of Robertson and of Hyma, who closely follows him. In so far as all these writers, among whom may be included Brentano, Sée, Pirenne, Brodnitz and von Schulze-Gävernitz, construe Weber's thesis as implying a necessary causal influence exerted by Calvinism on the evolution of capitalism, they have misread Weber.

Most animadversions on his thesis, even in works composed during the last decade, spring from a misunderstanding or oversimplification of his theory, for which he is only slightly to blame. Surely Weber, one of the foremost historians of jurisprudence and economics in his generation, needed no reminder that the origins of capitalism are complex and diverse, and are due to changes in economic process as well as in spiritual outlook. By and large most of his critics have simply not perceived the direction of his interest, the moderation of his purpose and the caution of his procedure.

Only a very few of his critics rose to the level of his argument and recognized that his errors or shortcomings were inherent in his particular method. And the handful who did attack Weber's method, such as Sée, Robertson, Walker and Borkenau, did so in ignorance of his writings on the nature of social science and the method appropriate to it. Weber's shortcomings were not due to ignorance, naivete or partisanship; on the contrary, he had a considered and subtle approach. An acquaintance with Weber's views as to the nature and goal of the social sciences — his view of theory as only ideal-typical, and his peculiar method of historical research committed to the interpretative understanding of historical atoms, of particular emergents chosen on the basis of their cultural significance and understood by means of a controlled intuitive method — might have clarified the reason for a whole range of errors or inadequacies in his *Protestant Ethic*. Certainly no validation of his method is here projected: clearly it has shortcomings; its usefulness has very plain limitations; and its employment is fraught with particular occupational hazards. But any essay avowedly composed under that method should be evaluated on its own terms, as an essay in interpretative understanding. From this view not a few of the strictures here listed would lose their point, or would at least appear in their proper perspective as the inevitable consequences of Weber's atomistic method.

His employment of the ideal-type method leads to various distortions, as in his overemphasis of the concepts of vocation and predestination. Here a bias in the choice of the historical atom to be interpreted and in the definition of its character and influence makes itself strongly felt. The oversimplification induced by the method also extends to his construction of the Protestant ethic as a component of Calvinism, Puritanism, Pietism, Methodism and the Anabaptist sects, and to his treatment of Puritanism. Another instance is his definition of modern capitalism, accentuating its novelty, rationality and ascetic character. Once he had so defined it he did not have much difficulty in discovering elements of congruity with the schematic construction of the Protestant ethic slanted in the same direction. To the empirical historian the whole procedure necessarily appears suffused by a tendency to idealization, with a comparative neglect of secular factors, economic, political and technological.

Weber's method of atomistic isolation necessarily leads to oversimplification of a complex historical entity through the accentuation and isolation of a particular component factor regarded as significant from a certain point of view; its tracing of alleged influences on the further course of historical evolution; and its tendency toward reifying the particular component factors of a given historical entity. In the nature of the case this method cannot serve for the illumination of a total historical problem, or the interpretation of a whole epoch or movement.

His pluralistic agnosticism, manifested in his refusal to pledge allegiance to any exclusive viewpoint lest it do injustice to the unique individuality of historical entities and the perpetual shift of cultural horizons, was laudable in intention. It seemed to be pointing the way to the functionalization of research and interpretation in the social sciences. Actually, however, Weber's isolative treatment led to inevitable distortions. His method entailed the breakdown of any complex phenomenon into its components, and then choosing each one seriatim as a constant, tracing its effects on the other variables. At the end of the process, he indicated, there would have to be a return to assess the varying force of each component in the actual historical composite, and to determine how closely the empirical phenomena approached the ideal types he had formulated. This he had planned to do for his problem of the relationship between the Protestant ethic and the spirit of capitalism, but he must have felt the infinite and impossible nature of the task. Moreover, his approach offers no method for determining the interrelation of factors, the degree of influence pertaining to each, or their temporal variations, thereby leaving room for the play of personal evaluation in the choice and characterization of the particular historical atoms.

For the historian concerned with determining the causes of a particular historical datum, the problem of timing historical phenomena and tracing temporal variations is one of the crucial difficulties arising out of the impossibility, inherent in Weber's method, of determining the degree of influence to be assigned to the various factors involved. The ideal-type method neglects the time coefficient, or at any rate impairs the possibility of establishing time sequences, because it involves a telescoping of data. Granted, for instance, that Weber's interpretation of Calvinist theology is correct and that it was of the type that would result in activism, dynamism, industry, etc., the question still remains whether these influences did not begin to exert a significant effect only after capitalism had already reached a dominant position.

Consequently, while there is readiness enough to accept the congruity between Calvinism and capitalism, it has been suggested that a consideration of the crucial question of timing will show that Calvinism emerged later than capitalism where the latter became decisively powerful. Hence the conclusion that Calvinism could not have causally influenced capitalism, and that its subsequent favorable disposition to capitalist practice and ethics is rather to be construed as an adaptation.

The development of the Weberian thesis by Troeltsch, and his American disciple, Reinhold Niebuhr, meets this criticism by tracing the modifications induced in later Calvinism by the various social factors impinging upon it after the first appearance of the original doctrine, such as religious wars, political pressures and the exigencies of acquisitive life. His rich analysis reveals how the social ethic was the net result of the particular religious and ethical peculiarities of Calvinism, which showed a marked individuality in its doctrine of predestination, its activism and its ethic, aiming at achieving what was possible and practical. On the other hand, Troeltsch emphasizes the importance in the evolution of the ethic of the republican tendency in politics, the capitalistic tendency in economics and the diplomatic and militaristic tendencies in international affairs. All these tendencies radiated from Geneva, at first in a very limited way; then they united with similar elements within the Calvinist religion and ethic, and in this union they became stronger and stronger, until in connection with the political, social and ecclesiastical history of individual countries they received that particular character of the religious morality of the middle classes (or bourgeois world) which differs from the early Calvinism of Geneva and France.

In the light of all this, Weber's thesis must be construed not according to the usual interpretation, as an effort to trace the causative influence of the Protestant ethic upon the emergence of capitalism, but as an exposition of the rich congruency of such diverse aspects of a culture as religion and economics. The essay should be considered as a stimulating project of hermeneutics, a demonstration of interesting correlations between diverse cultural factors. Although at the time of the republication of the essay Weber insisted that he had not changed his views on this matter at all, the whole intent of his later work does show an implicit shift of view, or at any rate of emphasis. No longer laying the basic stress on the causal factors in the economic ethic of radical Protestantism as related to the capitalist spirit, his later researches, culminating in the systematic sociology of religion, accepted rather the congruency of these diverse aspects of our culture, and their subsumption under the comprehensive process of rationalization. It is important to emphasize that some of the distortions involved in Weber's ideal-type method are neutralized in his later sociological studies of the non-Christian religions, to which all too little attention has been paid. In these mighty studies, which are cultural sociologies of the *Weltreligionen,* Weber traces the influence of material, geographic and economic circumstances on the religious and ethical ideas of different cultures. Yet though he treated religious norms, institutions and practices with cold detachment, he never denied the historical reality and power of the religious complex. His general view remained that human affairs are infinitely complicated, with numerous elements interacting; and it was his unshakable conviction that to attribute causal primacy is to be guilty of oversimplification.

In view of Weber's limited intention and the cautious demarcation of his task (including the frequently expressed indication of its incompleteness), his idiosyncratic method which would not permit statistical proof or disproof, and his later supplementation of the original effort by systematic studies in the sociology of religion, it must be concluded that his task was justified by its results. Although the discussion of his problem has not in itself promoted our knowledge of past economic life in proportion to the considerable effort it has evoked, it has greatly sharpened our appreciation of Catholic and Protestant doctrinal history; and it has also paved the way for the formulation of an adequate social theory of religion. Weber's essay on *The Protestant Ethic* is also in a peculiar sense an introduction to his massive system of sociology and his philosophy of history, and exemplifies in striking fashion the anfractuosities of his intellect and temper. As an illuminating tentative approach to a great problem, as an introduction to the domain of the sociology of religion which it served to stake out, as the stimulus to a generation of researchers in this new discipline, and finally, as the precursor of functional analysis in culture history, Weber's essay deserves a better fate than it has thus far enjoyed.

SUGGESTIONS FOR ADDITIONAL READING

The student interested in doing additional reading on this problem should, first of all, read more extensively in the works from which selections were taken for this volume. A thoughtful reading of all of Max Weber's *The Protestant Ethic and the Spirit of Capitalism* (London, 1930) should provide a clearer concept of Weber's methodology just as a wider perusal of Ernst Troeltsch's *The Social Teaching of the Christian Churches* (New York, 1931) will reveal how his comments on this problem fit into his major purpose of determining the effect of sociological conditions upon the origin, growth, and modifications of Christianity. Werner Sombart's *The Quintessence of Capitalism* (New York, 1915) offers the reader of the entire work an explanation of the role of Judaism, as well as of Protestantism and Catholicism, in the development of modern capitalism; Sombart also assigns biological factors a share of the responsibility for the emergence of capitalism. Sombart's views are further explained in his article, "Capitalism," in the *Encyclopedia of Social Sciences* and in F. L. Nussbaum, *A History of the Economic Institutions of Modern Europe* (New York, 1933). A complete reading of R. H. Tawney's *Religion and the Rise of Capitalism* (London, 1926, and later editions) offers a much better survey of the whole economic and political situation during the period than it is possible to provide in a brief extract (there is also a perfectly satisfactory paperback edition of this book published by The New American Library of World Literature, a "Mentor" book, New York, 1947, and later editions). The full text of H. M. Robertson's *Aspects of the Rise of Economic Individualism* (Cambridge, 1933) furnishes a materialist explanation of the development of capitalism including analyses of the effects of overseas discoveries upon capitalism and of the teachings of the Jesuits concerning the taking of interest in the 16th and 17th centuries. Robertson bases some of his findings concerning the Jesuits on the unscholarly writings of opponents of the order, and part of his conclusions were considerably modified by James Brodrick, S.J., *The Economic Morals of the Jesuits: An Answer to Dr. H. M. Robertson* (London, 1934). Amintore Fanfani's *Catholicism, Protestantism and Capitalism* (London, 1935) offers the reader of the entire study not only a more complete discussion of the views presented in the selection in this volume but also a presentation of the author's contentions concerning anthropological factors in the emergence of capitalism. The selection from Albert Hyma's *Renaissance to Reformation* (Grand Rapids, 1955) is only a small part of this work which surveys the whole period, including political and theological, as well as economic, views of leaders of both Catholic and Protestant reform movements. Hyma also wrote *Christianity, Capitalism and Communism* (Ann Arbor, 1937) of which the third through the seventh chapters are concerned with this controversy. Another aspect of the problem is presented in Professor Hyma's article, "Calvinism and Capitalism in the Netherlands, 1555–1700," which appeared in the *Journal of Modern History*, X (1938), 321–343.

Nearly all the best known biographies of the leading Protestant reformers offer some commentary on their economic views and social teachings. Particularly relevant to this controversy, however, is Georgia Harkness' *John Calvin: the Man and His Ethics* (New York, 1931). Part III of this work, "Calvinistic Conscience and Man's Duty to Man," offers a detailed and objective exposition of Calvin's social teaching; Chapter IX is devoted to a careful examination of the Weber thesis which, though not wholly rejected, is considered an inadequate explanation of the relationship of Protestantism and capitalism. "The Social Consequences of the Theological System of John Calvin" is a chapter written by Frank N. Hnik for a volume, *The Philanthropic Motive in Christianity* (Oxford, 1938); Hnik's chapter is largely dependent upon the works of Weber, Troeltsch, and Tawney. Very brief, but well-balanced and informed commentaries on the social effects of the Reformation are offered on the pages indicated of the three following works: Roland H. Bainton, *The Reformation of the Sixteenth Century* (Boston, 1952), pp. 244–256; V. H. H. Green, *Renaissance and Reformation* (London, 1952), pp. 398–401; and Harold J. Grimm, *The Reformation Era* (New York, 1954), pp. 578–581.

Studies on the origin and evolution of modern capitalism are naturally related to the Weber thesis controversy. The materialistic interpretations provided by the Marxist historians offer little support to any concept of a "spirit of capitalism." Such a view is presented by Maurice Dobb, *Studies in the Development of Capitalism* (London, 1946). Another Marxist more specifically concerned with the Weber thesis than Dobb is P.C. Gordon Walker whose article, "Capitalism and the Reformation," appears in the November, 1937, issue of the *Economic History Review*. Gordon Walker denies the conclusions of both Weber and his critics and asserts that the entire Reformation movement was a product of the price revolution. A widely recognized non-Marxist study of the history of capitalism is Henri Sée, *Modern Capitalism* (New York, 1928); Sée, like Dobb and Gordon Walker, concedes practically nothing to the view of a "capitalist spirit" as a guiding force of economic history. A Catholic interpretation of the economic changes of the Reformation period is presented by G. A. T. O'Brien, *An Essay on the Economic Effects of the Reformation* (London, 1923). In contrast to O'Brien's view is Conrad H.

Moehlmann's article, "The Christianization of Interest," *Church History*, III (1934), 3–15; Moehlmann offers evidence of the relaxation of prohibitions of interest by predecessors and contemporaries of Calvin. For a superior survey of the overall, long range economic development of Europe, the reader should refer to Herbert Heaton, *Economic History of Europe* (New York, 1936).

Probably the most complete bibliography of the controversy is provided by Benjamin N. Nelson, *The Idea of Usury* (Princeton, 1949). John T. McNeill's article, "Thirty Years of Calvin Study," *Church History*, XVII (1948), 207–240, offers a sound, brief, critical bibliography.

At least a few of the many additional titles available to those students who are able to read foreign languages should be mentioned here. Lujo Brentano, *Die Anfänge des Kapitalismus* (Munich, 1916) is regarded by many as one of the most effective attacks on Weber; Brentano asserts that Weber considers Protestantism the cause of many developments which had already occurred during the Renaissance. Henri Hauser's work, *Les débuts de capitalisme* (Paris, 1927), offers an excellent chapter, "Les Idées économiques de Calvin." The same author also contributed "A propos des idées économiques de Calvin" to the *Mélanges offerts à Henri Pirenne* (Brussels, 1926), I, 211–244. Among Hauser's other works is the article, "L'économie calvinienne," *Études sur Calvin,* vol. 100 (1935), 227–242. In the studies mentioned here, Professor Hauser is essentially opposed to Weber's view. Another aspect of the controversy is presented in an article by André E. Sayous, "Calvinisme et capitalisme: l'expérience genèvoise," *Annales d'histoire économique et sociale*, VII (1935), 225–244. Sayous finds Calvinist discipline so rigorous in its restriction of capitalism in Geneva that capitalism was prevented for many years from developing beyond a primitive form in that city.